Contemporary Minority Migration, Education and Ethnicity in China

Contemporary Minority Migration, Education and Ethnicity in China

Robyn Iredale
Associate Professor of Human Geography, School of Geosciences and Coordinator, Migration and Multicultural Societies Program, Centre for Asia Pacific Social Transformation Studies (CAPSTRANS), University of Wollongong, Australia

Naran Bilik
Professor of Anthropology, Institute of Nationality Studies, Chinese Academy of Social Sciences, China

Wang Su
Senior Researcher, China National Institute of Educational Research, Beijing, China

With contributions from

Fei Guo
Research Fellow, Migration and Multicultural Societies Program, Centre for Asia Pacific Social Transformation Studies (CAPSTRANS), University of Wollongong, Australia

Caroline Hoy
Lecturer in Human Geography, Department of Geography, University of Dundee, UK

Edward Elgar
Cheltenham, UK • Northampton, MA, USA

Published by
Edward Elgar Publishing Limited
Glensanda House
Montpellier Parade
Cheltenham
Glos GL50 1UA
UK

Edward Elgar Publishing, Inc.
136 West Street
Suite 202
Northampton
Massachusetts 01060
USA

A catalogue record for this book
is available from the British Library

Library of Congress Cataloguing in Publication Data

Iredale, Robyn R.
    Contemporary minority migration, education, and ethnicity in China / Robyn Iredale, Naran Bilik, and Wang Su ; in conjunction with Fei Guo and Caroline Hoy.
        p. cm.
    Includes bibliographical references and index.
        1. Migration, Internal—China. 2. Minorities—China. 3. China—Population policy. I. Bilik, Naran. II. Su, Wang. III. Guo, Fei. IV. Hoy, Caroline. V. Title.

HB2114.A3 I74 2001
305.8'00951—dc21

00–065450

ISBN 1 84064 443 5

Printed and bound in Great Britain by MPG Books Ltd, Bodmin, Cornwall

Contents

List of figures

List of tables

List of plates

Acknowledgements

The authors would like to acknowledge the Australian Research Council (ARC) and the University of Wollongong for supporting this research. The early research was conducted in 1996-98 on two small ARC grants from the University and in 1999 a large ARC grant enabled the completion of the research and the conduct of the workshop in Beijing. The Australian Academy of Social Sciences also provided financial assistance which enabled Robyn Iredale to visit Beijing for an extended period of time in 1998.

The Institute of Nationality Studies (INS) in the Chinese Academy of Social Sciences (CASS) organised and hosted the workshop. The authors wish to thank the INS for doing such a professional job and for supporting Naran Bilik at all times. The participation and contribution of Dru Gladney to the workshop was extremely insightful and valuable. For this we are very grateful.

The China National Institute of Educational Research (CNIER) has cooperated with the project and enabled Wang Su to devote a considerable amount of time to fieldwork, data analysis and writing up the results in both China and Australia. We especially appreciate the input on contemporary education issues and the work of Professor Liu in analysing the data from the *Sample Survey of Ethnic Minority Migration*.

Professors Zhang Tianlu and Wang Shu-xin from Beijing were instrumental in organising the fieldwork in Tibet and Professor Tsui Yan Hu from Urumqi conducted the fieldwork in Xinjiang. To them we owe a debt of gratitude. Jirgal, of the Cadre School in Hohhot, was vitally important in Inner Mongolia for assisting with the *Sample Survey of Ethnic Minority Migration*.

A number of people were crucial in the early stages of this project for linking up the researchers. John Elfink, formerly education consultant at the UNESCO office in Beijing, put the CNIER and University of Wollongong in touch with each other. Without his assistance it would have been virtually impossible to get started. Huang Ping, Institute of Sociology, CASS, was also instrumental in assisting in the early stages and at many other times throughout the project.

Li Youwen, of the Australian Studies Centre at Beijing Foreign Studies University, has provided invaluable assistance in many ways. She frequently acted as interpreter and translator and she was always a ready friend to assist when needed.

Many people at the Centre for Asia Pacific Social Transformation Studies (CAPSTRANS) and in the School of Geosciences, University of

Wollongong, have played a vital role in this project. In particular, the Director of CAPSTRANS, Stephen Castles, offered support and encouragement and the Executive Officer, Maureen Dibden, was always cooperative and helpful. Our sincerest thanks go to Jennifer Wark and Paola Crinnion for their efforts in preparing the manuscript for publication. Their hard work and cheerful nature made the task a pleasure. Richard Miller prepared the maps and made very good suggestions as to their format. Tim Turpin filled the vital role of independent reader of the manuscript and his suggestions helped tie all the parts together. Many other people, including graduate and undergraduate students and colleagues, acted as sounding boards on different occasions and for this we are grateful. In particular we thank Xiang Biao, Visiting Fellow at CAPSTRANS, for his comments on the manuscript.

Last but most importantly, to all the family members and friends who supported us throughout this research we say a big thank you.

Abbreviations

CAPSTRANS	Centre for Asia Pacific Social Transformation Studies
CAS	Chinese Academy of Sciences
CASS	Chinese Academy of Social Sciences
CNIER	China National Institute of Educational Research
CPC	Communist Party of China
ID	Identity card
INR	Institute for Nationalities Research
INS	Institute of Nationality Studies
LRNA	Law on Regional National Autonomy
PLA	People's Liberation Army
PRC	People's Republic of China
SEI	Socio-economic Index
SEZ	Special Economic Zone
SOE	State Owned Enterprise
TAR	Tibet Autonomous Region
TFR	Total fertility rate
TRC	Temporary Residence Certificate
TVE	Township and Village Enterprise
USSR	Union of Soviet Socialist Republics

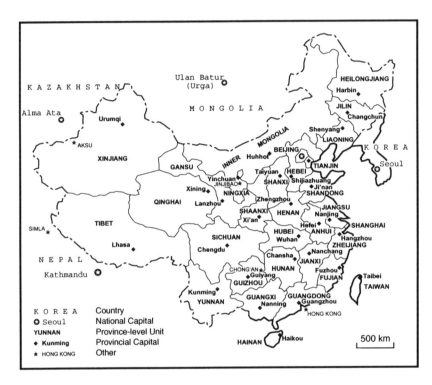

Figure 1.1 Provinces and major cities of China

1. Introduction

Urbanisation and rural-urban migration are important aspects in the development of countries. Up till the late 1980s, the People's Republic of China (PRC) and Vietnam were unique in the degree to which they were able to control both the process of urbanisation and peoples' movements. The mechanisms of control operated indirectly through the economic system and directly through migration control policies. Both countries are now undergoing major change and the study of new patterns and dynamics of internal migration is important for understanding the social change process from a centrally planned system to a more market-oriented one. In addition, the unique coexistence of planned and market-oriented economic systems make the study more significant, as the existing literature in migration studies has mostly been generated from the experiences of developing countries with market economies (Guo 1996a).

Internal mobility has been a feature of Chinese history. It has been seen as a normal event that occurred as a result of natural disasters, wars, marriage, population pressure, opening up new areas, exploitation of natural resources and seasonal changes. The revolution and formation of the PRC imposed a new set of circumstances whereby mobility came to be constrained except in certain limited circumstances. State planning and centralised control led to the introduction of various limits to movement during the 1950s to 1970s.

The role of 'marketisation' in speeding up movement while the continuation of controls over movement still exist makes for a very interesting situation in China. The government has placed a lot of stress on control or management of the population in the past but this is rapidly breaking down. Many people still see themselves as bound to stay in a particular place while others have no hesitation in moving elsewhere for work, business or other opportunities. The increased flow of people leads to increased communication, increased knowledge about employment, market and investment opportunities elsewhere and more rapid industrial, social and cultural transformation. Families are increasingly moving to find better education for their children or for themselves either within provinces or across provincial borders. Movement for educational purposes is often promoted by the central government both as part of preferential policies for minorities and

1

as part of wider policies of economic development.

The upsurge of movement within China has sped up the rate of interchange and the degree of interaction between different regions and different ethnic groups. This is posing particular challenges for China. Will it lead to the greater 'hybridisation', assimilation, amalgamation or integration of minorities? Minority regions are changing rapidly as a result of many new factors, including the in-migration of other nationalities and the out-migration and return migration of people traditionally belonging to the region. Predominantly Han regions are also changing as a result of inflows of new ethnic groups and their cultures. Is there a process of increasing diversification and 'hyphenisation', rather than 'hybridisation', going on? Will there be new dimensions to the old debates between universalism and particularism? Will widening disparities between regions become more evident and provide grounds for ethnic discontent, since most regions with high minority populations tend to be poor? Economic reform and the open-door policy are also leading to increased interaction with many outside countries. How does the government ensure one of its key goals — maintenance of the multinational state? What will be the effect of increased border movements, trade and communication? Will ethnic nationalism along the frontier regions of China escalate?

These are some of the pressing issues relating to mobility in China. This book addresses particular aspects associated with minority mobility, a topic that has so far received very little attention. The book takes existing census data as a starting point but then makes a new contribution to this field of study. It does this by drawing on a targeted survey in four regions. These data are then used as the basis for detailed case study analysis. We argue that while minorities have probably taken longer to start moving in significant numbers, they have now become part of this trend. This is manifestly an urbanisation phenomenon, motivated by economic, social, political and environmental factors. The impact on ethnicity and the relationship between education, ethnicity and migration is examined in depth. In the final analysis, it is argued that the internal mobility of minorities is both a product of and contributing to social transformation in China.

INTERNAL MOVEMENT IN CHINA SINCE 1949

Throughout the period from the founding of the PRC in 1949 to the introduction of reform measures in the early 1980s, net population movement was from rural to urban areas but the trend of this movement was neither smooth nor consistently in the one direction. Traditional peasant migration from one rural area to another or from a densely populated area to a less densely populated region in search of resources and land continued during this period (and still prevails). During the early to mid-1950s, however, cities and towns began to absorb large numbers of workers from rural areas — people who fled from rural collectivisation. It is estimated that rural-urban migration accounted for 60 per cent of the increased urban population from 1950 to 1957 (Zhang *et al.* 1998, p. 2). This 'blind flow' of population, especially into cities such as Shanghai, became a matter of concern for the authorities who responded with the introduction of measures designed to halt the expansion of the urban population.

In the early 1960s, the 'hard times of the Three Years of Natural Calamity [Great Leap Forward], the Movement of Simplification of Administration and the transfer of large numbers of demobilised military personnel into rural areas to take up agricultural activities' brought this urban-oriented movement almost to a halt (Wang 1994, p. 27). This situation was compounded by the events of the Cultural Revolution from 1966 to 1976 and the upheaval associated with this. During this ten-year period there was an attempt to stamp out class differences that had begun to become evident and to get rid of various 'olds' (customs, religions, superstitions). The period saw the widespread destruction of temples, shrines and monuments, especially those belonging to ethnic minorities. At the same time, there was a transfer of school graduates and government officials, administrative staff and educators to rural areas for re-education. Between 1969 and 1973, some 10 to 15 million urban secondary school leavers were resettled in rural areas, predominantly in the north and west. Their resettlement was designed to be permanent as they were deprived of the documents that were necessary to regain the right to urban residency.

With the death of Mao in 1976 and the rise of Deng Xiaoping in 1978, the situation began to change and the trend to urbanisation resumed. It is argued that much of the initial reversal of the flow, in the late 1970s and early 1980s, was the movement of people who had been sent to rural areas back to urban areas or 'policy rectification' (Ma 1994, p. 23). This flow gradually expanded to include other forms of migration. Current movements are rural-rural, rural-urban, urban-rural and urban-urban, across local, county and provincial borders. Some moves are seasonal and temporary while others are semi-permanent or permanent. As elsewhere, there is a high degree of crossover between temporary and permanent movement as actual outcomes often vary from expected outcomes.

The rate of urbanisation began to increase in 1982 as changes to the social and economic systems deepened. This was associated with the 'introduction of the rural responsibility system of family based units controlling production on land assigned to their care. ... The transformation of agriculture into a productive and wealth producing activity involved a rapid increase in labour productivity and the need to export labour surpluses' (Hoy 1996, p. 18). Some of these excess labourers (10 per cent by the end of 1985) gained employment in non-agricultural activities, primarily Township and Village Enterprises (TVEs). It was the surplus who began to move to urban areas in search of jobs. Some of the jobs that they sought were created by the official endorsement in 1983 of private enterprises.

Much of the movement was comprised of temporary migrants who were not required to comply with permanent registration requirements and for whom temporary registration was possible. Joint venture and township enterprises did not require permanent registration (*hukou*), only temporary registration.[1] Village and township committees also became involved in exporting surplus rural labourers on a temporary basis to other places either in China or overseas, as a development strategy to improve the local economy and help alleviate poverty. Movement to middle sized towns, unlike movement to large cities, was never tightly monitored and was even encouraged as part of a wider policy of channelling migration. The period of flexibility after 1984 is described as one of half-open migration which began as a result of legislation introduced in that year to allow peasants and their families to move to urban areas (below the county level). This option did not apply for other members of the population but it created a precedent for the migration of couples and families.

Table 1.1 shows the rate of urbanisation at each of the four censuses of the People's Republic of China. Data from the 1990 census were analysed under both a 'restricted' and a more 'extended' urban definition. The older restricted definition covers only that part of (1) the city population residing in districts of cities and in neighbourhood committees of cities without districts and (2) the town population in neighbourhood committees of towns under city or county administration. The newer extended definition includes all persons residing in places administratively defined as cities and towns: 'extra large' cities (over 1 million), 'large' cities (500 000 to 1 million), 'medium-sized' cities (200 000 to 500 000), 'small' cities (less than 200 000) and towns.

---

[1] *Hukou* is a household registration system in which everyone is registered at his/her place of birth or the place where they are permitted to move to. People who were born in rural areas are registered as agricultural *hukou* and people who were born in urban areas are registered as non-agricultural *hukou*.

Table 1.1 Rate of urbanisation in People's Republic of China, 1953, 1964, 1982 and 1990

Population	1st Census (July 1953)	2nd Census (July 1964)	3rd Census (July 1982)	4th Census (July 1990)	
				Restricted urban definition	Extended urban definition
Total (no.)	594.3	697.9	1008.2	1133.7	1133.7
Urban (no.)	77.3	130.5	206.6	296.5	601.3
% urban	13	19	20	26	53

Source: Day and Ma (1994, p. 2).

FACTORS RESPONSIBLE FOR AN INCREASE IN THE RATE OF INTERNAL MOBILITY

Many factors have sped up the rate of all internal mobility. First, average per capita land area is very small and an increasing number of rural labourers leave their villages to find non-agricultural jobs. Huang *et al.* (1995) found that the average amount of land available per household in eight villages in the provinces of Jiangsu, Anhui, Sichuan and Gansu was 1.3 *mu* or 0.08 of a hectare (15 *mu* in one hectare). Past policies (including unfair pricing policies and institutional arrangements) mean that returns to agricultural production, especially grain production, are low. Prices were kept artificially low to provide cheap raw materials for state enterprises so they could make a significant profit to enable increased capital investment. Thus, people were forced to leave rural areas and seek more profitable employment. If the 'villagers did not send some of their members out for non-agricultural jobs, it would not be easy for them even just to pay public collections and funds, not to speak of many other necessary costs such as medical care, children's education, and social or interpersonal costs' (Huang *et al.* 1995, p. 32).

Second, the differential between urban and rural incomes and between booming eastern cities and inland areas widened in the 1990s. This is a reversal of what happened in the late 1970s and 1980s, when China's economic development started with agricultural reform and the outcome was an improvement in rural incomes (Long 1999, pp. 61-62). Agricultural net output recorded a real growth of 7.4 per cent per annum from 1978 to 1984, compared to the pre-reform (1971-78) average of 1.8 per cent. There was a narrowing of the gap between rural and urban incomes but the early success with agriculture encouraged the state to extend the reforms to the urban industrial sector in late 1984. The engine of growth switched to the decentralisation process as control of many State Owned Enterprises (SOEs) moved from central to local governments. Economic decentralisation came about when local officials called for more autonomy and control over local affairs in the late 1970s and 1980s and this led to far greater autonomy for local government officials and individuals to promote local development. The fiscal contract system introduced at the end of the 1980s further increased the revenue share retained by localities and thereby enabled them to implement their own policies and priorities. The breakup of the communes and introduction of the household responsibility system provided the material basis for the emergence of private and collectively owned industrial enterprises. Local authorities encouraged the formation of owned TVEs as a means of generating employment and income for administrative purposes. TVEs mushroomed in rural areas but with much greater propensity in coastal regions. The pace of change of ownership of industrial facilities away from the emphasis on state ownership varied across provinces, and those in which the share of state ownership dropped most rapidly (Zhejiang, Jiangsu, Fujian, Guangdong, Shandong) became the fastest growing. Qinghai, Jilin and Tibet have seen little change in the ownership structure of industrial enterprises and this is reflected in their poor economic performance.

Thus since 1993 the income gap between coastal and inland (except for Xinjiang) regions in China has widened (Long 1999, p. 59).[2] The *Economist* (1996, p. 29) argues that this gap may be the 'biggest economic and political challenge now facing the Chinese government'. Thus decentralisation has resulted in widening regional and intra-regional disparities and to fresh calls in the 1990s by officials in poorer areas for a recentralisation of control (Zheng 1999, p. 58). The World Bank's *Poverty in China: what do the numbers say?* (1996) estimates that even though average per capita incomes have increased markedly the number living in poverty is around one third of the population. The figure depends on both how poverty is defined and the political will to address the issue. Lyons (1998, p. 412) notes that anti-poverty campaigns 'cooled off in the early 1990s, after announcements of near-total eradication of poverty in many keypoint areas' but they were revived in 1994.

The third factor, another impact of the decline of state control, is the lessening of controls over internal movement. From the 1950s to the 1970s there were three provisions for prohibiting the free movement of people. The household registration system (*hukou*) and the food ticket system strictly froze the possibility of moving from rural to urban areas while the work unit system operated indirectly by tying people's access to services to their place of work. The *hukou* system was introduced in 1955 for both rural and urban

---

[2] Xinjiang is among the fastest growing provinces in China for reasons that will be explained later.

households and its aim was the 'preservation of social order and the protection of rights and interests, in the service of the construction of socialism' (Zhang 1987, p. 2). It prevented the permanent movement of people out of rural areas by requiring permission from the local authorities for a permanent change of address of the household. It severely restricted movement up the urban hierarchy and in particular it prohibited migration to Beijing, Shanghai and Tianjin municipalities. Sideways migration from town to town and city to city was permitted but was difficult while rural-rural migration was generally unimpeded. Movement down the urban hierarchy was encouraged (Hoy 1996). Access to welfare services was contingent on possession of *hukou* and if people moved away from their place of *hukou* and their work unit they had no access to education, health, welfare and other services.

The food ticket system, also introduced in 1955, was another measure that was designed to limit the amount of rural-large city migration. The regulation identified the amount of food (grain and other essentials) that an urban dweller was entitled to buy and where it could be bought. Presentation of a person's *hukou* was required at the food station to purchase the supplies (with a coupon and the required cash). This limited the demand for food in urban areas and meant that people with rural *hukou* were unable to purchase food legally in urban areas. The food ticket system was not abolished until 1993.

The third provision for controlling movement, the work unit system, meant that education, welfare, security, housing, health care and other services were provided to employees by work units. Movement from one's work unit meant the loss of these services and difficulty in accessing them elsewhere. Since the reform, however, constraints imposed by this system have lessened as people have opted to pay for services in their new location or gone without some services.

While these three policies were not totally effective, increased industrialisation in China between the 1950s and 1970s did not lead to rapid urbanisation, as it did in many other countries (Goldstein and Goldstein 1994). More than 80 per cent of the population was still living in rural areas at the end of 1978. However, throughout the 1980s and early 1990s neither personnel nor budgets were sufficient to keep information up-to-date and comprehensive for monitoring people (Hoy 1996). The database that was developed in the early 1980s as part of the implementation and monitoring of the family planning policy was more comprehensive and began to threaten the *hukou* system. In addition, less regulation of food and housing supplies made it easier to survive without *hukou*.

As a consequence of the inability of the *hukou* system to deal with the amount of work associated with the growth of migration and the need to establish identities, link people to their origins and trace individual interactions, the identity card system was introduced in 1986. Temporary registration or temporary *hukou* (for 12 months) was introduced on a national basis, after it had been trialled in Wuhan, Hubei province. According to Hoy (1996, pp. 31-32), the 'identity card extended the remit of the household registration system, reflecting economic and social changes. Proof of identity would be required in litigation procedures, for credit loans and for individual business licences. Identity cards would be issued by the same offices which supervised the household registers: prior registration was to be used as initial proof of identity'. Though the *hukou* system still existed, rural people could now show their ID (identity) cards to employers/accommodation providers in their place of destination, instead of having to have the previous official stamped letter from their local authorities. This enabled migrants to rent houses in urban areas, and legitimised an already widespread practice. Registration details were held at a local police station and a charge was made for a card (and for renewal) and for monthly 'protection fees' (Hoy 1996, p. 23). Many migrants, however, ignored the new instructions, avoided any form of registration and sought jobs in the informal sectors. Thus, the identity card system failed to achieve its intended goal as a system of management. Corruption and non-acceptance by the public have been said to be the major reasons. The coverage of temporary registration amongst migrants continues to be limited, according to Davin (1999, pp. 43-44), but it introduced 'enough flexibility to allow the *hukou* system to survive, albeit in a modified form'. The 'purchase' of permanent *hukou* from local authorities was often available, for a fee of between 3000 and 6000 yuan (US$600-1200) per person, but this was outside the scope of possibilities for most people.

The fourth factor responsible for increased migration is the 'double structure', the institutional division between rural and urban, which means that two very different welfare systems have been operating in Chinese society since the 1950s. Urban residents have come to enjoy social welfare, security, health care, pension, housing, and other social infrastructure provisions that are superior to those in rural areas. Not surprisingly, the effect has been the development of a wide disparity between urban and rural living conditions. Better information and communication now mean that rural people are very conscious of the rural-urban split in quality of life and opportunities, with the result that many migrate.

Fifth, economic reform has transformed the system from a centrally planned to a market-oriented economy. Reform started in rural areas where the introduction of the household responsibility system (instead of the commune or collective) led to private ownership of land and the generation of surplus rural labour.[3] Initially these people worked in TVEs nearby but the inability of the TVEs to absorb the increasing amount of surplus rural labour led to increased rural out-migration. Urban reforms began in 1984 and rapid development and increasing large scale construction demanded labourers. The combination of urban employment opportunities and attractions of the urban environment acted as magnets. The introduction of the open-door policy and the creation of Special Economic Zones (SEZs) in 1979 had the greatest impact in the coastal areas. These regions have become magnets for rural workers and while the number of SEZs has increased from the early 1980s most are still in the coastal areas.

The move to privatisation has been a major part of the changeover from a centrally planned to a market economy. With the legalising of private business, people can be self-employed and meet their housing, food and employment needs outside of the official allocation system. This was made possible by the rapid development of urban free markets (Guo 1996a). Changing market conditions enabled migrants to stay and support themselves at the destination, even without local official household registration status.

> The collective, social responses to human needs characteristic of earlier periods are being replaced by more individual or, at most, household responses, instead. A prime mover in bringing this about, as with so much else in the People's Republic, has been government policy. The decline of state control and with it, the decline of social control has encouraged a return to family farming, the development of private businesses, movement towards the consumer society, and the development of a new (new to China, that is) disaggregation of society primarily on the basis of economic wealth instead of social function. (Day 1994, p. 4)

Finally, poor rural areas that began to export migrant workers as a means of earning income to fuel development and alleviate poverty pressed for policies to manage migration. For example, Sichuan Provincial government regarded the export of labour to coastal areas as a strategy for provincial development and in 1986 set up and implemented a set of structures and regulations to direct rural-urban migration (Zhang *et al.* 1998). A work registration card and work permit for out-going labourers would be issued by Sichuan officials and with this card migrant labourers could apply for jobs in urban areas. The Sichuan government also set up labour services stations within the province as well as labour services and management stations in receiving places (Shenzhen and Guangzhou), to help migrants find jobs, settle down and deal

---

[3] The move to the household responsibility system started informally, and against the law, among a group of villages in Anhui province in the late 1970s. The change was formalised nationally in 1984.

with difficulties.

Internal migration is expected to continue to increase. President Jiang Zemin's continuation of Deng Xiaoping's policies was confirmed in October 1997 with the announcement of privatisation of the SOEs. The Communist Party's 15th Congress voted to end its support of 118 000 SOEs, thereby forcing them to become competitive or cease to exist. At the moment this privatisation process has stalled, due to fears that many of the 130 million employees face the prospect of unemployment and that this would lead to protests and political backlash. This could also add to the potential 'floating' population (Higgins 1997, p. 5). One prediction has put the rural labour force in the year 2000 at 540 million, over half of whom will be unable to find work in the rural sector (Hoy 1996, pp. 18-19) but more recently this estimate has risen to 600 million. The importance of chain migration has escalated with increased information flows by word of mouth, letters, telephone and television. Out-migration has especially occurred from poor and ecologically damaged areas.

The central government's ability to curtail the movement of people now seems limited. The first centrally organised attempt to try to deal with rural-urban migrants was put forward by the Family Planning Commission in 1991 (Zhang *et al.* 1998). The Commission was concerned about migrants avoiding the 'one child' policy by relocating from one area to another. In 1994, the Labor Administration Ministry introduced 'Temporary Regulations for Interprovincial Migration of Rural Workers'. This set of regulations refers to migrant workers bringing work registration and work permit cards from their place of origin and then being entitled to social services and prolongation of their contracts. In 1995, central government regulations relating to the renting of houses were introduced. These measures are having limited effect and some people argue that the creation of a new system of registration, one which is compatible with the demands of the economy and the population, is urgently needed. For example, Cao (1995, p. 1) calls for controlling the moves so that they occur in an 'orderly manner'. Others argue for the free movement of people in line with the mechanisms that operate in market economies. Some regions, such as Shanghai and Beijing municipalities, have introduced their own forms of control. A 'blue chop' is now required by people wanting to move permanently to Shanghai but it is only available to those with large amounts of money to invest or with a skilled job offer. Temporary residence cards and work permits have been introduced for 'floaters' and there is a clear demarcation of the jobs that migrant labourers can do.

The real problem lies in the extent of the economic/social divide between urban and rural areas and the inferior services (schools, medical facilities, housing) that rural people experience. Mobile rural and other populations are voting with their feet in seeking out the superior opportunity structures and social advantages that urban and richer rural areas provide. Wide spatial variations have emerged in China in the process of economic reform, partly as a result of government economic policies and the emphasis on developing the east coast. The response has been similar to what would have occurred in most other nations and the question is now how to deal with this situation.

RESEARCH INTO MINORITY MOVEMENT

Increased mobility obviously includes the movement of ethnic minorities. However, this aspect has received little attention to date and migrants, on the whole, have been treated as an ethnically homogeneous group. Gladney (1996) argues that there has been an increased interest in ethnicity since 1991 but this is only just beginning to be seen in the study of migration. The census data allow analysis by nationality of most demographic and socio-economic aspects, including inter-censal inter-province and intra-province permanent movement, but these data have not been used by local or overseas researchers. Recent research that has been carried out on minorities' movement has been done by a few minority demographers, anthropologists and sociologists. One report on the movement of Uyghurs into Beijing was prepared at the Institute for Nationalities Research (INR), part of the Chinese Academy of Social Sciences, in 1996 but it was not published. Another project carried out recently by the Population Research Institute, Xinjiang University, on the health and other implications of the movement of Uyghurs into Beijing (Hoy and Ren 1996) again was not published.

At the same time, a review of Chinese and English literature reveals limited research into Han Chinese migration into primarily minority regions. Han migration into the northern regions has been researched by Li (1989) and Naughton (1988), into Xinjiang by Ren and Yuan (1999) and Mao (1999), to Tibet and Qinghai by Clarke (1994) and to Inner Mongolia by Pasternak and Salaff (1993) and others. The difficulty of conducting research into this topic is compounded by the absence of data on particular movements — for example, the movement of the armed forces and prison personnel for the purpose of setting up large scale agricultural organisations. The exact nature of planned resettlement movements of peasants is also difficult to understand and recent disquiet led the World Bank to delay funding large scale relocation programs of Chinese peasants into Qinghai and Tibet (World Bank 1999) until it was satisfied with the aims and intentions of the project.

Considerable research is being conducted into internal movement in general, by both Chinese agencies (Chinese Academy of Social Sciences,

Shanghai Academy of Social Sciences, Economic Restructuring Commission, Research Centre for Rural Economy, the State Science and Technology Commission, academic researchers) and overseas researchers. International funding sources (Ford Foundation, overseas governments, etc) are involved in many projects. However, it largely seems to be 'nationality neutral'. For example, one large study on occupational mobility being undertaken in the late 1990s by the State Science and Technology Commission in cooperation with the Norwegian government has involved consultation with 15 Chinese Ministries to elicit their policy concerns. The question of the movement of minorities did not emerge, according to a spokesperson, because 'their numbers mean that they constitute only a small part of the flows and their problems are no different to those facing other occupational migrants' (personal interview, 1995).

Thus, some see the nationality aspect of mobility as insignificant as minorities comprise only 8.04 per cent of China's total population, or less than 100 million people. Compared to the estimates of overall surplus rural labour, the potential movement of people belonging to minorities is numerically less significant. Nevertheless, the size of the minority population is large in terms of world populations and should be an important focus for research.

Another reason for the lack of research is the political sensitivity associated with the topic. The issue of minorities, in general, is highly sensitive given the separatist aspirations of people in both the Tibet Autonomous Region and the Xinjiang Uyghur Autonomous Region. The emergence of an organised secessionist movement in Xinjiang has generated a strong response from the central government and political activities are dealt with harshly. The recent movement of Inner Mongolia's former governor to Tibet has generated concern about the government's intentions regarding the maintenance of Tibetan identity. Other areas, including the Inner Mongolian Autonomous Region, also occasionally have political unrest that is perceived as destabilising. We also need to recognise that since China's opening up there have been more and more technocrats entering into the power structures who have little knowledge about Chinese ethnic minorities. To their way of thinking 'science always has the final say' and a homogeneous China, not a diversified one, will help promote the 'modernisation' process. They argue that in the face of inadequate resources, ethnicity and gender issues should sometimes give way to more urgent economic concerns. Some politicians say that 'human rights issues in China are no more than getting enough to eat', or the 'right to exist'.

But issues associated with minorities are crucial and occupy a critical place in the Chinese scheme of things for three reasons. First, minorities occupy 62 per cent of the land area. Second, over 90 per cent of the border regions of China are occupied by minorities. From a geopolitical perspective, Inner Mongolia, Tibet and Xinjiang are very significant and any separatist activities pose a major threat. Third, 'by far the greater proportion, sometimes even the whole, of forestry resources, mining resources, precious medical resources, tropical crops and bases of animal husbandry industries are located in national minority regions' (Postiglione 1992, p. 21).

The neo-classical orthodoxy that dominates economic policy ignores 'macro-social forces and local traditions, experiences and identities' (Castles 1999, p. 6). But we cannot ignore these aspects and all changes should serve human beings, not the reverse. In other words, for humanity's sake, ethnicity, local languages, rituals, performances, etc are all usable resources in the development or transformation process and they are not things to be conquered or eliminated. The latter approach was embodied in the 'modernisation' theory of development popular in the 1960s and 1970s but it has fallen into disfavour in many parts of the world. More complex processes are now seen as operating and there is scope for elements of the 'old' to survive while elements of the 'new' are added. Some groups are even opting to return to past ways of life as a means of survival.

The discourse on race did not emerge till the twentieth century in China but then it was officially abolished in 1949 and anthropology departments in universities were suspended. The official view was of equality and the views of anthropologists and others were criticised. Anthropologists were accused during the anti-rightist campaigns of the 1950s of having used disrespectful anthropometric methods that insulted the national minorities. It was also suspected that many of their studies were meant to prove racist ideas of minority inferiority (Dikotter 1992, p. 191).

Anthropology departments have re-emerged but anthropology is still treated very warily and more attention is focused on sociology. Mainstream departments shy away from minority issues. At a more practical level, Professor Zhang Tianlu, China's pre-eminent researcher on minority population issues feels that the lack of minority research has two explanations.[4] First, the lack of previous work in this area meant there is a lack of materials, both statistics and past examples of work on migration. Second, the difficulty of conducting migration research is widely acknowledged but in the case of minorities the often low levels of education and language complications make it even more challenging. This means that different techniques must be invoked to collect the data. To this end a *Sample Survey of Ethnic Minority Migrants* was conducted in 1996-97 and the data from the 1628 interviews form the basis of much of the discussion in

---

[4] Professor Zhang Tianlu stated this at the Minority Migration Workshop held as part of this project in Beijing on 5-6 October, 1999.

Chapters 5 to 8.

Initial inquiries for this project in 1994-95 revealed that there was some hesitancy to discuss the issue of mobility as minority populations in autonomous regions were expected to remain in the regions where special policies were in place to enhance their socio-economic status. Theoretically, as for the rest of China's population, minorities were not free to move without permission. However, market reforms have changed the official position. The most recent migratory flows of minorities have come about as a result of these reforms as well as the breakdown of the registration control system. There are seven or eight levels of administration in China for each location and this registration system is administered at the bottom level — the grassroots village level in rural areas and the street/district level in urban areas.

THE IMPLICATIONS OF MINORITY MIGRATION

Han Chinese started moving in increasing numbers, in response to the factors discussed above, in the early 1980s. This appears to have been earlier than for minorities. This is borne out by the 1990 census in relation to movement for a period of longer than one year or where there has been a change of *hukou*. These data show that between 1985 and 1990, minorities accounted for 6.5 per cent of the total number of moves, compared with their 8.04 per cent of the total population. Short-term movement is much harder to quantify, as it is not captured in the census. It may account for most minority movement and therefore reliance on census data may give an inaccurate picture.[5] The absence of other data makes it difficult to detect the patterns as will be discussed in Chapter 4.

The movement of minorities within regions and to other provinces will have major socio-economic impacts in the areas of education, health, employment, housing, welfare, the environment and intercultural relations. Movement from a region where identity is closely related to membership of an ethnic group and adherence to the group's values, language, practices, customs and religious beliefs to a region where this ethnic contact is altered or limited and where the socio-cultural environment is different will have consequences for the ethnic or national identity of minorities. People who move to an environment which is different from their traditional environment, may lose aspects of their culture, in favour of the prevailing

---

[5] This view was put by Professor Hao Shi Yuan of the Institute of Nationality Studies, Chinese Academy of Social Sciences, at the Minority Migration Workshop conducted in Beijing on 5-6 October, 1999.

culture of the destination, through the process of acculturation or through intermarriage. On the other hand, their ethnic identity may be strengthened by the very fact of being removed from their homeland. The latter is a common trend in the era of globalisation as improved communication and travel enable people to maintain links with their homeland.

In addition, enclaves of minority ethnic groups have sprung up in large cities and towns and they act as reservoirs of minority cultures. There were 414 036 people belonging to minority nationalities in Beijing in 1990, compared with 285 000 in 1982. Enclaves may serve to reinforce minority cultures and identity, especially if members are excluded from services such as education, health and welfare. At the same time, social transformations occur within enclaves as people begin to intermarry and the influences of the surrounding environment infiltrate. Even without enclaves, the very presence of increasing numbers of ethnic minority people within China's large cities is often coming as an unwelcome change. Migrants have the potential for alienating the existing residents of towns or cities as the latter resent the intrusion of other people whose culture, especially language, religion and values, they do not understand. The response from the authorities in terms of access to education and other services, as well as scope for the emergence of ethnic institutions, are important aspects to be investigated in China's cities.

At the same time, the movement of Han Chinese into minority regions may assist in the process of economic development but it may also operate to weaken the culture of minority groups. On the other hand, some Han Chinese have changed their nationality, to become part of a minority nationality, in order to benefit from special minority policies or for other reasons. Intermarriage and social and economic interaction may operate over time to bring about integration. The culture that emerges may be a hybrid of a number of cultures or the culture of the majority. Where little mixing occurs, for reasons of ethnic, religious or cultural difference, the minority culture is more likely to survive and flourish. Thus, the impact of economic development on minority identities is an important aspect in the social development of China.

The nature of government policies in relation to the administration of areas where minorities prevail will be a strong determinant of what happens to minority groups and their cultures. Policies that are universalist in scope may lead to homogenisation and unification. Alternatively, they may lead to greater unrest and a stronger push for independence. Policies that are flexible and that provide for local autonomy may be seen as allowing or promoting differential levels of economic and social development, which in turn may also fuel unrest and secessionist aspirations. Alternatively, autonomy and localised policies, which acknowledge and provide for cultural diversity, within a framework of sustainable development, may lead to less unrest and a greater level of satisfaction with the central government. These are all issues that need to be examined within the context of the rapid social as well as economic transformations that are occurring within China. How these issues are dealt with will be an important indicator of the future direction of the nation as a whole.

AIMS OF THIS BOOK

The Chinese Government is permitting the increasingly free movement of people for both economic development and the improvement of individual living standards. This is manifested in the loosening of controls over movement and the overt policies adopted by some administrators to promote movements for economic gain. Many movements are essential for the economic survival of people living in poverty stricken areas but other movements are not of low-income people but of people at the upper end of the income spectrum. They are moving to increase their income, for better opportunities and/or for a better quality of life.

Neo-classical theory predicts that people will only move if they are better off but this theory is now outdated. It is inevitable that not all the outcomes will be positive. This research is designed to analyse some of the processes at work in internal migration and to discuss policies and conditions conducive to the development of positive and healthy social, economic and political outcomes. The focus is on the movement of minorities from a social, economic and ethnic identification perspective. Migration is only one of the elements leading to social transformations. The development of high speed communications, new technologies and goods, consumerism, tourism and trade are all opening up areas that were previously relatively closed in China. So separating the impacts is not easy and not even desirable. Migration is just one of the forces at work, in this period of globalisation, that is bringing major changes to many societies.

It is neither possible nor desirable to treat minorities as a homogeneous group. There are 55 identified minority nationalities and they differ in terms of many factors including population size, location and patterns of livelihood, nature of identification of the group, proportion in autonomous regions, proximity and relationships to other nationalities including Han, history of migration to the region and contacts with nationality members outside of China, and culture, especially religion, language and literacy. The three national minorities, Mongols, Tibetans and Uyghurs, that form the core of this work were selected for quite specific reasons. First, they are located in the north and west, border areas that have attracted little attention from minority researchers. Second, they are all groups where there is a considerable degree of instability and therefore there is particular interest. Third, they are very diverse in terms of the factors identified above, particularly levels of education, lifestyle, degree of historical interaction with other nationalities, especially Han, and interaction with other regions. Therefore, they cover a spectrum of minorities and will illustrate a range of forces at work in relation to migration, ethnicity and education. Fourth, they are three of the five early peoples recognized by Sun Yat-sen, the revolutionary pioneer of modern China. Therefore they have important historical implications as well.

The aims of this book are as follows:

- to attempt to quantify the overall level of minority movement *vis à vis* total mobility — a complex task given the range, scale, direction and timing of movements, problems of definition and absence of adequate data on short term moves;
- to analyse the relationships between migration and educational processes;
- to consider conditions and policies conducive to the development of positive and healthy outcomes for minority migrant households;
- to increase understanding of the effect of movement on the social, economic and ethnic status of migrant family households.

Macro- and micro-structures interact with each other at all levels and together they can be examined 'as facets of an overarching *migratory process*' (Castles and Miller 1998, p. 27). In order to understand all aspects of the migratory process it is important to ask the following types of questions:

1. What economic, social, demographic, environmental and/or political factors have changed so that people want or are forced to leave their area of origin?
2. What factors have led to opportunities opening up in the destination area/s?
3. What role does education policy play in patterns of movement? Education is given a deliberate focus as it is commonly a vehicle through which ethnic groups seek to achieve social and occupational mobility even while preserving their own linguistic and cultural identities.
4. How do social networks and other links develop between areas providing information, means of travel and other cultural capital?
5. What legal, political, economic and social structures and practices exist or emerge to regulate/manage migration and settlement?
6. How do migrants settle/become integrated and what are the impacts on the receiving area?
7. How does out-migration change the sending area and what links develop

between sending and receiving areas?

These questions formed the starting point for our research. As it turned out they were over-ambitious and some aspects have so far not been addressed. In particular, issues of social networks and impacts of out-migration on sending areas remain almost untouched and need to be the subject of further research.

DEFINITIONS AND CONCEPTS

Movement rather than migration

The focus on movement, rather than migration which implies permanent movement, is consistent with the emerging literature on migration systems and processes. Much of this literature does not attempt to differentiate between permanent and temporary movers as there is often a high level of crossover between the two. Any distinction may be arbitrary and this is the case in China, though the different policies for the two groups are extremely important. Many people have called themselves temporary migrants to circumvent the administrative *hukou* system but had the intention of being or becoming permanent.

The Chinese census and other data sources use various definitions which are included in the text and therefore require clarification. Permanent migrants are defined in the 1990 census as those who have changed their place of official registration (*hukou*) or who have been in the destination for more than 12 months. Temporary migrants are defined as those who have been away from their place of official registration for more than one year. All other people who are not in their place of official registration are not counted as migrants but are counted at their place of official registration, though they may have moved. Thus a clear distinction still remains in China between permanent and temporary and this is reflected in Hoy's approach (1996).

Migrant and non-migrant households

The term migrant households is used to define households that have relocated to their current address. Households were selected as migrant households if they had moved, regardless of their original intention or their pattern of movement. Salt (1996) stresses the need to include non-migrants in studies of migration and to ask the crucial question — 'why don't more people move, especially from poor areas?' In order to be able to understand the operation of networks, continuing links with the source and the impact of movements on non-migrant family members, households that have not moved should be included.

Ethnic and national identity

It is necessary to take into account two important facts when discussing the concept of ethnicity. First, China has a long history of literature that has lasted thousands of years and second it has a highly centralised state form. Pre-Opium War Chinese cosmology centres on the very traditional version of *wenhua* (moral and cultural transformation) which emphasises the levels and process of excellence as well as the embellishment of literacy, humanity and tranquillity (Ping 1995, pp. 127-54). From the classical mentor Confucius to the Ming Emporer Zhu Yuanzhang, Han Chinese mainstream advocates have tended to judge people in terms of their cultural accomplishments and obedience to social norms, rather than their ethnicity. The *zhongguo* or Central Kingdom (the literal translation for China) means to be at the centre of Chinese culture and in a position of 'moral authority', without any reference to racial purity or superiority.

It was only after the defeat of the Chinese naval fleet in the Sino-Japanese War in 1894 and other humiliating historical events, that western notions of 'ethnicity', together with 'race', 'nation', 'state' and 'citizenship', began to enter into Han Chinese social discourses and give agency to social transformations that followed. The Chinese notion of 'ethnicity' has been chosen for groups of people by rulers and literati in the modern discourse of the nation-state, with regard to both Sino-foreign (external) and Han-minority (internal) relations. This 'nativisation' process of a genealogy of foreign notions and concepts is well advanced and is very much in a mode of directed imagination and practices. That is, it is informed by decisions and instructions from, and policies made and movements launched by, the central government.

The definition of ethnic identity is an even more complex issue than usual in China as there are two definitions: self-definition by the ethnic group itself and definition by the state. To take an example, in his discussion of the Hui people, Gladney (1996, pp. 66-78) describes three bodies of theory that have been put forward to explain how the Hui regard themselves as an ethnic group and why the state chose to recognise them as a nationality despite the wide cultural and religious diversity of Hui communities. The typology of theories is the Chinese-Stalinist, the cultural-primordialist and the circumstantialist-instrumentalist.

Under the Chinese-Stalinist approach, common language, economy, locality and culture should be co-present, though in reality this does not apply to any of the Chinese minority groups. Actually, what Stalin was talking about was 'nation', which is a capitalist phenomenon, rather than 'ethnicity' (Stalin 1953, p. 349).[6] Second, while minorities were seen as equal to the Han, and hence they were called 'nationalities', they were also seen by Han Chinese as representatives of earlier forms of society or 'living fossils', the cultural-primordialist approach, and they were perceived as aiming to achieve the level of the Han Chinese. Third, the circumstantialist-instrumentalist approach sees ethnicity as a 'dependent' variable where ethnicity is reactive to factors in the environment, economy and political atmosphere, but it fails to acknowledge the power that ethnicity possesses of itself.

Gladney (1996, p. 76) concludes that none of these three bodies of theory accurately describes the situation facing the Hui nationality in China and he poses a dialogical interpretation. For ethnicity to be a reality in China, Gladney argues that it requires two elements. First, it requires a primordial loyalty to one's ethnic group that stems from a group's basic agreement upon and attachment to an idea of shared descent which constitutes the basis of an ethnic group's identity. Second, interaction with the socio-political context causes these loyalties to become explicit, salient and empowered — the socio-economic and political context affects ethnicity.

A similar process can be seen to have occurred with the formation of the Uyghur nationality. The Uyghur are descended from Mongol migrants and various Turkic-speaking Muslim groups but the widespread use of the term Uyghur did not occur till the 1930s. The term conceals a great deal of diversity and factionalism based on religion, geography, location and politics. The Uyghur nationality is, in effect, an artificial construct of the Communist state but, having assumed the title, Uyghurs are now modifying this identity for themselves (Hoy 1996).

Minority nationality/ies

The Chinese word for nationalities is *minzu,* meaning 'a people' and 'an ethnic group'. The word was taken directly from the Japanese term *minzoku* at the start of the twentieth century. The long stay by the leader of the republican movement, Dr Sun Yat-sen, in Japan was largely responsible for the widespread adoption of the term. He categorised 'Five Peoples of China': the Han, Man (Manchu), Meng (Mongols), Zang (Tibetan) and Hui (including all Muslims in China, now divided into the Uyghurs, Kazaks, Hui, and so on) (Gladney 1993, pp. 171-92). Mackerras (1994, pp. 6-7) incorrectly argues that *min* and *zu* were combined by Westerners in 1882 and that the term was a 'product of Western notions of nation and nationality'.

---

[6] The Soviet version of *nacia* is outlined by Joseph Stalin as the four commons: common language, common territory, common economic life, and common psychological makeup.

According to Mackerras, nationality or *minzu* means an ethnic group 'forming part of one or more political nations'.

In all of the nation-states of China in the twentieth century, Han have been the most populous ethnic group/race/nationality but there have also been a number of much smaller groups of people living inside China's borders. These are defined as minority nationalities.[7] By 1979, 55 groups had been recognised as having minority nationality status, along with the majority Han Chinese. Over 400 groups actually applied for recognition as a minority nationality after 1949 and while many were not successful they still have features which identify them from other groups. Their national/ethnic identity while not officially recognised is still evident in many aspects of their lives.

Assimilation/absorption/pluralism/fusion/integration/ amalgamation/hybridisation

A wide range of terms are used in various countries to describe both the status and functioning of ethnic groups. *Assimilation* is at one end of the spectrum and describes a situation where members of minority ethnic groups 'have absorbed the characteristics of the dominant group to the exclusion of their own and become indistinguishable from members of the majority' (Dreyer 1976, p. 2). There are various degrees of assimilation but on the whole it is perceived as a negative phenomenon, especially where it is forced. In China, the corresponding term *tonghua* means 'to make the same'. *Absorption*, a similar concept, is resisted in a state in which ethnic groups exist freely in a situation of mutual respect, equality and interdependence. *Pluralism* characterises the other, more liberal, end of the spectrum.

Fusion exists somewhere in between the two and implies a 'process whereby two or more cultures combine to produce another, that is significantly different from the parent cultures' (Thornberry 1987, p. 4). It contrasts with assimilation as the process is voluntary and non-exploitative of all groups. The Chinese word for fusion or amalgamation is *ronghe* and represents the 'highest formation in the development of nationalities and relationships among nationalities' (Alatan *et al.* 1989, p. 205). This is very 'much in line with the Marxist concept of an eventual disappearance of different nationalities after the establishment of communist society', when nationality demarcations will no longer exist (Mackerras 1994, p. 8). This concept pertained until the 1980s and its continued existence is debated later in the conclusion.

---

[7] The process of identifying minority nationalities will be outlined in Chapter 3.

The term *integration* is widely used in other countries in the study of minorities and its equivalent in Chinese is *zhenghe* (literally means 'to come together as a whole'). The term implies a maintenance of ethnic identity and even boundaries, within a wider context of willingness and ability to participate, equally, in the overall social system. Integration is not necessarily a one-way process and political or social events may lead to a reversal of an apparent move towards integration. Both Dreyer (1976) and Seymour (1976) address the need for coherence in a large nation-state such as China and they see integration as the means by which this could occur. In fact, either explicitly or implicitly, both recognise that the 'degree to which the performance of a system corresponds with the will and willingness of a people to take part in it is one criterion for evaluating the extent to which integration has occurred' (Mackerras 1994, p. 10). Changes in the relationships both within and between nationalities in China are an important part of this study as migration is one means of bringing about rapid changes in ethnic/nationality identity and inter-ethnic/nationality relationships.

Amalgamation is a commonly used term in China and Chinese scholars sometimes talk about successful *amalgamation*. This is not a term used in this book as both it and *hydridisation* imply the development of static mixtures of ethnicity/culture and the subjugation of one to another. Cultures and ethnicities are constantly changing and adjusting and are highly individualised. Moreover, people may choose their ethnic identity — as a result of intermarriages, location or other factors (such as government policies).

Autonomy/autonomous regions

China currently has five autonomous regions (Guangzi, Inner Mongolia, Tibet, Xinjiang and Yunnan), 30 autonomous prefectures and 113 autonomous counties in other provinces. Together they cover around 64 per cent of China's territory and the total population of these regions constitutes about one tenth of China's population, though less than half of these belong to minorities. In all approximately 70 million people belonging to minorities live in autonomous areas.

The notion of autonomy stems from imperial times in China. Early Muslim settlers residing in Tang and Song China for the purposes of trade 'were allowed or required to live in separate, discrete quarters known as *fan fang* (foreign zones)'. These zones elected their own Arabic officials who in turn exercised 'considerable autonomy in judicial matters' (Dicks 1990, p. 355). The practice of granting autonomy to minority groups continued under the Ming dynasty and there is evidence that Muslim, Tibetan and Mongol communities operated fairly autonomously provided they accepted Qing rule and did not threaten the integrity of the imperial state.

Autonomy as an 'institutionally vague concept' was re-introduced by Mao Zedong in 1949 when he changed his mind about minority people having the right to independence (Zheng 1999, p. 70). Articles 50-53 of the constitution of the Chinese People's Political Consultative Congress of 1949 spelled out the conditions of autonomy, and subsequent constitutions of 1975, 1978 and 1982 elaborated on the first constitution. Some form of independence for autonomous regions is implied but the degree of autonomy has fluctuated with changing politics. Phan (1996, p. 107) traces the development of policies on autonomy since 1949 and concludes that in spite of the changes to the constitution and the Law on Regional National Autonomy (LRNA) 1984 the powers of autonomous regions 'vis-à-vis the central Party-state are quite weak'. The LRNA is restrictive in effect and is designed to 'curb any potential excesses in the exercise of autonomy' (Phan 1996, pp. 95-96).

The creation of autonomous regions/areas acknowledged cultural, ethnic and linguistic diversity and enabled the appearance of independence in the determination of local policies and priorities. Autonomous administrative bodies have been required in their administration and many day-to-day activities to fall into line with party policies and principles. This is the case at all levels — regions, prefectures and counties (banners) — even though they are classed as independent. This is ensured in a variety of ways: only nine (one-third) of the articles in the 1984 law are without restrictive clauses that limit autonomous regions' self-government to state plans and/or other forms of administrative restrictions; the appointment of a Han person as party secretary to autonomous regions where he or she is number one in terms of political position; and the provision for sending in technical and skilled personnel gives the state the 'necessary pretext for relocating Han Chinese and PLA [People's Liberation Army] units' into geopolitically strategic areas (Phan 1996, p. 100).

The nine articles that do allow for autonomous policies deal with innocuous or 'soft' issues (Phan 1996, p. 107). These issues include education, cultural development, family planning, management of the floating population, technological/scientific advancement, health care and disease prevention, sports and physical fitness, interregional cultural exchanges and environmental protection. Laws regarding age at marriage, property rights, family patterns and educational participation, for example, can be developed to suit the region but increasingly central influence is being felt in these as well. While most autonomous regions were set up in the 1950s, there were at least eight new counties established in the 1990s (in Qinghai, Sichuan and Guizhou). According to Gladney (1993, p. 186), this reflected 'a real desire for greater independence from central jurisdiction'.

The Communist Party of China (CPC) also established Han cities for administrative purposes in autonomous regions as part of leadership and assistance from state organs at higher levels as specified in articles 54 to 66 of the 1984 law. More advanced eastern regions were also enlisted to assist with economic and technical development. The aim was to further the development of roads and other infrastructure and to provide an administrative layer, which included varying proportions of minority nationalities. The argument was often put in the early years that Han Chinese were required as administrators as there were insufficient educated people belonging to ethnic minorities to train and hire as cadres. Cadres had to be party members and so a commitment to the CPC and selection for membership of the party were both required. These articles gave the central government the authority to send in professionals, managers, teachers and trainers, doctors, scientists and technicians. The PLA supplied many of these professionals.

The movement of Han Chinese, other than government officials, skilled workers and army personnel, into autonomous regions has also occurred. This often involved people lacking *hukou*. Many of these people had trouble surviving elsewhere, while others moved as a result of natural catastrophes. Still others moved to take advantage of business opportunities in newly developing regions. All have had the effect of changing the nationality mix of the population in autonomous regions.

Modernisation and social transformation

What is the relationship between integration and modernisation, as many minority nationalities move between geographic areas and especially to cities such as Beijing, Shanghai and Guangzhou? Seymour (1976) wonders whether the factors involved in integration are a gauge of the success of 'modernisation'. Modernisation is usually defined as the process by which societies are transformed as a result of the impact of the scientific and technological revolution. The term was originally used to imply notions of increased human control over the natural landscape and the displacement of traditional beliefs and values by 'truths of utility, calculation, and science' (Rudolph and Rudolph 1967, p. 3). Both of these notions have now fallen by the wayside as, for example, many industrialised societies strive to redress issues such as the environmental damage caused by their populations and economic activity, and as religions continue to flourish in 'modern' societies such as the United States. Value judgments about what is 'modern' and what constitutes 'modernisation' were made much more warily in the late 1990s than in the heyday of development studies and theory in the 1960s and 1970s.

Moreover, modernisation was often linked with homogenisation whereas a very noticeable feature of the late twentieth century was the strength of local forces and the emergence of culture and ethnicity as vital elements for many communities. Localisation and increasing heterogeneity, rather then homogeneity, are now acknowledged as common trends resulting from globalisation. Thus, today, a more useful and appropriate substitute concept is that of *social transformation* where societies are not seen as moving from a static 'tradition-bound' state at one end of the spectrum to a 'modern' state at the other end. Instead the process of social change is complex, convoluted and multi-directional. Political, economic and social forces interact to affect groups in different ways and some elements may remain unchanged while other aspects of the life of the society may alter. Aspects that existed in the past may re-emerge in response to current needs and pressures, such as various forms of worship in China.

Migration represents a process of speeding up the interactions and change processes as not only the movers but also the people left behind become drawn into a new web of factors that affect their lives. The term *social transformation* has been around for a long time but its use in relation to the changes in communities/individuals, in place of the term 'development', began to occur in the 1980s and 1990s. The term *socialist transformation* has been in use in China since 1949 and is quite different. For example, as Shaw (1989, pp. 55-57) points out, ethnology in China, after the founding of the People's Republic, contributed to:

> the identification of nationalities and the democratic reform and socialist transformation in ethnic regions. ... In the regions where a lot of remnants of the primitive commune were retained, the ethnic minorities were helped to develop their economy and culture and transit to socialism directly, with no social reforms being introduced.

OUTLINE

Chapter 2 addresses the theoretical background on migration theories and reviews the literature on internal migration in China. It also provides a profile of the demographic and spatial background of minorities, covering their identification, numbers, location and overall patterns of movement. Chapter 3 on the social and political background of minorities outlines the major policy developments, including education policies, since 1949. Chapter 4 provides a background to minority mobility by analysing the data from the 1990 census on minority and Han movement (as defined in the census) between 1985 and 1990. It describes the broad trends and sets the scene for the case studies.

The following three chapters are largely based on the *Sample Survey of Ethnic Minority Migrants* and focus on patterns of mobility and the outcomes for Mongolians, Tibetans and Uyghurs. Chapter 5 covers the Inner Mongolian Autonomous Region and discusses the complexity of the situation that has emerged from extensive Han in-migration over the last 100 years. Mongolian identity has undergone a revival especially since 1976 and the end of the Cultural Revolution, and the struggle between these forces and the forces of 'sinification' is ongoing. Economic change and migration are adding new dimensions. Chapter 6 investigates the movement of Tibetans. The Tibet Autonomous Region was created in 1965, much later than the Inner Mongolian Autonomous Region (1947). Economic and social changes began to occur in the 1980s and early forms of migration were largely organised and military movements. In the last decade, in particular, spontaneous movement has escalated as well as more organised outward movement of Tibetans for education and training. Education is being used by the central government as a means of integrating Tibet into China and the impacts will be considered. Chapter 7 provides an overview of Xinjiang Autonomous Region, the interaction between Han and minorities since 1950 and the increased internal movement of minorities since 1980. This has now spilled over into inter-provincial movement of Uyghurs, in particular, to various parts of China where a process of 'colonisation' is occurring. The movement of Uyghurs into Beijing in recent years is evident and this is taken up in greater detail in the next chapter.

Chapter 8 provides an overview of the growth of Beijing, the role of migration in this growth and the socio-economic impacts of minority mobility to Beijing. This chapter draws together material from the sample survey as well as other material collected by the authors over the last few years. The discussion of educational outcomes provides a glimpse into the ways in which policies are changing to cope with migrant children and the incremental way in which major policy adjustments are brought about.

The concluding chapter analyses the findings of this study and discusses the major educational and identity issues emerging as a result of mobility. The dynamic nature of identity will be highlighted and the role of migration and education in contributing to this dynamism will be discussed. This will provide a new direction for research in China as it moves away from the static type of anthropological study that is normally undertaken in relation to ethnic minorities and provides a template for an interdisciplinary approach to the role of migration in social transformation.

2. Migration research background

The study of human migration has been undertaken in the past by geographers, sociologists, economists, demographers and others. Each discipline brings a particular orientation but most of the work has been carried out within the context of an empirically-based, hypothesis-testing approach to social science (Cadwallader 1992). The study contributing to the present book incorporates sociological, ethnographic and geographic angles. We argue that an interdisciplinary approach is essential for understanding complex migration flows. Disciplines look at different aspects of population mobility, and 'a full understanding requires contributions from all of them' (Castles and Miller 1998, p. 19). The Institute of Nationality Studies (INS), Chinese Academy of Social Sciences (CASS) and the China National Institute of Educational Research (CNIER) joined with researchers from the Centre for Asia Pacific Social Transformation Studies (CAPSTRANS), University of Wollongong, Australia, to conduct this research.[1]

THEORETICAL FRAMEWORK

The theoretical framework is based on a number of perspectives: social mobility, modernisation and spatial analysis of migration flows. These perspectives have, generally speaking, been developed from studies in social, political and cultural contexts quite different to that prevailing in contemporary China. While each provides valuable insights and starting points for the design of the present study no single approach adequately explains the transformation process involving minority mobility in China. They do, however, serve to guide the analysis and findings presented through this book. But first, the major theories of migration are considered and their applicability discussed.

---

[1] The project falls under the Migration and Multicultural Societies Program of the Centre for Asia Pacific Social Transformation Studies at the University of Wollongong and the UNESCO Management of Social Transformations (MOST) project, being coordinated by Wollongong University.

1. Neo-classical equilibrium approach

In the neo-classical equilibrium or social structural approach, migration is conceptualised as an individual response to unevenly distributed opportunities. Internal migration and international migration are seen as caused by geographic differences in both supply and demand of labour and other resources. Regions with a large endowment of labour relative to capital have a low equilibrium market wage, while regions with a limited endowment of labour are characterised by a high market wage. The resulting differential in wages causes workers to move from low-wage regions to high-wage regions (Todaro 1969, 1976, Massey *et al.* 1993).

This theory pre-supposes freedom of movement which of course was not the case in China till the 1980s. By the late 1990s there were still controls but people either got around the controls or ignored them. The dual-economy concept is used within this perspective to categorise areas or countries by their level of development: the modern sector (urban areas) and traditional sectors (rural areas). Dual-economy theorists assert that internal migration is caused by a demand for labour that is inherent in the economic structure of developed regions or nations (Brown and Sanders 1981, Piore 1979). Unable to meet the demand from within their own boundaries, they must attract migrants to fill positions left vacant or unwanted by local residents. Thus, the demand for migrant labour may spring from a shortage of local people wanting to undertake the employment that is available and/or from the unwillingness of employers to offer higher wages, as this will upset the wages hierarchy and lead to structural inflation.

Migrant workers often move in to fill these bottom-level jobs. They do not consider themselves to be at the bottom of the occupational hierarchy, even if they are working at the lowest level in the labour market, since they often compare themselves with people in their place of origin or their own situation prior to migration. Thus, Goldscheider (1987) argues that the motivation to migrate from rural to urban areas is primarily to find work and the relative absence of employment opportunities in the place of origin, compared with the destination, is the major explanatory factor for migration patterns. In the case of minorities, this may be an overwhelming factor as many minority groups inhabit poor areas in the northern, western and southern areas of China. But other research has already shown that it is not necessarily the poorest, the least educated or the unemployed who are migrating in China (Sun 1998).

2. Migration as a means of pursuing higher social and economic status

Sociologists emphasise social mobility as the most important motivation for migration (Lipset and Zetterberg 1967, De Jong and Gardner 1981). They see frustration with the educational and occupational opportunities that are available in rural areas or less developed regions as a major motivation for migration to urban or more developed regions. The possible improvement in social status may be one element but there may also be the desire to improve both income and consumption levels.

Prior to the introduction of economic reform in China, peasants were at the bottom of the job hierarchy. Their aspirations for improved social status were frustrated by the lack of opportunities for advancement, including educational and occupational advancement, in the rural areas. However, they were unable to move due to tight government control policies. Since the early 1980s, the loosening of controls and improved information flows have stimulated the desire among many people for improved social status. Migration may offer the prospect of social mobility. For others in China it may simply provide a means of survival in an otherwise dire situation. Alternately, it may be a planned move to achieve some wider economic or political objective.

For minorities, migration may provide the opportunity for personal social and economic advancement, especially from areas that are generally perceived as 'backward' by the rest of the Chinese population. The provision of opportunities for education elsewhere and the desire to acquire better paying jobs in more affluent coastal and urban regions, may provide the motivation for some individuals. The promise of a better future, within the framework of the Han Chinese society, may be enough to encourage some people to take up opportunities elsewhere. For example, the provision of high school, cadre and tertiary education for many Tibetan young people in Beijing and other places outside of Tibet is prevalent. Some parents may see this as a means of ensuring that their children have a better future in the current system of government. The possible 'assimilationist' aspect of such a policy may be barely questioned by them and the opportunity for 'outside' experience may prevail as the strongest motivating force.

The actual ability to relocate may often be conditioned by the structural context and the behavioural response of individuals. In the case of minorities, the cultural context is crucially important as migration may involve a diminution of their culture, language, customs, religion, etc. The political and legal framework of the society, as well as social structures, operate to promote or discourage migration — more often the latter. Social structure both constrains and enables, while simultaneously being reproduced and transformed by individuals.

3. Migration as a part of the modernisation process

Modernisation theorists point out that one of the important factors in the modernisation process is the contact between relatively modernised societies and relatively non-modernised societies through which information and technologies are transferred from the former to the latter (So 1990). Sending areas of migrants are often relatively less developed than receiving areas. Modernisation results in the enhancement of personal freedom, which in turn engenders the breaking of ties with traditional areas of origin (Zelinsky 1971). Thus, personal preferences and the enhancement of personal freedom become the major motivations for a desire for spatial mobility.

In the case of minorities, the tension between wanting to remain with the ethnic group and retain the cultural, linguistic and other elements that this entails and the pull of a modern environment, liberated from the cultural baggage of one's ethnic group, may be enormous. On the other hand, migration may not represent a break with tradition and culture but patterns of movement may be established that strive to ensure the maintenance of tradition as well as absorption into the 'modern' world.

The migration of some individuals of a minority group may lead to the development of the origin as well as the personal advancement of migrants at the destination. The links that are established, the remittances and information that are returned to the origin and the return of migrants intermittently or permanently after a period, may all lead to the development of the source region or of households in the source. Conversely, the departure of young workers may adversely effect development in the place of origin and dependency theorists see the emergence of a cycle of stunted development in sending areas. The balance between these two sets of forces and the way to maximise the gains from out-migration is growing as an important area of study.

4. Migration systems approach

The migration systems approach incorporates a wide range of factors and takes into account the role of history, institutions, family networks and migration chains and political and social structures, as well as individual motivational factors. This approach lays great stress on historical and institutional factors as well as individual and social factors. It has developed in response to criticisms of the neo-classical approach, with its undue emphasis on the individual and its disregard for structural and historical factors. A migration system is constituted by a number of regions which exchange relatively large numbers of migrants with each other. It might consist of only two regions (or countries), but it is more useful to try to include all regions (or countries) linked by large migration flows.

The migration systems approach sets out to provide a conceptual framework which includes both ends of the flow and studies all dimensions of the relations between emigration and immigration countries/regions. The model recognises the close links between flows of capital, commodities, ideas and people, and that such flows rise out of historical linkages (such as military presence, political influence, trade or cultural penetration). The links can be categorised as state-to-state or region-to-region relations, mass culture connections and family and social networks. The conceptual model goes through the main stages of migration (the emigration decision process, the exit process, the entry process and the adjustment process) and indicates the main factors to be considered at each stage. These include such matters as legal barriers, labour market conditions, settlement opportunities and community formation. It provides a list of the factors and relationships that need to be investigated in order to analyse a specific migratory movement. This theoretical approach to migration most informs this research. The contemporary migration of minorities cannot be seen in isolation from the past. However, emphasis will be placed on the present patterns of movement in order to explain the impacts of market reform and structural factors on a selection of minority groups.

5. Migration and ethnicity

Though little study has been conducted on 'ethnicity' in China, there is an impressive amount of literature on this topic in the United States, Great Britain and elsewhere. Theories of ethnicity have centered on the following aspects: the individual versus the group; the contents of an ethnic group's identity versus its boundary; the primordial 'gut' feeling of an identity versus its instrumental expression, and ethnicity as an all-inclusive general theory versus ethnicity as a limited approach to particular problems (Banks 1996). A wide range of studies have examined the impact on ethnicity of a range of processes, one of which is migration.

In China, no such studies have been conducted and therefore this research is exploratory in both content and scope. Most work carried out in China on ethnicity has been conducted in particular locations, and while ethnicity is far from static, the study groups have been stationary. The Barth (1969) approach to ethnicity is useful in China's case as it emphasises 'the social organization of culture difference'. This has been reconfirmed by other work on the anthropology of ethnicity 25 years later: '(1) ethnicity is a form of social organization; this implies that (2) the critical focus for investigation becomes the ethnic boundary that defines the group rather than the cultural stuff that it encloses; the critical feature of ethnic groups is (3) the characteristic of self-ascription and ascription by others' (Vermeulen and Govers 1994, p. 1). Ethnic minorities must reorganise their sociocultural and economic 'differences' in interaction with the local Han Chinese and other minority groups in a rapidly changing world. As a consequence of migration, ethnic boundaries are even more fluid.

Though the 'boundary' approach merits our attention and has added an important dimension to the study of ethnicity, some important modifications are required. Since China has long been under highly centralised control, official versions of ethnicity exist and continue to find their way into folk memories and daily practices (Connerton 1989). To what extent an ethnic group in China can socially organise their own community still calls for detailed fieldwork reports. All 55 Chinese minority peoples have been formally recognised by the central government and their status is constantly reconfirmed and solidified by political, educational and other affirmative actions and policies. The boundaries of the 55 are very rigid. This fact together with strong media propaganda over many years has built up a framework within which ethnic groups and individuals do not negotiate boundaries freely. People have adjusted to this situation. We may expect some cognitive changes with the ever-deepening information revolution in China, but this will take some time yet.

These five theoretical approaches to migration are drawn upon in both the method and the interpretation of data. No one approach is adequate for explaining what is happening in China and elements of all theories are needed to explain the processes of minority mobility as well as the outcomes.

ISSUES, DEBATES AND PROBLEMS

Population movement in China in the 1980s and 1990s

There is a growing body of literature on internal migration in China generally (Banister 1987, Day and Ma 1994, Goldstein and Goldstein 1994, Goldstein and Wang 1996, Guo 1996a, Hoy 1996, Solinger 1999, Davin 1999). The literature describes the overall trends in internal migration, in particular the prominence of movement to small and medium-sized towns, the impact of government controls throughout the 1960s and 1970s and the freeing up of these controls and economic development in the 1980s. Popular sources of data for these studies have been the 1987 one per cent sample survey (State Statistical Bureau 1988), the 1985-86 study of 74 cities and towns (Day and Ma 1994) and the 1985 and 1990 population censuses. The

1985-86 survey showed that migration rates were higher into large cities (0.5 to 1 million), medium-sized cities (200 000 to 500 000), small cities (less than 200 000) and towns (more than 2 000) than into extra-large cities (Wang 1994, p. 29). The 1990 census is the most comprehensive as it covers the entire country and is the most up-to-date. Various subsamples, 10 per cent and 1 per cent of the national census, have been used by researchers for looking at internal migration.

According to Guo (1996b), much of the permanent movement between 1982 and 1987 was brought about by three main policy processes which were associated with family reunification: workers were reassigned to be with their families rather than in distant locations where they had been sent; army personnel were re-deployed back home, and intellectuals who had been sent to outlying areas during the Cultural Revolution were able to return home (many after more than 10 years). Guo's analysis of household census data shows that it was not till after 1987 that permanent movement became driven largely by economic factors when working in a business or employment became the prime reasons for movement.

The official level of migration between 1985 and 1990 is measured by the two categories of migrants defined by the census. Permanent migrants were those who changed their place of official registration (*hukou*) between 1985 and 1990, irrespective of the time they had been at the destination. Information was collected about their place of permanent registration (*hukou*) and the major reason for moving. Temporary migrants were defined as those (aged five and over) who had not changed their place of official residence registration (*hukou*) between 1985 and 1990 but who had been away from their place of usual residence of 1985 for more than one year. All other people who were not at their place of official registration at the time of the 1990 census were not counted as migrants but were regarded as short term movers. They constitute the 'floating population' who are still classed as 'rural'. Because of the definitions used in the census the figures clearly underestimate the number of migrants.

From the 1990 census it was estimated that 33.8 million people aged five and over moved between 1985 and 1990, or 3 per cent of the total population. Among these, 46.2 per cent were temporary migrants and 53.8 per cent were permanent migrants, according to the above definitions. Table 2.1 is derived from the one per cent sample of the 1990 census and shows the number of permanent and temporary inter-provincial migrants by province/autonomous region/municipality of destination. Guangdong province received by far the largest number of inter-provincial migrants (43 984) as defined by the census, between 1985 and 1990. Sixty per cent of them were temporary migrants (no local *hukou*). Shandong received 30 225 migrants during this period with 70 per cent being classed as permanent

Table 2.1 Percentage and number ('000) of inter-provincial migrants by destination, 1985-90, and SES index

Destination	Permanent migrants (%)	Temporary migrants (%)	Total migrants (No)	SES index(a)
Beijing	47.9	52.1	7 963	27.0
Tianjin	54.6	45.4	10 098	24.1
Hebei	63.1	36.9	12 809	17.4
Shanxi	39.4	60.6	6 147	18.0
Inner Mongolia	42.5	57.5	9 774	14.3
Liaoning	59.0	41.0	14 930	24.6
Jilin	60.1	39.9	8 618	22.9
Heilonjiang	34.1	65.9	14 500	19.4
Shanghai	40.9	59.1	11 763	26.1
Jiangsu	45.6	54.4	15 717	18.0
Zhejiang	40.8	59.2	12 904	17.0
Anhui	51.1	48.9	14 460	11.6
Fujian	37.4	62.6	11 970	13.9
Jiangxi	69.5	30.5	13 190	9.9
Shandong	70.1	29.9	30 225	17.1
Henan	65.6	34.4	19 447	10.9
Hubei	61.9	38.1	16 688	15.6
Hunan	72.2	27.8	15 743	11.7
Guangdong	40.9	59.1	43 984	18.9
Guangxi	62.1	37.9	10 124	11.6
Hainan	36.1	63.9	2 808	18.9
Sichuan	64.3	35.7	25 733	6.9
Guizhou	50.6	49.4	3 739	4.3
Yunnan	54.1	45.9	9 548	3.9
Tibet	n.a.	n.a.	n.a.	n.a.
Shaanxi	57.1	42.9	11 997	10.0
Gansu	74.6	25.4	9 810	6.6
Qinghai	36.4	63.6	2 436	4.0
Ningxia	74.0	26.0	739	8.4
Xinjiang	24.2	75.8	5 744	12.1
Total	53.8	46.2	361 608	n.a.

Note: (a) SES index = socioeconomic index, developed by Mauldin and Berelson (1978) was constructed for each province of China in 1988. Seven variables comprise the index: percent adult literacy, primary and secondary school enrolment ratio, life expectancy, infant mortality rate, percent of male labour force not in agriculture, gross provincial product per capita and percent urban population. Provinces were ranked from high to low on each variable, the ranks were summed and divided by 7. The scores range from 27 for Beijing to 3.9 for Yunnan.

Source: Yang and Guo (1996, p. 777).

migrants. Sichuan received the third largest number, 25 733, but in the case of this province 64 per cent were permanent. The propensity to obtain *hukou* clearly varies by province or region. The province which received fewest inter-provincial migrants was Ningxia Hui Autonomous Region, one of the poorest regions of China.

The last column of Table 2.1 gives the socio-economic (SES) index for each province, autonomous region or municipality. The SES index is derived from a number of indices as described under the table. Beijing, Shanghai and Tianjin ranked highest on this score, demonstrating the superior facilities and environment offered by these major urban areas. Regional disparity is a major issue in China and partly explains the large scale movement from the west to the east. Scores of 3.9 for Yunnan, 4.0 for Qinghai and 4.3 for Guizhou (all significant minority areas) are extremely low and point to the potential for high levels of out-migration.

Yang and Guo (1996, pp. 785-6) focussed on long-term rural to urban temporary economic migrants identified by the 1990 census. They found them most likely to enter the industrial and tertiary sectors, predominantly on the east coast. In the industrial sector, they were 'more likely to work in those occupations which were physically demanding, required low skills, and were potentially hazardous. In the tertiary sector, over half were private retailers in sales business, and a large proportion of them served in restaurants or as housemaids in the service sector. Those who engaged in ... agricultural production were most likely to grow cash crops and raise domestic animals or poultry where there were free markets for their products in cities'. Yang and Guo maintain that if government policies permitted, temporary migrants would prefer to be permanent migrants.

Table 2.2 shows the total level of inter- and intra-provincial migration and the proportion of the population registered elsewhere, from the 1990 census. The data are by region — eastern, central and western — in order to clearly illustrate the overall trends in internal migration. Table 2.2 provides figures in columns (1), (2) and (3) for population and both in-migration and out-migration by region. This means that there is double counting but Fan has done this to show the spatial pattern of the flows. Column (4) gives the level of net inter-provincial migration and (5) gives the rate by area. Columns (6) and (7) give the number and rate of intra-provincial migration. Overall, the number of people moving within provinces (intra-provincial migration), from the census data, is about double the rate of between province (inter-provincial) migration. This is shown in the total line that has been inserted in the second row from the bottom of the table. Column (8) shows the number of people with *hukou* elsewhere — a figure of almost 24 million in 1990 or 2.3 per cent of the total population.

Guangdong, Beijing and Shanghai have the highest proportions of migrants without *hukou* in the place of destination.

Table 2.2 Population and size and rate of inter- and intra-provincial migration, and population registered elsewhere, by province ('000)

Area	Population (1990)	Inter-provincial migration (1985-1990)				Intra-provincial migration (1985-1990)		*Hukou* elsewhere (1990)	
	No.	In	Out	Net	Rate (%)	No.	Rate (%)	No.	Rate (%)
	(1)	(2)	(3)	(4)	(5)	(6)	(7)	(8)	(9)
Eastern (mean)	39 005	515	354	161	1.02	799	1.84	883	2.63
Beijing	10 819	673	132	541	5.00	84	0.78	517	4.78
Tianjin	8 785	245	72	172	1.96	35	0.40	182	2.07
Hebei	61 083	520	646	-125	-0.21	813	1.33	727	1.19
Liaoning	39 460	541	295	246	0.62	883	2.24	821	2.08
Shanghai	13 342	666	133	533	399	173	1.30	542	4.06
Jiangsu	67 057	791	620	171	0.25	1 189	1.77	1 303	1.94
Zhejiang	41 446	336	632	-296	-0.72	800	1.93	723	1.74
Fujian	30 048	251	238	13	0.04	723	2.41	795	2.65
Shandong	84 392	609	535	75	0.09	1 190	1.41	835	0.99
Guangdong	62 830	1 258	250	1 007	1.60	2 671	4.25	3 315	5.28
Guangxi	42 245	143	589	-446	-1.06	888	2.10	617	1.46
Hainan	6 558	150	106	44	0.67	143	2.18	220	3.35
Central (mean)	44 905	323	420	-96	-0.22	900	2.16	787	2.01
Shanxi	28 759	307	218	89	0.31	627	2.18	760	2.64
Inner Mong.	21 547	254	303	-49	-0.23	578	2.69	612	2.85
Jilin	24 660	237	356	-118	-0.48	611	2.48	509	2.07
Heilong-jiang	35 216	367	607	-240	-0.68	056	3.00	1 257	3.57
Anhui	56 181	338	533	-196	-0.35	870	1.55	767	1.37
Jiangxi	37 710	225	294	69	-0.18	734	1.95	588	1.56
Henan	85 534	478	590	-112	-0.13	1 239	1.45	919	1.07
Hubei	53 971	431	346	85	0.16	1 088	2.02	934	1.73
Hunan	60 658	272	529	-257	-0.42	1 298	2.14	738	1.22
Western (mean)	32 013	247	373	-126	-0.03	667	2.27	483	2.11
Sichuan	107 218	470	1 316	-846	-0.79	2 345	2.19	1 208	1.13
Guizhou	32 391	190	313	-122	-0.38	465	1.43	457	1.41
Yunnan	36 973	250	277	-27	-0.07	732	1.98	541	1.46
Shaanxi	32 882	315	362	-48	0.15	706	2.15	485	1.47
Gansu	22 371	199	281	-82	0.36	450	2.01	317	1.42
Qinghai	4 457	116	102	14	0.31	151	3.39	183	4.10
Ningxia	4 655	92	57	35	0.76	123	2.64	98	2.12
Xinjiang	15 157	342	277	64	0.42	361	2.38	576	3.80
Mean	38 907	382	380	2	0.34	794	2.06	690	2.30

Notes: Tibet was omitted from the table due to poor quality data.

Source: Fan (1996, p. 34).

Fan used the data to illustrate the broad flow of the 11 065 361 inter-provincial migrants to and within the three economic belts constituted according to column 1 of Table 2.2. Figure 2.1 shows that the largest flow of 2 626 620 inter-provincial migrants was between provinces within the eastern region, followed by the flow of 2 263 270 from the central to the eastern region and the flow of 1 238 890 from the western to the eastern region. In summary, the eastern region is the most attractive as well as retaining most of its inter-provincial migrants. In net terms, the western region lost 1 078 460 people and the central region lost 876 470 to inter-provincial migration.

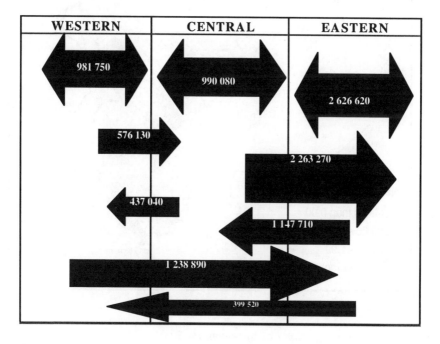

Source: Fan (1996, p. 32).

Figure 2.1 Inter-provincial migration by region, 1985-90

At the regional level, Figure 2.2 shows the net migration rate for each province. The grey regions all experienced a net loss in terms of internal migration while Beijing and Shanghai municipalities experienced more than 5 per cent and 4 per cent net migration gain, respectively, followed by Guangdong with a 1.6 per cent gain. Fan (1996, p. 42) attributes Guangdong's gain to its rapid economic growth since the economic reform and to the fact that it has 'received large amounts of foreign investment that created and promised to create plenty of jobs, suggesting that both existing and expected economic opportunities are at work'.

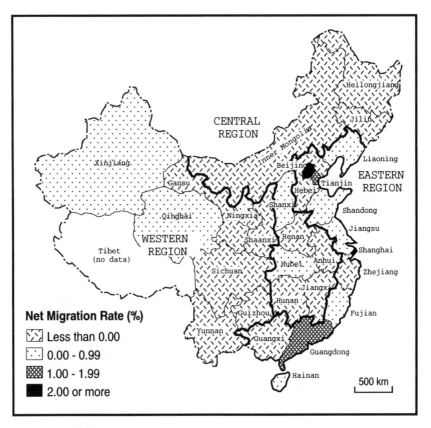

Source: Fan (1996, p. 33).

Figure 2.2 Net migration rate by region, 1985-90

Nevertheless, Figure 2.1 shows that movements were multi-directional and, therefore, other factors beside economics are at work. To understand migration in China, the role of governments, in terms of the constraints and interventions that they use to encourage or deter internal migration, and the role of traditional culture and values in affecting the desire to migrate are very important and need to be studied (Li and Li 1995).

While the census provides valuable information on macro trends it under-enumerates, quite considerably, the real level of movement. The 1990 census required a minimum of one year in the 1990 place of residence for non-registered migrants to be counted as residents at that destination. Survey data from Beijing and Shanghai show that up to 80 per cent of temporary migrants had been there for less than one year (Davin 1999). A number of official attempts have been made recently to more accurately measure the real level of overall movement. The 1995 one per cent census tried to overcome the previous problems by framing a question which addressed *hukou* and movement together. The census defined migrants as those who had moved for six months or more, rather than for one year as before. The results, therefore, are not comparable with the 1990 census. Table 2.3 from 1995 data shows that 95.5 per cent of the population were living in the place where they had permanent registration. They may have moved earlier or been born in this place. For the remaining 4.5 per cent, 3.9 per cent (48 377 400) had been living for more than six months in a place where they did not have *hukou*. Beijing, Tianjin, Shanghai and Guangdong stand out as having the highest proportions of people without permanent registration. The estimated temporary or floating population for the Beijing municipality was 1 891 100 and for Shanghai, the non-permanent registered population was 2 241 100 from the 1995 one per cent census.

These figures are not regarded as proper estimates and both Beijing and Shanghai have recently undertaken migrant censuses. On 1 November 1997, the Beijing Statistical Bureau conducted a full census of the city's temporary population. This census counted the size of the floating population (including migrants and visitors) or number of temporary migrants (defined as people without *hukou* in Beijing) as 2.86 million (Beijing Statistical Bureau 1998). These data will be discussed further in Chapter 8.

The major focus of internal migration research in China is labour migration. The size of this phenomenon makes it of crucial importance to the Chinese government as well as to many international bodies that are concerned about possible future emigration from China. The exact scale of these movements is extremely difficult to quantify for both definitional reasons and problems of surveys/censuses. First, as shown above, the definition of what constitutes a 'migrant' and 'labour migrant' vary according to whether the data are collected in a government census or survey or in another form of survey. As we have seen, the census defines as an 'official' migrant a person who has registered with the authorities and, therefore, changed their place of official registration or *hukou*. A person who has been in the current destination for more than 12 months but who has not changed their place of official registration is captured in the census as a non-official or temporary migrant. All other movers (seasonal, circulatory) are not captured in the census. All but official migrants are classed as the 'floating

Table 2.3 Number and percentage of population by region, hukou *and length of residence, one per cent census, 1995*

Province/ region	Hukou here and living here	Hukou elsewhere, living here > 6 months	Left hukou place > 6 months, living here < 6 months	Hukou uncertain, living here	Hukou was here but gone abroad	Total
	No.	No.	No.	No.	No.	No.
Beijing	109 881	17 978	303	630	217	129 008
Tianjin	86 668	9 535	130	663	43	97 040
Hebei	643 496	16 707	373	1 575	9	662 160
Shanxi	301 667	12 710	199	1 909	3	316 488
Inner Mongolia	217 446	14 590	347	2 518	16	234 917
Liaoning	398 898	20 391	377	1 643	57	421 365
Jilin	251 816	13 387	256	1 301	125	266 885
Heilonjiang	356 675	20 655	531	2 927	154	380 941
Shanghai	128 416	15 723	635	684	360	145 818
Jiangsu	675 381	45 160	1 031	5 613	150	727 334
Zhejiang	421 337	20 041	479	2 714	100	444 671
Anhui	603 450	13 438	354	1 175	18	618 435
Fujian	312 969	13 744	781	4 729	662	332 885
Jiangxi	400 101	13 175	337	3 721	9	417 343
Shandong	864 197	29 963	474	1 475	143	896 252
Henan	917 961	16 088	401	931	57	935 439
Hubei	571 501	20 133	388	1 539	21	593 582
Hunan	639 714	17 185	514	1 224	17	658 654
Guangdong	634 340	57 775	2 685	10 291	72	705 163
Guangxi	456 895	9 851	266	715	15	466 843
Hainan	70 926	2 745	93	480	6	74 249
Sichuan	1 122 441	34 183	655	6 006	58	1 163 343
Guizhou	350 722	8 505	287	902	3	360 419
Yunnan	395 861	12 375	338	926	6	409 506
Tibet	23 947	603	32	62	3	24 647
Shaanxi	350 880	8 519	236	1 279	19	360 934
Gansu	241 852	6 776	168	1 378	5	250 179
Qinghai	46 248	2 456	64	628	1	49 396
Ningxia	49 701	2 006	68	714	1	52 490
Xinjiang	161 358	8 278	377	545	10	170 567
Total No.	11 806 744	483 774	13 181	60 897	2 360	12 366 955
Total %	95.5	3.9	0.1	0.5	0.02	100.0

Source: State Statistical Bureau (1996, pp. 538-9).

population'. These and other problems partly explain variations in the estimates of internal migration.

Wu and Li (1996) reviewed the literature on the magnitude of permanent rural-urban labour movement and reported wide variation in the findings, though there is a consistent finding of increasing permanent flows. The 1987 one per cent sample survey and the 1990 census estimated a flow of 3.9 million per annum in 1982-87 and 4.2 million per annum in 1985-90, respectively. As Wu and Li (1996) point out, however, these migration data underestimate the total migration rate of China because they do not take account of multiple moves, return migration, migrants less than five years old and people who died in the intercensal period.

Wu (1994) and Chan (1994) used another technique, the residual method, to estimate permanent rural-to-urban migration. This technique is based on the total and natural growth of an urban population, with the difference between the two being attributed to rural-urban migration. Using this method, Wu's estimate of the average annual rate of net rural-to-urban migration was 4.7 million for 1978-83 and 8.7 million for 1984-90. Chan's estimates were 7.3 million and 8.4 million, for the same periods. On top of these figures, data for the 'floating population' or temporary migrants, mostly farmers, are patchy and often 'guesstimates'. Goldstein (1990) estimated the total floating population to be 50 million in 1990 but by 1996-98 it is thought to have reached 80 to 100 million (Karmel 1996, Bu 1998).

Mobility to particular regions has begun to be addressed recently, as a result of improved data available for analysis (Fan 1996, Huang *et al.* 1995, Ma 1991). Fan (1996), as shown, focused on Guangdong province and attempted to address some of the imbalance between national and regional studies by analysing the scale and direction of internal migration and then describing the migration system that is operating between Guangdong and elsewhere within China.

Migration, settlement and the role of government

Little attention has been devoted in China to the study of the consequences of migration and the role for government in the resettlement of migrants. The 1990s saw a realisation of the impact of the out-migration of young, often male workers on rural areas as well as the welfare provision implications for immigrants in urban areas. Urban unemployment, overcrowding or lack of housing and a shortage of public amenities (such as schools, medical and health care facilities, water and sewerage systems, transport, etc) are all being felt to various degrees in urban China. Social issues, such as class differences, homelessness, crime and intercultural relations, are emerging as issues for the nation. According to Fan (1996, p. 43), 'the relationship between migration and social segmentation will likely be an important issue in China and needs to be further researched'.

The need for government intervention to restrain, regulate or manage internal migration, and to mitigate its adverse consequences, is divided in the literature both nationally and internationally. Some argue that population movements need to be managed to ensure a more even distribution of economic activity, more efficient use of natural resources and more adequate provision of urban infrastructure. Others argue for a *laissez faire* approach.

Internal migration-influencing policies and programs have been categorised by Oberai (1983a) into the following groups:

- direct controls on mobility (as in China, Indonesia, Poland);
- policies for redirecting migrants to other areas, through land settlement schemes (Indonesia, India, Malaysia, Nepal) and growth pole and dispersed urbanisation strategies (Japan, Republic of Korea, India);
- policies for reducing the flow of migrants, through rural development programs and preferential policies for minorities that have as part of their preview the discouragement of inter-regional migration (China, Japan, Sri Lanka); and
- policies that influence urban in-migration, such as limiting access of immigrants to education and housing, non-provision or curtailment of water and other services to shanty areas (Philippines, China).

Oberai (1983b, p. 24) concluded that planned economies, such as China and formerly Poland, were reasonably successful in managing movement 'partly because of the way planning and implementation [took] place in those countries'. This was in the period when 'public ownership of the means of production and complete command over the allocation of resources facilitated the manipulation of investment decisions over national space'. Now that the level of public ownership is diminishing in China it will be somewhat harder to achieve this spread of investment. Already, the establishment of SEZs in the east and their attraction for foreign investors has led to the movement of people to seek out better economic opportunities.

According to Oberai (1983b, p. 26), 'policy instruments available to governments will have little impact on internal migration until the basic factors responsible for wide rural-urban and inter-urban differences in wages, employment opportunities, and amenities are modified'. The increasing amount of research in China into widening income differentials highlights concern about this trend (Cai 1998). The need for an over-all development strategy, linking and harmonising policies on population, industrialisation, agriculture, and social welfare has constantly been an issue for the central government but is increasing in importance as the differentials widen. Ethnic integration and national unity are also likely to be a concern in heterogeneous societies and often lead to attempts to bring about more mixing of groups. At the same time, appropriate spatial policies may be required to meet demands for autonomy (Oberai 1983a). These two issues exist in China where the push for autonomy and even self determination exists side by side with an increasing level of movement of minority peoples in recent years.

The identification of minorities or minority nationalities, as alluded to in Chapter 1, has been part of an official process. This will be described as it forms the basis for the discussion of the number and distribution of minorities.

IDENTIFICATION OF MINORITY NATIONALITIES IN THE PRC

The project of nationality identification started on the basis of visits by Chinese central delegations to the minority regions from 1949 to 1951. Three major investigations followed in the 1950s and 1960s and these helped to determine the status and number of nationalities in China. From 1952 to 1956, six investigation teams were organised by the Central Institute of Nationalities (now the Central University of Nationalities) and sent to the northeast and Inner Mongolia, Gansu and Qinghai, western Hunan, Guangdong, Yunnan and Guizhou. From 1956-58, eight teams were organised by the Ethnic Committee of the National People's Congress and sent to the northeast and Inner Mongolia, Xinjiang, Tibet, Sichuan, Yunnan, Guizhou, Guangxi and Guangdong. From 1958-63, another eight teams were organised by the Chinese Academy of Social Sciences (CASS) and sent to Heilongjiang, Jilin, Liaoning, Ningxia, Gansu, Qinghai, Hunan and Fujian. The teams consisted of linguists, ethnologists, archaeologists, economists, and experts in literature and the arts, and they were expected to live, work and relax with the people they were investigating. By 1979, officials had designated 55 minorities, which with the majority Han, made a total of 56 nationalities in China. Han Chinese comprised 91.96 per cent of the population in 1990. The 55 recognised minority nationalities comprised the remaining 8.04 per cent of the total population.

The Stalinist definition of *nacia* was used with important modifications in relation to 'Chinese characteristics.' In a lecture given by Professor Li Yifu at the People's University in Beijing during the 1950s, the Soviet expert and ethnologist Kozlov was quoted as saying that 'none of the ethnic groups in China had reached the level of a *nacia* (nation) according to the Marxist-Leninist five-stage social development scheme'. This comment aroused great indignation among Chinese scholars and they refused to use the Soviet ethnic classificatory system in nationality identification. According to Chairman Mao's instructions, all ethnic groups, no matter how large or small, developed or undeveloped, are 'nationalities.'[2] All of the four criteria were supposed to be present but in reality for some groups, such as the Manchu and the Hui, some elements are missing. The process of identification is itself the subject of considerable discussion that will not be taken up in detail here but will be dealt with later.

GEOGRAPHICAL LOCATION OF MINORITIES

Minority nationalities have traditionally been located mainly in the north, west and southern parts of China, in areas bordering other countries. Table 2.4 shows the total population of each of the 30 provinces/autonomous regions/municipalities at the 1990 census and the number and proportion of each region's population that belong to a minority nationality. In the last column, the regions are ranked in terms of their minorities' component with Tibet ranking first with 96.3 per cent and Jiansu 30th with 0.02 per cent. Table 2.4 groups the regions by geographic location so that the overall spread of minorities stands out clearly. The west and parts of the south and north are home to the majority of minority peoples. The eastern regions have extremely low proportions of minorities, with Hubei being highest among them at 4 per cent.

Xinjiang Uyghur Autonomous Region, on the northwestern frontier adjoining India, Pakistan, Turkestan and Kazakstan, is the largest administrative region in China. It had a population of over 15 156 883 in 1990 and ranked second to Tibet, with 62.6 per cent of its population belonging to a minority nationality. Uyghurs make up the largest component but many other groups (Tujias, Kazaks, Tatars, etc) are also found in Xinjiang.

Qinghai ranked third in terms of proportion of the population belonging to a minority nationality, and contains a range of minority nationalities. Qinghai is followed by Guangxi Zhuang Autonomous Region. The Zhuang, as seen in Tables 2.5 and 2.6, are numerically the largest minority nationality group in China. Guizhou and Yunnan ranked fifth and sixth in terms of their minority component. Guizhou is home to many Miao, and Yunnan contains many of the Yi people. The region with the

---

[2] Discussion of the concept of *minzu*, a seminar held by the Institute of Nationality Studies, Chinese Academy of Social Sciences, March, 1999.

seventh largest minority component is Ningxia, home to many of the Hui people.

The Inner Mongolian Autonomous Region is the third largest administrative region in China and in 1990 19.4 per cent of its population of 21 456 518 belonged to a minority nationality, giving it the eighth highest ranking.

Table 2.4 Importance of minorities by region, 1990

Province/Region	Total population	Minority population		Rank
	Number	Number	Proportion (%)	(1-30)
North				
Beijing	10 819 414	414 063	3.8	19
Tianjin	8 785 427	202 666	2.3	20
Hebei	61 082 755	2 309 093	3.9	18
Shanxi	28 758 846	82 295	0.3	28.5
Inner Mongolia	21 456 518	4 166 523	19.4	8
Liaoning	39 459 694	6 165 912	15.6	10
Jilin	24 659 790	2 525 365	10.2	11
Heilongjiang	35 215 932	1 998 632	5.3	14
East				
Shanghai	12 341 852	2 235	0.5	26.5
Jiangsu	67 056 812	153 343	0.2	30
Zhejiang	41 446 015	212 752	0.5	26.5
Anhui	56 181 005	324 352	0.6	24
Fujian	30 048 275	466 800	1.6	21
Jiangxi	37 710 177	101 288	0.3	28.5
Shandong	84 392 104	505 900	0.6	24
Henan	85 534 200	1 009 521	1.2	22
Hubei	53 970 501	2 140 579	4.0	17
South				
Hunan	60 657 992	4 823 837	8.0	13
Guangdong	62 829 741	355 317	0.6	24
Guangxi	42 244 884	16 577 766	39.2	4
Hainan	6 558 075	1 116 582	17.0	9
West				
Sichuan	107 218 310	4 890 024	4.6	15
Guizhou	32 391 051	11 242 295	34.7	5
Yunnan	36 972 587	12 358 054	33.5	6
Tibet	2 196 029	2 115 192	96.3	1
Shaanxi	32 882 286	1 857 478	4.5	16
Gansu	22 371 085	2 217 478	8.3	12
Qinghai	4 456 952	1 878 040	42.1	3
Ningxia	4 655 445	1 549 068	33.3	7
Xinjiang	15 156 883	9 461 474	62.4	2
Total	1 130 510 638	91 323 090	8.04	30

Source: State Population Census Office and State Statistical Bureau (1993), Vols. 1 and 4.

RESEARCH METHOD

Given the number of minority nationalities (55) in China it was decided to focus on three case studies. The patterns of migration and consequences vary for each group and so the groups chosen can best be seen as examples that may bring some light to bear on the overall changes that are taking place. Table 2.5 shows the estimated number of people in each of the recognised minority nationalities in 1953, 1964, 1982 and 1990. Data are missing for some groups in the early censuses as they had not been identified at that time. Two small groups, the Mongren and Sharen, were not enumerated after 1953. In 1990, there were 749 341 people who claimed to belong to ethnic minorities but did not have recognised minority nationality status and were classified as 'not yet identified nationalities' (Mackerras 1994, p. 143). Table 2.5 shows that the number of people enumerated as belonging to a particular minority nationality has fluctuated significantly at the censuses.

Table 2.5 Population of China's nationalities, 1953, 1964, 1982 and 1990

Nationality	1953 Census	1964 Census	1982 Census	1990 Census
Han	547 283 057	651 296 368	940 880 121	1 042 482 187
Zhuang	6 611 455	8 386 140	13 388 118	15 489 630
Manchus	2 418 931	2 695 675	4 304 160	9 821 180
Hui	3 559 350	4 473 147	7 227 022	8 602 978
Miao	2 511 339	2 782 088	5 036 377	7 398 035
Uygurs	2 775 622	3 996 311	5 962 814	7 214 431
Yi	3 254 269	3 380 960	5 457 251	5 572 173
Tujia		524 755	2 834 732	5 704 223
Mongols	1 462 956	1 965 766	3 416 881	4 806 849
Tibetans	2 775 622	2 501 174	3 874 035	4 593 330
Bouyei	1 274 883	1 348 055	2 122 389	2 545 059
Dong	712 802	836 123	1 426 335	2 514 014
Yao	665 933	857 265	1 403 664	2 134 013
Koreans	1 120 405	1 339 569	1 766 439	1 920 597
Bai	567 119	706 623	1 132 010	1 594 827
Hani	481 220	628 727	1 059 404	1 253 952
Kazaks	509 375	491 637	908 414	1 111 718
Li	360 950	438 813	818 255	1 110 900
Dai	478 966	535 389	840 590	1 025 128
She		234 167	368 832	630 378
Lisu	317 465	270 628	480 960	574 856
Gelao		26 852	53 802	437 997
Lahu	139 060	191 241	304 174	411 476
Dongxiang	155 761	147 443	279 397	373 872
Va	286 158	220 272	298 591	351 974
Shui	133 566	156 099	286 487	345 993
Naxi	143 453	156 796	245 154	278 009
Qiang	35 660	49 105	102 768	198 252

Table 2.5 (continued)

Tu	53 277	77 349	159 426	191 624
Xibe	19 022	33 438	83 629	172 847
Mulam		52 819	90 426	159 328
Kirgiz	70 944	70 151	113 999	141 549
Daur		63 394	94 014	121 357
Jingpo	101 852	57 762	93 008	119 209
Salar	30 658	34 644	69 102	87 697
Blang		39 411	58 476	82 280
Maonan		22 382	38 135	71 968
Tajiks	14 462	16 236	26 503	33 538
Primi		14 298	24 237	29 657
Achang		12 032	20 441	27 708
Nu		15 047	23 166	27 123
Ewenkis	4 957	9 681	19 343	26 315
Gin		4 293	11 995	18 915
Jino			11 974	18 021
Benglong or Deang		7 261	12 295	15 462
Uzbeks	13 626	7 717	12 453	14 502
Russians	22 656	1 326	2 935	13 504
Yugurs	3 861	5 717	10 569	12 297
Bonan	4 957	5 125	9 027	12 212
Monba		3 809	6 248	7 475
Oroqen	2 262	2 709	4 132	6 965
Derung		3 090	4 682	5 816
Tatars	6 929	2 294	4 127	4 873
Hezhen		718	1 476	4 245
Gaoshan	329	366	1 549	2 909
Lhoba			2 065	2 312
Others	1 380 745			
Others not identified		32 411	881 838	749 341
Total	582 603 417	691 220 104	1 003 937 078	1 133 682 501

Source: Mackerras (1994, pp. 238–9).

Table 2.6 shows the rate of population change of the Han nationality and the nine largest minority nationalities between the four censuses. The Tujia were not recognised till after the 1953 census and so are not included till the 1964 census.

Table 2.6 China's ten largest nationalities, 1953-1990

Nationality	1953 Census	1964 Census	1982 Census	1990 Census
	Number	% Growth	% Growth	% Growth
Han	547 283 057	19.00	43.82	10.80
Zhuang	6 611 455	26.84	59.53	15.70
Manchus	2 418 931	11.44	59.48	128.18
Hui	3 559 350	25.67	61.39	19.04
Miao	2 511 339	10.78	80.83	46.89
Uygurs	2 775 622	43.98	49.07	20.99
Yi	3 254 269	3.89	61.30	20.43
Tujia	-	524 755*	439.82	101.23
Mongols	1 462 956	34.37	73.55	40.68
Tibetans	2 775 622	-9.89	53.73	18.57

Note: * Tujia not enumerated in 1953 Census, therefore, number given for 1964 Census, not % growth.

Source: Mackerras (1994, p. 238).

The differences over time are partly due to changes in the number of people willing to identify themselves as belonging to a minority nationality. Perceptions of minorities in different periods have influenced willingness to identify. Between 1953 and 1964, there was significant increase in the number of Uyghurs and Mongols, due predominantly to this phenomenon. During the Cultural Revolution many people hid their minority status for fear of persecution but by the 1982 census there was a 74 per cent increase in the number of Mongolians and a 49 per cent increase in the number of Uyghurs. The Miao also experienced a major increase in numbers between 1964 and 1982. The number of Tibetans declined between the first two censuses but since 1964 they have continued to increase in number. Another explanation lies in the rate of natural increase of minority nationalities compared to Han Chinese. Fertility has remained higher among minorities, as until fairly recently the state's family planning policies have not been as rigorously applied.

Figure 2.3 shows the distribution of the major minority nationalities. Most research into minorities in China has focussed on people in the more hospitable and accessible southern parts, with the exception of Gladney's work on the Hui. Mongols, Tibetans and Uygurs were selected for this study as they are located in the north and west areas. The three groups represent quite significant differences in terms of lifestyles, ways of earning a living and religion. It is also known from the census and other surveys that they are relatively recent arrivals to Beijing and this makes them interesting case studies of how ethnic minorities are settling and integrating into a city in the current context.

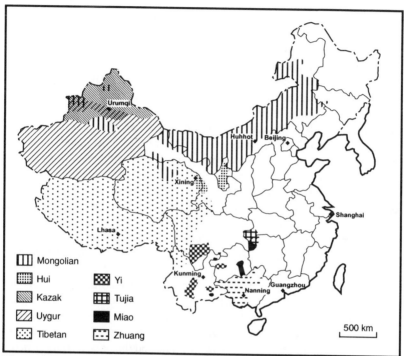

Figure 2.3 Distribution of major minority groups

The *Sample Survey of Ethnic Minority Migration* was undertaken in two stages. A pilot study was conducted with migrant and non-migrant households in Hohhot and Bayan Bulag (Inner Mongolia), Urumqi and Turpan (Xinjiang) and Beijing in 1996-97. Interviews were also conducted with key informants, including researchers at the Inner Mongolia Academy of Social Sciences, the principal of the Mongolian School in Hohhot, and scholars of the Inner Mongolia Normal (Teachers') University. In Xinjiang, interviews were conducted with a range of academics and government officials, involving the Institute of Cultural Anthropology, Xinjiang Normal University; the People's Government of Shayibake District and two school principals and their staff, Urumqi; the Population Research Institute and History Department, Xinjiang University; the Education Affairs and two Family Planning Unit officials, Turpan, Xinjiang; the principal of Turpan No. 1 Nationality Middle School, and the Xinjiang Education Commission.

As a result of stage 1, the feasibility of the research team conducting the fieldwork was questioned. First, the technique of conducting in-depth household interviews proved quite difficult. Interviewees were relatively easy to gain in the *som* in Inner Mongolia, because of the assistance provided by a local official, but in other places the technique of approaching people directly often led to suspicion and unwillingness to cooperate. Locals could sometimes be used to explain the purpose of the study and at other times the offer of a fee to cover their time encouraged cooperation. It was decided that a much longer time period is often required, a number of informal meetings rather than a formal interview may be necessary to collect the data and questionnaires are best completed out of sight of the interviewees. Interviews with some key informants, especially government officers, are difficult when a foreigner is involved, especially on sensitive topics.

Based on stage 1, the two pilot questionnaires were revised and the samples were drawn and interviewed by local teams of experienced researchers. The criteria for selection of the samples to be drawn were as follows: males and females to be included (equal numbers if possible), a mixture of age groups, households to be the key focus and migrant households that had moved after 1986. The data were coded, entered and analysed by the research team at the China National Institute for Educational Research.[3] A workshop was held with key ethnologists, demographers, educationalists and others in Beijing in October 1999 to discuss aspects of the project. The workshop enabled the presentation of major findings, critiquing by key researchers working in China and the presentation of papers on related topics by other researchers.[4]

---

[3] Professor Liu is to be thanked for her meticulous work in relation to data analysis.
[4] The papers presented at the *Minority Mobility Workshop* are being published separately.

3. Ethnicity and minority education policy

The story of minority mobility in any country is embedded in a cultural and material policy context. Education policy, in particular, provides an important social foundation for the maintenance, reconstruction or transformation of ethnic identity. This chapter provides a review of the history of China's policies in relation to cultural and ethnic identity. It then reviews education policies and finally deals more particularly with minority education policies. The chapter concludes by arguing that these policies have focussed on minority participation. While they reflect a recognition of the existence and acceptance of ethnic diversity they do not appear to reflect a 'valuing' of such diversity as national capital. The value of diversity in cultural capital is only now being realised in many societies and a similar trend towards this position may emerge in China.

CULTURE AND ETHNICITY IN CHINA BEFORE 1949

Any discussion of social policy involving China's minority nationalities needs to be undertaken within the context of China's overall perception of its culture, and perceptions of ethnicity and of 'others'. According to Pasternak and Salaff (1993, p. 3), 'ever since the Chinese state unified the populace 5000 years ago, spread a script and consolidated rule, we have recognised a common "Chinese Way" of life. The features of this singular way of life seem timeless and uniform'. The closest hint of 'ethnicity' in ancient China is cultural identity. A notion of continuity, embedded in a spectrum of philosophical writings, ethical qualifications and artistic achievements, starts from the Xia dynasty (2100-1600 BC), lingers through the Shang dynasty (1600-1027 BC) and the Zhou dynasty (1100-221 BC) up till modern China. It is civilisation that sets up the configuration of identities: the 'civilised' Chinese Kingdom sits right in the middle between heaven and earth while those barbarian peoples (*yi di*) spread away in the peripheral areas. Ping (1995) believes that the notion of the Chinese as a race crystallised in the

Han dynasty (206 BC-220 AD). He apparently confuses the lately much borrowed western notion of 'race' with what at that time we may call 'communities' that are distinguished by 'cultures' rather than phenotypical appearance. The notion of 'race' came into China during the discourse of 'nation-state' and 'nationalism' in the modern history of China (Dikotter 1996). It was after the humiliating defeats in wars with foreign powers from 1839 – 42 that the discourse of the community of Chinese civilisation versus barbarian peripherals was replaced by that of confrontation between races that are ordered hierarchically in a phenotypical map.

The Chinese equivalent of 'culture' is *wenhua*. As early as 3500 years ago, the character *wen* 'appears as a pictograph of a man with a tattoo on his chest, and as a man adorned with a string of shells on his chest' (Ping 1995, p. 129). From this origin *wen* derived a set of ideas. It could denote a process of embellishing one's inner self or feelings, a body of ideas, achievements and practices in terms of excellency, literacy, humanity and tranquillity, as well as a civilised state and 'the accomplishments or characteristics resulting from the embellishment' (Ping 1995, p. 130). The character *hua* derives from the character *bi* as a pictograph of a person standing upside down, 'signifying a human being at the beginning of his life in the womb'.

> [I]t eventually came to designate a dynamic, emergent process of the pattern of life, and also the process of cultivating, a human being's inner self and outer behaviour through education and indoctrination, as conveyed by the phrase *jiaohua*. The origin and the various meanings of the character *hua* convey an image of the human life cycle, his birth, and his gradual maturing into adulthood through genetic and nongenetic influences. (Ping 1995, p. 130)

Thus the earlier meaning of *wenhua* lays emphasis on self-perfection by 'studying the classics, practising poetry, reading and writing, participating in rituals and music, etc.' (Ping 1995, p. 130). The classical Central Kingdom is a cosmos of rituals and symbols with a civilisation of continuity and perfection. This static texture of civilisation is after all a myth that is constructed by the ruling class and literati and is brought into play with the help of an ideographic script. However, we can hardly underestimate its dynamic force in shaping identities. In Chinese modern history, the central government was always aiming to 'civilise' those remote and peripheral 'barbarians'. This can be evidenced by names of places in borderland areas as illustrated in the following two examples. The former Chinese name for Urumqi, capital of the Xinjiang Autonomous Region, was *dihua*, meaning 'to come into a state of renaissance'. The previous Chinese name for the old quarter of Hohhot, capital of the Inner Mongolian Autonomous Region, was *guihua,* meaning 'come to join civilisation'. Chinese culture has absorbed and reshaped the cultures of those with whom it has come in contact. There have been times when some or all of China's minorities 'were partially or fully assimilated' (Postiglione 1992, p. 23). Harrell points out that this has not been a static situation and those who constituted the core changed on many occasions. Two of the present minorities, the Mongolians and the Manchu, ruled China for hundreds of years. Therefore, the concept of 'Chineseness' has also changed.

> There has never been a rigid boundary around the category 'Chinese'. Since earliest times, the people who have called themselves Hua or Xia or Zhongguo ren (people of the countries in the middle) or, of late, Han, have held an ideology of both cultural superiority and inclusivist expansion, conducting what I have elsewhere called a 'civilizing project' (Harrell 1994), an attempt to bring the benefits and responsibilities of their own purportedly superior civilization to the presently inferior people around their periphery ... The core has consisted of those culturally closest to the literati ideal of civilization or, in more recent times, to the 'advanced culture' of the Han. Those around the periphery, if they approached closely enough to the centre's cultural ideals, might be included in the category of *shufan,* or 'cooked barbarians', those whose foreign ancestry was not in doubt, but who had come far enough in the civilizing process to participate in the civilized order. (Harrell 1996, p. 6)

The strong sense of superiority among Han Chinese was voiced earlier by John King Fairbank (cited in Bodde 1959, p. 61).

> The Chinese were impressed with one fact: that their superiority was not one of mere material power but of culture ... So great was their virtue, so overwhelming the achievements of the Middle Kingdom in art and letters and the art of living, that no barbarian could long resist them. Gradually but invariably the barbarians in contact with China tended to become Chinese. ... After centuries of solitary grandeur as the center of Eastern Asia, the Chinese developed what may be called, by analogy to nationalism, a spirit of 'culturism'. Those who did not follow the Chinese way were *ipso facto* inferior.

Over time, there has been a history of ethnic groups gradually changing their identity to become 'Chinese'. As occurs elsewhere, through intermarriage, migration and changes in habits and customs from one generation to the next, individuals and groups gradually adapted to become like the core group. Assimilation or cultural adaptation have occurred so that ethnic groups have become subsumed in the 'superior "Chinese" culture' of the time. This process was 'often accentuated by a process of genealogical construction whereby individuals were given a Chinese ancestry by means of giving them a single character surname and a genealogy tracing that surname to remote historical or proto-historical periods' (Ebrey 1996, p. 26).

The influence of Western 'orientalism' in helping to form the perceptions of minorities cannot be underestimated. Ethnic groups in remote areas of China were described by European missionaries and anthropologists as 'barbarians' and 'uncivilised', as they had no written history. The Christian civilising project had found fertile ground among the peripheral peoples of China for a number of reasons. One of them may have been 'as a useful counterweight to the Han' (Harrell 1994, p. 21).[1] What prevailed in China was an overriding notion of 'scientific racism'. This was based on the genetic or physical superiority of some 'races' over others but 'other' races did not include China's minorities. This view was the conventional wisdom of the western biological and social sciences up till the 1940s. Physical continuity with minorities precluded the development of such theories in relationship to minority nationalities and 'culture' was the justification for seeing some minority groups as inferior to others. That is, phenotypical differences provided the explanation for the superiority of Han Chinese over white and black races (or their equality with white, or lower than white but higher than black) while cultural explanations provided the basis for explanations for superiority in relation to internal minorities. Socio-economically disadvantaged minority groups were seen as disadvantaged because of their cultural values that were perceived to be backward and inappropriate for technological advance and economic development. As Castles (1996, pp. 28-9) points out:

> The acceptance of cultural pluralism is compatible with a belief in the superiority of the dominant culture. The very idea of tolerance for minority cultures implies a belief in the superiority of the dominant one: immigrants and ethnic minorities can keep their own values and cultures, but they cannot complain if this leads to their marginalisation.

Under the Guomindang, the minorities received poor treatment and the priority of the government was to maintain national unity. Mackerras (1994, p. 144) points out that, as a result, before 1949 'many members of the minorities [even] tried to hide their identity'. Some minority areas in the

---

[1] We have not tackled the whole question of Han identity and whether the 92 per cent who were identified as Han in the 1990 census is in fact correct. Gladney's discussion of this issue suggests that there has been a significant amount of classification of non-Han people as Han and their Hakka, Subei or other identity has been explained away as 'sub-ethnic' or 'regional' (Gladney 1998, pp. 162-3).

north-eastern part of China were controlled by the CPC before 1949 and the Inner Mongolian Autonomous Region, the first autonomous region, was set up in 1947.

POLICY DEVELOPMENTS UNDER CPC

In 1922, the CPC declared that federalism would be used to unify China and integrate different ethnic groups into a Chinese nation. In 1931, the CPC constitution went further and stated in Article 14 that the party 'recognises the right of self-determination of the national minorities in China, their right to complete separation from China, and to the formation of an independent state for each minority' (Brandt *et al.* 1952, p. 220). This policy was supported up to October 1949 when the Central Party Propaganda Office of the New China News Agency to the Northwestern Branch Office issued an important cable:

> Today the question of each minority's 'self-determination' should not be stressed any further. In the past, during the period of civil war, for the sake of strengthening the minorities' opposition to the Guomindang's [KMT's] reactionary rule, we emphasized this slogan. This was correct at the time. But today the situation has fundamentally changed. The KMT's reactionary rule has been basically destroyed and the party leaders of the New China have already arisen. For the sake of completing our state's great purpose of unification, for the sake of opposing the conspiracy of imperialists and other running dogs to divide China's nationality unity, we should not stress this slogan in the domestic nationality question and should not allow its usage by imperialists and reactionary elements among various domestic nationalities ... The Han occupy the majority population of the country; moreover, the Han today are the major force in China's revolution. Under the leadership of the Chinese Communist Party, the victory of China's people's democratic revolution mainly relied on the industry of the Han people. (Gladney 1993, pp. 178-9)

This change of policy was in line with what the former Soviet Bolsheviks argued — the revocation of the right of complete separation for non-Russian peoples. In the early Soviet years, however, the revolutionary government, headed by Lenin, was under severe pressure from reactionary forces both within and outside. For the sake of stability at the time, non-Russians were allowed to have their own independent state if they wanted to. After the situation was under control, the central government formed the Union of Soviet Socialist Republics (USSR).

Chairman Mao was not sure what system the CPC should follow immediately after the founding of the PRC. He considered the Soviet-style confederacy but Li Weihan, the number one ethnic policy maker of the CPC, told Mao that the Chinese case was very different from the Soviet Union in terms of history, population ratio between the majority and minorities, and international timing. He argued that two factors were crucial in calling for a different response in China. First, China had a much longer history of highly centralised unification. Second, China's minority population was less than 7 per cent in 1949. So it was determined that the central government would grant national minorities the right to autonomy rather than confederal choice.

After the formation of the PRC

The new government directly encouraged pride in minority status and equality of all ethnic groups from the 1950s. The first constitution stated that all nationalities were equal and regional autonomy applied in areas where a minority nationality lived in a compact community. The two principles emphasised were equality and autonomy, but autonomy did not include the right to secession. Like the Guomindang, the CPC came to power with a strong determination to prevent secession and any subsequent disintegration of China. The policy, as spelled out in 1954, was basically one of 'integration', somewhere between 'assimilation' and 'pluralism' according to Mackerras (1994). Minorities' rights to the maintenance of their own culture, language and religion were the basis of this policy. In fact, as Chapter 1 indicated, the groups that were sent out in the 1950s to identify minority nationalities were required to make their decisions on such criteria, along with the criteria of common territory and common economic life. Most of the five autonomous regions, 30 autonomous prefectures and 123 autonomous counties (banners in Inner Mongolia) were established between 1950 and 1958.

The government under Mao Zedong attempted to counter notions of Han superiority with pronouncements about equality and the right of nationalities to use and develop their own languages and to preserve or reform their own customs and ways. From the beginning, Chinese leaders also asserted the principle that Han people should assist the other nationalities economically and culturally. This was because the Han had 'a comparatively higher political, economic, and cultural level than the others', according to Government Deputy Chairman Liu Shaoqi in 1954. Liu believed that this superiority did not entitle the Han to 'put on airs' towards other nationalities, but rather imposed on Han an obligation to help in their development. The Eighth Congress of the Chinese Communist Party when it met in 1956 reasserted that special attention needed to be paid to the prevention and correction of tendencies of 'great-Hanism' (Mackerras 1994, pp. 146-7).

Changes, such as major land reforms, were introduced more slowly in some autonomous regions (such as Tibet) than in others. In Xinjiang (particularly among the Uyghurs) they were completed between 1951 and 1953. In Inner Mongolia, softer approaches were adopted towards land reform in pastoral areas. Herd owners were not humiliated in front of the masses and were not categorised into classes, nor were their herds confiscated for reallocation, as in the case in other Han populated areas. There were few problems for the new government in either Xinjiang or Inner Mongolia on account of either the history of contact and/or the policy of incorporating minority leaders in the change process. This relatively smooth transition did not occur in all regions and in some areas the reform met with violence from anti-CPC guerrillas or outright opposition from the masses, as in Tibet in 1959.

A range of bodies was set up to handle national minorities work. At the national level it has primarily been carried out through two organs — the Nationalities Committee under the National People's Congress (the highest organ of state power) and the State Nationalities (now Ethnic) Affairs Commission under the State Council (the highest administrative organ). The former puts proposals relating to autonomous regions and minority issues up for deliberation and ratification by the People's Congress while the role of the Commission is to implement national policy in national minority regions. At the national level, there are also divisions of ministries or commissions concerned with minority affairs. At the local level, the People's Congress in some provinces and autonomous regions has a nationality committee or section. Governments of provinces, regions and major cities have a nationalities affairs committee.

The retreat from integration between the late 1950s and the late 1970s

The Great Leap Forward, from 1958 to 1962, was a period when Mao was on a path of radical 'leftist' programs and reforms, such as the formation of communes. In some autonomous regions these were introduced in 1958, at the same time as for the Han, but in other regions change proceeded more slowly. Nevertheless the changes were implemented and opposition to Han socialism was suppressed. This was especially the case in Inner Mongolia, Xinjiang, and Tibet. Consequently this was a much more assimilationist period, rather than one of integration.

Even before the commencement of the Cultural Revolution in 1966, the CPC had specified two basic premises for the resolution of nationality problems: the need for equality within each nationality and the need for revolutionary struggle by the broad masses of exploited people. The period of the Cultural Revolution, from 1966 to 1976, became the most assimilative in the history of China. All social contradictions were seen in class terms and nationality leaders were condemned. Autonomy was retained in principle but in reality many cultural relics, symbols and institutions were destroyed. Nationality leaders were imprisoned and ill treated. Many religious temples were damaged, minority schools shut down and people tortured to death after being falsely charged with 'attempting to split from the motherland'. Han Chinese cadres became high-handed in their treatment of what they perceived as 'backward' minority groups. The events of the Cultural Revolution, with the general move to assimilation and the destruction and violence directed towards many nationality cadres, marked a temporary abandonment of the policy of cultural pluralism.

'During the heyday of the Maoist orthodoxy', according to Harrell (1996, p. 16), questions of ethnicity were muted and 'everybody inside was Chinese'. Some reformers inside China had advocated former Yugoslavia-like decentralisation but this was rejected as being politically destabilising. In the 1960s, the difference on issues associated with ethnicity/nationality was the major reason for the split with the former USSR. The CPC did not go as far as true Marxists believed and Mao Zedong 'soon found that the Marxist paradigm of nationalism was in serious conflict with the goal of the Chinese nationalists; that is, a strong and independent nation-state' (Zheng 1999, p. 69).

Aside from the Cultural Revolution, several events mar the national minority situation in China during this period. The Tibetan uprising of 1956-59 resulted in the departure of the Dalai Lama and many Tibetans and in 1962 70 000 Kazaks crossed the border from Xinjiang into the former Soviet Union. Increasing Han migration into minority regions was also leading to the emergence of bitter feelings (Postiglione 1992, p. 25).

After Mao Zedong's death in 1976

The death of Mao Zedong in 1976 led to a softening of policies and an acknowledgment that the assimilationist period had been oppressive and exploitative towards minorities and that minority regions had fallen behind in terms of economic and social development. Deng Xiaoping's leadership placed renewed emphasis on nationality and autonomy, as long as there were no moves to secession. According to Soled (1995, p. 256), the party 'cautiously returned to a revival of autonomous rule and at least a rhetorical commitment to equal treatment and development priority for minorities'. The 1980s saw a return to the policy of integration and to resources being directed towards minority cultures. Defaced monuments and religious symbols and buildings began to be restored and religious practices were permitted, though the number of religious leaders was closely monitored. Ethnic dances and other performances began to be showcased at major events and in the media. There was a rebirth of national ethnic identity after the Cultural Revolution.

The process of market reform and the open-door policy began in 1978 after Deng Xiaoping came to power. Deng Xiaoping and his comrades put the highest priority on economic modernisation in order to strengthen the nation-state that Mao had built. Mao's 'politics in command' approach had resulted in economic disasters and 'posed a serious threat to everything the Party leaders had fought for: that is, a strong Chinese nation and people's loyalty to the state' (Zheng 1999, p. 91). The communes were dismantled in the 1980s and there was a return to a family-based contract system in 1984, with all land still belonging to the state. The open-door policy enabled foreign investment and the exchange of ideas, technology and people. Learning from the West was seen as the means of achieving economic growth and modernisation. International migration increased and by 1991 the level was 3.4 times higher than in 1978. It was acknowledged that the

> closed state of population caused a bad impact on the social, economic and cultural progress of China — low level of economic development, low living standard of people, poor medical conditions, little absorption of foreign advanced scientific, cultural knowledge and scientific research methods, lack of innovation, etc. (Yan 1996, p. 3)

Thus, a revival in the early 1980s of an emphasis on equality and autonomy coincided with a push for economic, social and political development, but economic development was not undertaken evenly. Coastal areas were opened first to the outside world and SEZs were created around Shanghai, Guangzhou and Tianjin and then expanded to other areas. This was the so-called 'East-Central-West' strategy of favouring East China over the Western sectors in the allocation of development funds. This decision was based on the view that investment in the east would bring better returns than investment elsewhere due to the existence of better infrastructure, more educated population, easier access to export markets and greater knowledge in dealing with the outside world. Pressure from local officials in these regions for decentralisation of control soon led to these regions becoming much more autonomous and setting their own rules.

On the whole, less economic development occurred in minority areas in spite of massive state allocations to overcome inequalities in outcomes. There was a significant expansion in industry and agriculture in many areas, and communications, health and education services improved markedly, but on the whole minority regions experienced lower rates of economic and social development than the rest of China. The regions where minorities live are often mountainous, inaccessible and difficult to farm. Some areas are rich in oil, coal and minerals but minorities are not the principal beneficiaries of these deposits. Difficulties such as long distances to markets and ports and the high cost of transport meant that mining and other activities were gradually taken over by non-minority interests. As a consequence, inequalities with Han Chinese widened.

Economic growth may constrain or fuel ethnic nationalism. In the case of China, economic change has often brought the development of media, better transportation, higher school enrolment and increased mobility and urbanisation.

> These factors do not necessarily favor a homogenization of society. On the contrary, they objectively unify styles of living while providing minorities with the means of subjectively recognizing themselves as conscious entities. (Dogan and Pelassy 1984, p. 52)

Minority nationalities began to stress the maintenance of their languages, culture, institutions and relics. The state demonstrated its tolerance by producing books during the 1980s on the culture, especially the costumes, dance and traditional life styles, of minority nationalities. The rise in ethnic consciousness was also partly a response to growing inequalities, and local officials in minority regions voiced their concern that they were being left out of the economic modernisation process. But a trip to Tibet in 1980 by two top ranking Chinese officials, Hu Yaobang and Wan Li, and the resulting six-point plan that was to assist Tibetan culture and economy and spark greater tolerance for Chinese rule led to the opposite of what was expected (Zheng 1999, p. 35). Ethnic nationalism manifested itself in rebellions and increased pressure for secession, especially in Tibet and Xinjiang. Inner Mongolia did not manifest a desire to join with the Mongolian People's Republic and later the State of Mongolia, though there was discontent and some 'separatists' were arrested in the 1980s.

The central government responded by introducing the *Law on Regional National Autonomy (LRNA)* on 1 October 1984. It was designed to enable greater nationality representation in local administration, some choice as to whether central government laws be adopted or not and greater autonomy in education and culture. One of the resulting outcomes was less development of education in some regions, partly because of lack of funding for school facilities, especially in remote areas where there were limited resources. The policy also enabled autonomous regions to be exempted from the one-child policy introduced in 1979. This birth control waiver was designed to stop the emergence of further discontent in autonomous regions.

By the mid to late 1980s and 'in recognition of the inadequate number of nationality cadres in proportion to their populations, and of the serious and continuing problems in nationality areas, the State Nationalities' Affairs Commission decided to establish the Minority Nationalities Research Centre in order to offer advice, information, and suggestions on how to improve the economy and welfare of minority nationalities' (Mackerras 1994, p. 159). The centre was set up in 1988. In the same year the central government expressed serious concerns about minority problems, especially due to events in Tibet. The effectiveness of the autonomy law and of autonomy itself was being questioned. Events in Tibet and elsewhere in the late 1980s led in 1989 to a reduction in the extent of autonomy allowed, though there was not a corresponding move to increased assimilation. The Tiananmen event of 4 June 1989 was to lead to a reversal of the move away from leftism as well as a return to more central government control from 1990. The inclusion of two minority students on the 21 most wanted student leaders list, after 4 June 1989, signalled the government's concern about minority separatist issues.

Minority policies of the 1990s

In spite of policy statements, economic development has been relatively slow in minority regions. Agricultural incomes generally have not kept pace with urban incomes and the growth of TVEs in inland and minority regions lagged behind that in other areas. Lack of communication and transport facilities and distance from the coast all imposed substantial hurdles to be overcome. By the early 1990s, minority regions still had a low degree of self-sufficiency and 'poverty [was] the continuing burden of the minorities in border regions' (Soled 1995, p. 257). Table 3.1 shows two measures of the comparative standard of living in 1992 in a number of locations. Average wages as a percentage of the national average and sales per person as a percentage of the national average are collected by the State Statistical Bureau as markers of living standards. These figures indicate the situation that applied more than ten years after the introduction of economic reforms and the open door policy.

Table 3.1 shows that wages in Beijing and Shanghai municipalities were considerably higher than for Shandong, Guizhou and Inner Mongolia in 1992. The last two have high proportions of minorities while Shandong was a poor overcrowded province on the coast south of Shanghai. Guangdong on the south coast incorporated rapidly growing economic areas and had become a magnet for people from all over China as already discussed. While Yunnan's figures for wages are average, when figures for sales/person are used as an indicator of living standards it comes out as being much poorer, as do Inner Mongolia and Guizhou. Guizhou is one of the poorest areas of China

Table 3.1 Wages and total sales per person, selected regions, 1992

Region	Population 1991 ('000)	Wages per person as % of national average	Total sales per person as % of national average
Municipalities			
Beijing	10 819	128.2	408.7
Shanghai	13 342	156.6	377.2
Provinces			
Shandong	84 393	94.7	97.0
Guangdong	62 829	141.0	173.6
Yunnan	36 963	100.0	65.3
Guizhou	32 392	88.2	38.4
Inner Mongolia	21 457	81.1	89.6
Xinjiang	15 156	117.3	106.9

Source: Euromonitor (1994, pp. 197-204).

and is also home to a large number of minorities. Fears about economic disadvantage leading to ethnic uprisings and increased ethnic nationalism stem from the picture portrayed in this table.

Xinjiang had higher than national average for wages and sales, though many people's incomes were low. The average figures were inflated by the incomes of wealthy traders, businesspeople and agriculturalists. Large scale infrastructure developments, such as roads, railways, air transport and other facilities (irrigated farming areas) have also been undertaken in recent decades in Xinjiang to provide the basis for economic development. Xinjiang has experienced a rapid upsurge in its Han component, partly to operate and take advantage of the new facilities. In spite of the economic developments in Xinjiang there has been an upsurge in ethnic nationalism. Outside influences have come to play a major part in various parts of China. The collapse of the Soviet Union enabled separatist groups in Xinjiang to seek support from the newly independent states of Central Asia 'leading to over 30 reported bombing incidents in Xinjiang in 1994' (Zheng 1999, p. 36). Groups pushing for an 'Independent East Turkestan' claimed responsibility for these activities (Gladney 1995, Wang 1998a). Inner Mongolia also reportedly had an independence movement that was crushed by the regional government in 1991 (Zheng 1999, p. 36).

In February 1990, a meeting of the State National Minorities Affairs Commission was held in Beijing because of concern about 'calls for autonomy in border regions' (Postiglione 1992, pp. 25-6). The meeting agreed on ten tasks to defuse the 'racial problem', including

> strengthening of unity and [the] maintenance of stability in minority areas, more funds for infrastructure development, a token number of promotions for cadres of minority origin, and more flexible economic and trading policies to help local people attract foreign investment. (Postiglione 1992, pp. 25-6)

In 1994, Mackerras (pp. 165-6) argues that the curtailment of administrative autonomy in minority regions in the late 1980s was 'reversed in the 1990s'. Soled (1995, p. 256) also maintains that administrative autonomy 'is not assured but it has been taken seriously in the interests of an inter ethnic united front and the security of China's frontiers' and that the party has 'cautiously returned to a revival of autonomous rule and at least a rhetorical commitment to equal treatment and development priority for minorities'.

This view is debatable. Minority regions have increasingly been brought into line with central government policies. For example, while family planning policies were implemented for minorities in 1982 the central authorities in Beijing 'gave autonomous administration units the right to develop their own policies' (Heberer 1989, p. 81). In 1984 it was ruled that the one-child family should be encouraged for minorities comprising more than 10 million members (the Zhuang minority only) and in the early 1990s minority populations were brought more into line with the Han family planning policy. Couples belonging to minority nationalities in urban areas could now have two children and those in rural areas could have three. Han Chinese are confined to one child for urban dwellers and one/two children for rural residents (two if the first child is a girl). Other social changes enable only a limited amount of tinkering with 'soft' autonomy. Phan (1996, p. 103) questions whether even these small concessions have been meticulously executed. For example, the under-representation of minority cadres at all administrative levels, to practice 'pro forma autonomy', is still very noticeable. In reality, the lack of economic development seriously challenged the practical implementation of autonomy.

Many local officials began to argue in the 1990s that there needed to be a strengthening of the state through recentralisation to ensure both continued economic growth and survival as a nation-state. The fear that China as a nation-state could be endangered by economic decentralisation became prevalent not only in intellectual circles but also among government officials at different levels.

> Local officials, especially those in minority areas, are afraid that the weakening of central power will result in national disintegration. Many argued that if the central government is not able to promote economic development in poor and minority areas, conflicts between nationalities and socio-political instability will follow. (Zheng 1999, p. 41)

Thus the emphasis at the end of the 1990s was on unity and a new form of nationalism. The new form of nationalism was promoted as something much more than patriotism. It stemmed from a range of factors but most importantly from: the need for all citizens to believe in the nation-state as a multinational state; pride in the economic achievements of the past 20 years especially in light of the fact that China has not followed the western model of economic development; and pride in the great tradition of China which has enabled its economic success. It is argued by the Chinese that economic reforms in the Soviet Union and eastern Europe led to the collapse of communist regimes due to the decline of their ideology. They argue that once 'all ideas, values, and "isms" embedded in that ideology could no longer provide the political legitimacy for the government, the collapse of the empire became inevitable' (Zheng 1999, p. 71).

Throughout the 1990s there has been pressure from within China to develop a new 'ism' or ideology, to fill the gap left by the demise of traditional communist ideology (which is no longer attractive to Chinese or outsiders) and to ensure the non-disintegration of the country. Many 'new' nationalists believe that China's survival as a multinational state depends on whether a new 'ism' or ideology can be created and whether a process of recentralisation can be put in place. Anti-westernisation also became a major theme of this group. On the other hand, liberal forces have been pushing for a freeing up of markets, greater freedom and less state control. They argue that China will only continue on the path of economic development if it liberalises more institutions while at the same time maintaining strong central fiscal power. But central power must be constrained or it will be abused. Liberals also emphasise the importance of increased integration into the globalisation process. This debate continues in China and is reflected in many of the anomalies that occur.

Minority issues in 2000

The state attitude continues in the post-Mao tradition of officially representing China as a nation of many nationalities with the emphasis on the image of internal ethnic diversity, in contrast to the Mao period of active suppression of ethnic difference. This re-imagining of the nation 'has fostered an expectation of a new order of social experience' that will encompass both harmony and the official promotion of diversity (Chao 1996, p. 211). Chinese literature on minorities, however, is still generally of the 'celebration' type whereby cultural differences such as dance, diet, dialect, customs and dress are seen as the only real manifestations of difference. The portrayal of minorities by using pictures of women and children as images of subordination continues, according to Harrell (1994). Minority groups are showcased at many events including the 1 October 1999, 50th Anniversary Celebrations of the formation of the PRC. A special folder of stamps depicting the 56 nationalities, under the title *National Unity*, was released on the occasion of the 50th Anniversary Celebrations. Prior to the celebrations, minority games were held in Beijing and received a great deal of media coverage, and a nationalities conference was held in Beijing from 30 September to 3 October 1999 'to solve nationality problems' (Hao 1999). This was the first major conference for many years.

The above is not unlike the way that many governments seek to promote ethnicity or multiculturalism. That is, they emphasise difference but don't grapple with the policy implications that follow, such as equitable access to resources, opportunities, dignity and rights. In China, material on the literature, music, socio-economic status, science and technology, business ventures and other cultural aspects of minority nationalities and on special policies directed towards them is generally lacking. While national minority languages have been strengthened, national minority literature is still strictly censored. Religion has been increasingly tolerated, and even encouraged when it helps tourism, yet 'limited when it threatens national sovereignty' (Postiglione 1992, p. 36). Academic debate or writings within China about ethnic interaction, ethnic conflicts, ethnic nationalism or ethnic movements are absent. Ethnic nationalism is referred to as 'narrow nationalism' and destabilising for China and therefore not a field in which patriotic Chinese would be engaged. According to Zheng (1999, pp. 70-71), 'the Government and Chinese intellectuals believe that if ethnic nationalism is to be avoided and separatist movements are to be kept under control, the issue of ethnic nationalism should not be brought to any public debate'.

Contemporary books by foreign authors are more diverse but few deal with the sensitive issue of ethnic nationalism. *China's Minorities Integration and Modernization in the Twentieth Century* (Mackerras 1994) provides the most complete overview and covers aspects of history, population, policies, economic conditions and social trends. However, it tends to put an official line and shows little indication of grassroots attitudes and aspirations. Poston and Yaukey's *Population of Modern China* (1992) includes a comprehensive coverage of minority nationality population issues from a demographic viewpoint. Other works concentrate on particular groups, such as the Hui or Muslim Chinese (Gladney 1991, 1996), the Yi (Harrell

1988, 1993) and the Bai (Wu 1990). The more recent *Negotiating Ethnicities in China and Taiwan* (Brown 1996) provides a valuable series of papers on the creation and subsequent reproduction of various identities, including Tibetans, Mongolians, Hui, Dongba, Prmi, Naxi and Ge. Dikotter's 1992 and 1996 work on race and racial identities in China provides a westerner's view on some of these aspects. *Unity and Diversity: Local Cultures and Identities in China* (Liu and Faure 1996) provides very interesting analysis of various groups, ethnic, rural and urban, both in contemporary China and throughout history. Most recently, Kaup's *Creating the Zhuang: Ethnic Politics in China* (2000) provides an in-depth discussion of many of the definitional issues around ethnicity and the strengthening of ethnic nationalism in particular political and economic environments.

Classification as a minority brings certain privileges in China today, including subsidies for education and special educational opportunities (for example, access to higher education through the National Minority Institutes). Special policies also support publications in minority languages and the dissemination of information, through TV, radio and the press, in minority languages. These are all valuable strategies for helping to improve the educational status of minorities, and therefore their employment opportunities. They may also improve access to better information on health, nutrition and other aspects that will improve their quality of life.

Education was chosen as the field to be investigated in depth in this book as a means of understanding the role and value of special policies. It is one aspect of social policy that has been generally supported throughout the communist period and has come to be seen as the major means by which groups raise their socio-economic status. At the same time it has been an area of research that has attracted very little attention, especially minority education. The development of education policies will be traced here in order to provide an understanding of the current situation in relation to minorities' education.

EDUCATION POLICIES

Under Mao Zedong and Deng Xiaoping

Since the formation of the PRC, there have been two major periods in the development of education — the period 1949 to 1976 dominated by Mao Zedong and the post-1976 period dominated by Deng Xiaoping. 'In retrospect, there exists a sharp difference in educational practices' due to the differences in their political agenda and personal experiences (Xiaodong 1996, p. 61). While both recognised the significance of education in society, they viewed the function of education differently.

Between 1949 and 1976, Mao Zedong 'emphasised that education should be combined with productive labour' (Xiaodong 1996, pp. 69-70). The education system and way of learning were characterised by schools, colleges and universities run by factories, education was to be a life-long process and much of it was to occur in informal settings in a China that was closed to the rest of the world. Thus, Mao's aims were closely related to his political agenda of serving proletarian politics and cultivating thousands of successors for the proletarian cause. During the time of Mao's leadership Deng Xiaoping attempted to promote higher education but as the latter was later to comment, 'Mao Zedong ... made a big mistake ... [he ignored] the development of economic productivity' (Deng 1987, p. 103).

The first priority in Deng's era was economic development rather than political struggle. Deng regarded educational institutions as key places to train experts and he stressed the combination of university scientific research with industry from an economic perspective. Deng also opened China up to educational exchanges and the borrowing of foreign intelligence to accelerate economic development. Under Deng Xiaoping:

> ... [t]he overriding aim of education in the post-Mao era was to serve the needs of the modernization program. In terms of the dual objectives of revolution and development, the post-Mao leadership gave first priority to development and demanded an education program that would speed up the 'four modernizations' by providing and fostering the personnel and knowledge needed for this development. (Chen 1990, p. 153)

At the same time, Deng Xiaoping 'was committed to the preservation of the Party's organizational identity and hence its monopoly on power. ... For him, it is the basis of order at home which alone ensures that the economic policies of reform and openness can be carried out without undermining Communist Party rule through the spread of liberal influence' (Xiaodong 1996, p. 72). This combination of elements led to a huge increase in both the number and diversity of education institutions and training modes in China. Universities were encouraged to engage in a wide range of teaching and research, especially with an emphasis on science and technology. Agricultural, specialised middle schools, professional and technical schools were established at the secondary level, and primary schools were encouraged to develop. The emphasis on achieving 100 per cent literacy came to the fore.

The *Decision of the Central Committee of the Communist Party of China on the Reform of the Educational Structure,* 1985 was basically about decentralisation (Cheng 1995). School reforms made the financing of schools increasingly dependent on locally generated revenue, accelerated the introduction of nine years compulsory education with the aim of reaching 100 per cent by 2000 (later amended to 85 per cent by this date with different targets for each of three broad regions) and introduced means of making education accessible to all. The latter was to be achieved by provisions to exempt families from school registration fees, to provide free textbooks and exercise books and to provide girls-only classes where required (Pepper 1990, Lewin *et al.* 1994). At the same time, principals were granted greater autonomy for decision-making and alternative systems of bilingual education were promoted. Policies to increase autonomy within the existing system of higher education, to develop occupational education and to improve the quality of educators were also implemented.

It is not clear how much improvement there was by the early 1990s. The decline of the government's financial capacity (due to the decentralisation of fiscal power and lack of taxes coming to the central government) meant that it was not able to provide support for basic education, especially in poor areas. Schools became highly dependent on the local economy for a large proportion of teachers' salaries, capital construction and other non-recurrent expenditure. The model for funding became known as 'sponsorship at three levels' — primary schools are sponsored (operated and owned) by villages, junior secondary schools by townships and senior secondary schools by counties (Cheng 1995, p. 70). This meant a rise in disparity between regions as economically more prosperous regions were able to fund good basic education while poor areas, including many minority regions, experienced an inability to provide salaries and equipment, or to build and maintain schools. The inability of poor farmers to pay became increasingly more evident and was manifested in unpaid salaries and an increase in dilapidated buildings in rural areas. The amount of dilapidated floor space in primary schools ranged from virtually none in Heilongjiang to 7.12 per cent in Ningxia and 4.94 per cent in Xinjiang (Department of Development and Planning 1999, p. 81). So the outcome was increased disparity and led 15 provinces in 1993 to make a representation to the central government 'requesting a reversion of the decentralization policy, so that the financial responsibility for basic education goes back to county governments' (Cheng 1995, p. 76). On the positive side, decentralisation led to increased diversity. Local administrations and community groups were able to develop education according to their perceived needs instead of it being centrally controlled. This is important for understanding some of the developments that will be documented in later chapters.

The decline of state financial power 'had a very negative impact on higher education, with professional educators and researchers increasingly shifting their focus to profit-making in order to improve their incomes', according to Zheng (1999, p. 121). About 60 per cent of all tertiary educators show up in the yearbook statistics as having more than one source of income. To some extent this trend has been encouraged by the government as one way of disseminating research activities and outcomes to the private sector and to SOEs and TVEs (Harvie and Turpin 1996). At the same time, many academics have left the state sector to work in joint ventures and private companies or have gone overseas and not returned. Much of this movement is driven by the low incomes (600 yuan per month) earned in state educational and research institutions compared to the incomes offered elsewhere. Commercial activities not only became prevalent among educators but also among educational institutions. Schools were forced to set up income generating businesses (such as car repair sites, factories, shops, orchards) on their grounds just to be able to pay teachers' salaries. One institution of the Chinese Academy of Sciences (CAS) instigated a scheme of sending local peasants to grow vegetables in Siberia every summer as a means of earning income. The income generated was split between the institution (60 per cent) and the farmers (40 per cent) (Wang 1997).

In the 1990s, the emphasis on education increased even more. In order to strengthen 'comprehensive national power' (*zonghe guoli*) or 'national interest', which replaced Maoist internationalism in the post-Mao era, there has been a concentration on four major strategies. The Fourteenth Party Congress (1992) stressed: increasing China's economic power, facilitating progress in technology; raising the educational level of the population, and strengthening military power. Education has become a major focus for achieving economic growth through the enhancement of human resources. At the tertiary level, market forces have come into even greater play with the trial introduction of fee paying arrangements in 37 universities in 1994 and with students having the free choice of jobs on graduation (rather than being assigned to a workplace).

The major change in minority education during the post-June 4 1989 period has been the intention to give special emphasis to education in border regions as education is seen as having a special role in maintaining stability. At the same time, state economic plans to defer mass economic development in the northwest and southwest till the late 1990s meant that one faction was pressing for increased state contributions to education in minority regions in the interim. They argued that the state should take on the larger share of education expenditure in these regions to ensure certain fixed educational targets were met in the short term (Postiglione 1992).

According to Zheng (1999, p. 121), at the end of the 1990s China's human resource development is the weakest in the Asia-Pacific region. There are still 200 million illiterates, only 2 per cent of the relevant age group are receiving a tertiary education (compared to 42 per cent in Korea and 45 per cent in Taiwan) and compulsory primary and junior secondary education is a long way from being achieved. Part of the explanation lies in the high dropout rate as children opt out of school to earn income for themselves or their families. Education also has other roles, however, and may be used as a means of implementing affirmative action policies to achieve equal opportunity and economic development and to encourage the interaction/integration of people of different ethnicities. The particular policies directed at minorities will be analysed within this framework.

EDUCATION FOR MINORITY NATIONALITIES

Minority education has attracted increasing attention and two major purposes have been stated: the maintenance of nationality languages and culture, and the economic development of outlying regions. There have been four national conferences on education for minorities to develop special policies and measures (1951, 1956, 1981 and 1992). The long gap between the second and third conferences is indicative of the lack of attention to minority issues during this period. The principles and special policies/measures that have emerged over time have been outlined in a special paper prepared by the China National Institute for Educational Research (Wang 1998b). Minority education can have the effect of invigorating ethnic diversity. It can also contribute to providing a broader range of employment opportunities and access to social and economic resources. Minority education policies can therefore be both a stimulus to and consequence of increased minority mobility.

1. Minority nationalities enjoy equal rights

The Constitution of the People's Republic of China promulgated in 1954 regulated that 'All nationalities in the People's Republic of China are equal. The State protects the lawful rights and interests of the minority nationalities and upholds and develops the relationship of equality, unity and mutual assistance among all of China's nationalities'. It also stipulated that it 'preserves the outstanding traditional culture of minority nationalities and promotes the cause of education for minority nationalities'. The *LNRA 1984* also made it clear that

> in accordance with the guidelines of the State on education and with the relevant stipulations of the law, the organs of self-government of national autonomous areas shall decide on plans for the development of education in these areas, on the establishment of various kinds of schools at different levels, and on their educational system, forms,

curricula, the language used in instruction and enrolment procedures. (Wang 1998b)

The law states that 'the organs of self-government of national autonomous areas shall independently develop education for the nationalities by eliminating illiteracy, setting up various kinds of schools, spreading compulsory primary education, developing secondary education and establishing specialized schools for the nationalities. Schools where most of the students come from minority nationalities should, whenever possible, use textbooks in their own languages and use these languages as the media of instruction. Classes for the teaching of Chinese (the Han language) shall be opened for senior grades of primary schools, or for secondary schools to popularize *putonghua*, the common speech based on Beijing pronunciation'.

Similar policies and measures are also clearly defined in the Education Law and the Compulsory Education Law of the PRC. Thus, through legislation, the equal rights of the minority nationalities are protected. However, nine years of schooling became mandatory in minority regions later than for the rest of China — for example, in April 1996 in Turpan, Xinjiang.

2. Flexibility in education provision

Autonomous areas and organisations can decide for themselves on the development of local education. There is provision for choosing various forms of education according to specific regional conditions and special characteristics of different minority nationalities. This may include setting up boarding primary schools, secondary schools and special classes in the boundary and remote mountainous areas and pastoral areas. In 1995, there were 6000 such schools and classes enrolling a total of one million students. This includes special classes and schools for female students in areas where inhabitants are Muslims and specialised schools for the offspring of the herdsmen (opening morning and evening sessions or classes that open every other day).

At the post-school level, this includes providing special classes and preparatory classes for students of minority nationalities in institutes of higher learning and in vocational schools. Preferential treatment has been provided to attract students of minority nationalities to institutes of such categories. This treatment includes: setting quotas for the number of minority students to be enrolled; permitting students of minority nationalities to enter universities and colleges with lower marks achieved during the national college entrance examinations; offering special training to such students; and assigning the graduates to work in areas where they came from. In 1998, the number of registered students of minority nationalities studying in such special classes and taking preparatory courses totalled nearly 10 000.

The state also operates the Central University for Minority Nationalities and 12 other colleges for minority nationalities. These are open only to students of the 55 minority nationalities. At the moment, the number of registered students of minority nationalities in these universities and colleges totals 22 839. The purpose is for training special personnel for national autonomous areas.

3. Training teachers of minority nationalities

A total of 157 normal universities, colleges and special secondary schools have been established in 19 provinces and autonomous regions mainly for the training of teachers of minority nationalities. Apart from these, there are also 124 colleges of education and schools for advanced studies. Teachers' training centres have also been established in the northwest and southeast for the polishing of teachers of minority nationalities.

4. Language teaching and learning

Two principles exist: all students may study both Chinese and their nationality languages and provision exists for compiling and publishing textbooks and teaching materials in languages of minorities. Eight provinces and autonomous regions (Inner Mongolia, Xinjiang, Jilin, Qinghai, Sichuan, Yunnan, Guizhou and Guangxi) have established organisations for compiling and translating textbooks and teaching materials and have set up publishing houses to produce books in languages other than Chinese. Under the guidance of the relevant departments of the State, supervision committees for teaching materials in Mongolian, Korean, Tibetan and Yi languages have been set up. The establishment of such compiling organisations, publishing houses and supervision committees is designed to guarantee bilingual teaching and studying.

5. Assisting autonomous regions

Institutes of higher learning throughout China that boast good teaching facilities and qualified faculties are matched up with universities in autonomous areas. Under this arrangement, mutual assistance is provided in the training of teaching and management personnel, in scientific research, in academic exchanges, in school management and in logistic administration. In 1998, 52 universities were engaged in training minority personnel in

Xinjiang. The program involves a total of 6000 undergraduates, post-graduates, teachers and company managers from the region.

Between the early 1950s and mid-1980s, thousands of university and secondary school teachers from other parts of the country were sent to Tibet to help develop education in that region. Starting from 1985, 26 provinces and municipalities with qualified teachers and advanced teaching facilities were arranged by the State to open special classes or schools for primary school graduates from Tibet. An accumulated 13 000 Tibetan students have graduated from or are receiving education in these schools and classes. Many of the graduates from these schools and classes are now studying in institutes of higher learning, with the aim of assisting in the economic construction of Tibet.

Since the fourth national conference on education for minority nationalities in 1992, the state has organised the economically and culturally developed coastal provinces and cities and other more developed areas to support educational development in 143 poverty-stricken counties inhabited by minority nationalities. Beijing was matched up with Inner Mongolia, Shanghai with Yunnan, Tianjin with Gansu, Liaoning with Ningxia, Shandong with Qinghai, Guangdong with Xinjiang, Jiangsu with Guangxi and Fujian with Guizhou. This matching-up program has brought new momentum to the development of education for minority nationalities.

6. Preferential treatment is offered by universities and secondary technical schools for enrolling minority students

Lower entrance marks are required for students of minority nationalities in entering such schools and when a minority nationality student is at the same level as a non-minority student, the former is to be given first consideration for enrolment. Such treatments ensure that more students of minority nationalities having the opportunity to enjoy higher education.

7. Special state subsidies to autonomous areas for education

A special subsidy is offered to assist with the development of education for minority nationalities and to help overcome education problems. Efforts have also been made to win World Bank loans and to attract donations from home and abroad in supporting the development of education for minorities.

8. Special central and local government monitoring mechanisms

At present, the Ministry of Education maintains a department of education for minority nationalities while the relevant provinces and regions all keep a similar division under their respective education commissions. These departments and divisions concentrate on education for minority nationalities. Provinces and regions that do not have a big population of minority nationalities usually have designated personnel in charge of such education.

9. Improving and administering education for minorities

Since opening up began in the late 1970s, many methods have been used for training administrative and management personnel in the education of minorities — training sessions, assigning government officials to teaching posts for training and sending teachers and officials for study tours abroad. From the mid-1980s to 1989, leaders in minority areas were sent overseas to study labour market and affirmative action programs, human resources management, the status of first nations people in North America and other models of autonomous government. Soled (1995, p. 258) argues that the Chinese 'started to try to find a balance between autonomy and economic and social integration' but that these moves were curtailed in 1989. This is in line with Postiglione's view (1992, p. 36) that 'cultural autonomy within authoritarian socialist systems has always been more a matter of degree than anything else'.

In recent years, with the support and guidance of the Ministry of Education, studies have been conducted on theories and major practices in education for minorities. This had been a neglected area of research but attempts are now being made to overcome some of the gaps in knowledge. Moves are also being made to involve religious and other minority leaders in educational provision and in encouraging increased participation and literacy.

10. Education of minorities for local economic construction

There has been significant progress in spreading compulsory primary education, and more emphasis is now being laid on developing vocational education and adult education, improving the quality of workers and training primary-level and secondary-level technical personnel. These reforms and adjustments are targeted at better serving the economic and social developments in the minority areas and making education more relevant and attractive.

DISCUSSION OF MINORITY EDUCATION POLICIES

The situation in relation to the education level in 1990 of four ethnic groups (Han, Mongolian, Tibetan, and Uyghur) is summarised in Figure 3.1. The figure shows that Mongolians had the highest education levels among the four groups followed by the Han. Uyghurs and Tibetans trailed a long way behind but considerable efforts have been made since 1990 to begin to rectify this.

International literature (see Iredale, Fox and Sherlaimoff 1994, p. 19) suggests that there are four major areas that need to be considered in relation to minority education: individual performance and requirements — access, participation and equity; language policy and programs; curriculum and instructional development; and teacher requirements. Each of these cannot be evaluated extensively but some general points about the current situation will provide an overview.

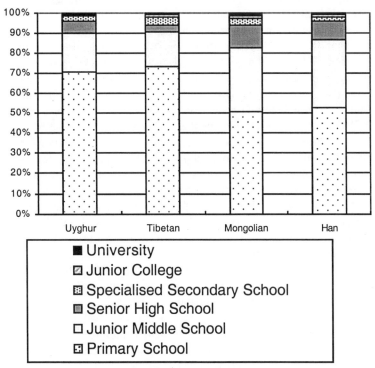

Source: Compiled from State Population Census Office data (1993).

Figure 3.1 Education levels of Uyghurs, Tibetans, Mongolians and Han, 1990

Individual performance and requirements — participation, access and equity

In 1985 the decision was made by the central government to institute nine years compulsory schooling for the whole country by 2000. In 1994, and in line with progress at that time, this was amended to the achievement of 85 per cent in 2000. The reality of the 'challenge the new economic system has posed to the cultural tradition' — of seeing education as a means to social and geographic mobility — has brought about this change (Cheng 1995, pp. 78-89). It is doubtful 'if this tradition could hold out against the tides of money making during the reform'.

The overall growth of participation in primary school education has been greater for minority nationalities (increased by 16.5 times) since 1950 than the national average (increased by 6.4 times). Further evidence of the expansion of primary education to minorities is the fact that the proportion of minority students surpasses their proportion in the relevant age group (China National Institute for Educational Research 1999). This figure conceals, however, significant differences amongst minority groups in terms of participation. The 1998 data show an overall participation rate in primary education of 98.93 (that is 98.93 per cent of primary aged children were enrolled at the time of the data collection). Beijing and Inner Mongolia have above average rates of 99.96 and 99.54, respectively, while the rate for Xinjiang is just below average at 97.68. Tibet has the lowest rate of all of 81.25 (Department of Development and Planning 1999, pp. 72-3).

These figures do not indicate the rate of completion of primary schooling. Figures quoted in Postiglione (1992, pp. 31-2) for 1987 show high drop out rates for minorities in Xinjiang and Yunnan but the 1998 figures for primary schools show a better than average situation in Xinjiang. On the other hand, the drop out rate for Tibet is well above the average rate of 0.93 per cent as it is in other minority regions such as Guangxi, Guizhou and Yunnan. This will be dealt with further in Chapters 5 to 7. The drop out rate at the junior secondary level is higher all over (3.23 per cent) and is of growing concern. It is almost double this average in Tibet (6.08 per cent) and it is high in some other minority regions but these do not include Inner Mongolia (2.30 per cent) and Xinjiang (1.15 per cent).

At the senior secondary level, there were two types of vocational schools (specialised secondary and craftsman) that trained students and directed them into state employment prior to 1980. But economic reform and the subsequent emergence of job markets has led to a major change (Cheng 1995, p. 82). Vocational high schools have been set up to cater for the needs of private enterprises, joint ventures with foreign investments, free recruitment, self employment and tertiary sector employment, and in 1993 they accounted for more enrolments than either of the other two former types of vocational schools. Many of the vocational high schools are joint ventures between employers and local education and labour authorities and the outcome is a situation where the supply of vocational schools varies significantly by location. Students in highly developed urban centres such as Shanghai and Tianjin often choose vocational high schools as their priority, rather than general senior secondary schools (that lead to university). Whereas in less developed areas fewer vocational schools are available and students still opt for the more traditional technical schools where employment is guaranteed on completion. In the early 1990s, vocational education surpassed general education at the national level as the preferred option at the senior secondary level. This represented a change in mentality among students and parents as 'short term economic returns [became] more attractive than academic studies' (Cheng 1995, p. 82). By the late 1990s the situation had changed again, according to the CNIER, so that senior middle schools or general secondary education had again become more popular, especially in cities and areas that have undergone more economic change. The growth of privately funded 'elite' senior middle schools and the increased emphasis being attached to a university education are responsible for this change at the national level.

The impact of these changes for minority students is clear. Many of them do not have access to the types of senior schooling that are available elsewhere in China and if they proceed to senior secondary education they are restricted to the traditional vocational types with tied or guaranteed employment or to general education. Enrolment rates at traditional vocational secondary schools are equivalent in Beijing and Inner Mongolia (91 per 10 000 inhabitants) but much lower in Xinjiang (30) and Tibet (18). But Beijing has 89 students per 10,000 inhabitants enrolled in specialised technical schools, while the figure for Inner Mongolia is 28, for Xinjiang it is 37 and for Tibet it is 12. The national average is 33 (Department of Development and Planning 1999, p. 69). These figures are not standardised by age and therefore only give a general picture of enrolment patterns — they are not participation rates.

Only a very small percentage of China's population is able to attend college as Table 3.2 demonstrates very clearly: 0.54 per cent of China's population in 1990 had attained a college level education.[2] The population of Beijing is a strong exception: more than ten times the national average has been to college. Xinjiang demonstrates a college-educated component which is slightly above the national average while this component in Inner

---

[2] College attendance in this section is defined as students who have attended four years of a degree course or *Daxue Benke*.

Mongolia is slightly below average. Tibet and Yunnan, another important minority region, have figures that are well below the national average.

Table 3.2 Provincial population with college education, 1990

Region	%
China	0.54
Beijing	5.58
Inner Mongolia	0.50
Tibet	0.21
Xinjiang	0.65
Yunnan	0.32

Source: State Population Census Office (1993, Volume 1, p. 5; Volume 2, pp. 32-3).

At the university and college level, minority nationality students comprised 6.4 per cent of the enrolled population in 1995, below their proportion in the total population but much more importantly below their proportion in the relevant age group (China National Institute for Educational Research 1999). Nevertheless, the number of minority students in higher education has increased by 106 times since 1950. This was starting from a very low base and a great deal of emphasis has gone into tertiary education. Article 64 of the *LNRA 1984* makes it incumbent upon the higher state organs to help train minority nationalities in various professions and trades. In autonomous areas, there are 12 National Minorities Institutes (one in Tibet but none in Inner Mongolia or Xinjiang), over 100 universities and colleges and an increasing number of national minority classes in many of the key universities. Special colleges of Tibetan and Mongolian medicine have also been set up.

The influence of market forces is also evident in the tertiary sector. A new strategy of fee payment and free job choice on graduation was introduced in 37 universities in 1993. This concept was not favourably received in less developed regions where the returns to higher education are low and employment options are limited. Therefore, in many regions the policy has remained the same as before with graduates being assigned to employment on completion of their tertiary studies.

One way of trying to overcome the low participation of minority students in education has been through the development of specialist universities, schools or other centres. According to 1994 statistics, there were 103 139 primary schools, 11 563 high schools and 105 institutes of higher learning in the autonomous areas across the country. About a quarter of the primary schools, some of the high schools and 303 vocational secondary schools were open only to minority nationality students. One problem with these, however, is that they may be 'enclaves'. They develop out of the need for cultural support and maintenance and they are places where minority languages and culture survive and flourish. But contiguously there may be questions about standards and entry levels, and even perhaps about the quality of the degrees/diplomas/certificates awarded. Their occurrence as separate structures highlights the fact that the dominant culture prevails. There is considerable debate about the advantages and disadvantages of segregated schools. In most countries, they are seen as detrimental to the development and improvement of minority populations. At best some authors argue that they should be transitory, a stage in the progression towards the full integration of minority cultures in all educational institutions. The advantages and disadvantages in China need to be weighed up against the background of what different minorities prefer and no universal solution should be either expected or sought. Groups with strong economic and cultural foundations (Russian and Koreans, for example) or those with more cultural similarities to the Han (Manchu) often exceed the national average in educational attainment.

Postiglione (1992, p. 32) attributes low school enrolment and retention among many minority groups to poor facilities, untrained teachers, irrelevant curriculum, low family socioeconomic background, cultural traditions and religious beliefs. However, he states that 'non utilisation could also be a form of cultural resistance on the part of national minorities to being integrated into the dominant status culture of the Han. It is most likely that a combination of factors is operating'.

Special measures have been taken to facilitate access by minority students to tertiary institutions, in particular. Since 1980, institutions in minority autonomous regions, which teach in minority languages, have been permitted to have their own entrance examinations (arranged by the region) and admit students directly. Minority students are also admitted to mainstream institutions on the basis of quotas and lower scores at the universal examinations apply than for Han. The groups identified above are most likely to take advantage of these affirmative action strategies so the gap between themselves and other minorities is wide. Interestingly, a number of Han families presented preferential policies as the explanation for changing their identity. In fact it is quite common for the children of minority and Han people to be registered as belonging to a minority so that they can take advantage of preferential policies.

Increased tertiary participation by minorities is a double-edged sword for the government. On the one hand, it prepares people for becoming ethnic officials (mouthpieces of the state) or ethnic scholars. According to Harrell (1994, p. 34), the participation of ethnic leaders is an essential part of minority regional policy. But it has also resulted in increased activism among minority students. Many of them participated in the democracy movement of 1989 in Tiananmen Square and minority university students have also been active in nationalist movements in Tibet and Xinjiang. Thus, further increasing university enrolments among minorities may impact on political activism and the question of national integration. When minority peoples are given a chance to pursue tertiary education without a concomitant granting of equality and the sharing of power, this can lead to discontent. In Harrell's words (1994, p. 35) when there is 'advancement without equal empowerment, revolts can be the result'.

Language policy and programs

The modernisation process may have a profound effect on minorities and their willingness to identify with their ethnic group. Many see it as simply more economically and socially expedient to abandon their ethnic identity for a more Chinese identity, at least in terms of Chinese language proficiency, in order to have a more prosperous future. Others maintain that economic reform and the household responsibility system will lead to a rebirth of cultural practices. Hinton (1990, p. 20), an agronomist, unfortunately refers to this as 'cultural regression' and says:

> ... the most striking consequence of reform was the far-reaching cultural regression. Privatization . . . brought with it, a revival of all the worst features of the old society . . . old customs, old habits, old ideology and old superstitions, all bearing a distinctly feudal flavor, also surfaced.

Both 'sinification' and a revival of folk cultures are occurring. Globalisation and disruption due to migration are leading many people to find new ways of affirming their cultural and ethnic identity. This may include decisions to send children back to the area of origin for their schooling, searching out minority schools where children can learn or re-learn their national language and heritage and interact with children of the same ethnicity, or, in the extreme situation, establishing their own schools in a new environment. These actions are a response to both globalisation and the exclusion of migrants from many of the services of urban environments.

Issues of language policy, curricula and parental choice of children's education are all important. In 1994, there were 13 times as many teachers of minority nationalities as there were in 1950 and 3000 textbooks were published in 30 languages other than Chinese. National minority languages are taught at all levels. Again it was starting from a low base but the state's emphasis on strengthening minority groups languages has been notable. This is seen as one way of restoring some degree of cultural autonomy and winning back support that was lost during the Cultural Revolution (Postiglione 1992).

Curriculum and instructional development

A common (Han) curriculum has progressively been implemented throughout all schools in the 1990s and curriculum texts have been translated into many minority languages. Whereas there used to be only one set of textbooks, since 1991 there has been 'one syllabus, multiple textbooks' (Cheng 1995, p. 74). The are now at least eight versions of the textbooks following the national curriculum. The common curriculum is a result of 'consensual bias' among educators, according to Cheng, and attempts at diversification have been resisted on the whole. Only a few areas, such as Shanghai and Zhejiang, have created their own curricula. Shanghai has also created a new subject called *career guidance*. The Department of Education started reforming the national curriculum in the late 1990s and in the future there will be three curricula: the national curriculum, local curriculum and school curriculum. This will enable curricula to be more diversified and be adaptable to different local and individual needs.

In minority schools, special subjects on minority cultures and histories may be taught but are rare. For example, the Mongolian primary school in Hohhot ran special subjects in Mongolian history. Family and religious institutions have been the main purveyors of this type of education in the past and this continues in some regions. For example, among the Hui people of Ningxia Autonomous Region 60 per cent of the children attend public schools and 40 per cent go to mosques for their learning.

At the tertiary level, special emphasis has been placed on teaching ethnology and minority historical traditions, culture and arts, though it would appear that only minority students take these subjects. Textbooks, reference books, newspapers and journals have all been translated under the supervision of the state. Students can major in minority languages with specialties in 21 minority languages including Mongolian, Tibetan, Uyghur, Kazak, Yao, Yi, Zhuang, Va and Jingpo.

Teacher requirements

The supply of adequately trained, appropriate teachers is obviously crucial in relation to educational outcomes. The system for teacher training relies heavily on Normal Universities, which are teacher training institutes. However, there is a shortage of teachers, especially minority teachers who had low enrolment rates in these institutions in the past. Consequently many teachers are undertrained or untrained. The shortage of teachers in many minority areas has resulted in groups of teachers from coastal and other regions being sent to frontier regions, such as Tibet, to set up and staff schools and higher education institutes. Such inter-regional educational (and cultural) exchanges were in accordance with Article 42 of the autonomy law in order to assist minority regions. But one Chinese commentator puts it as being to further consolidate 'the motherland's unity and border defense' (Phan 1996, p. 99).

There is a two tiered system for paying school teachers' salaries. Many teachers in rural primary schools are 'community' teachers who receive some subsidy from the state (the amount varies by a factor of seven) but they are mainly paid by an educational surcharge levied from local tax or by the community in cash or in kind. This often results in teachers receiving below subsistence pay or going unpaid for considerable periods and consequently there are high rates of turnover and separation in poor rural areas. In 1993 the central government decreed 'sanctions against local leaders unless they paid up' (Cheng 1995, p. 75). The proportion of community or *minban* teachers in a province is an indicator of the supply of properly trained teachers and will be looked at in Chapters 5 to 7 in detail. Most teachers in urban areas, on the other hand, are properly trained and paid by the state and the quality of teachers is much higher.

Table 3.3 shows that while Beijing and Shanghai have no *minban* teachers, minority regions rely on them to varying extents. Yunnan and Qinghai, in particular, have a heavy reliance at the primary level on these teachers and compared to these regions Xinjiang has low proportions of *minban* teachers. Pupil-teacher ratios are an indicator of the adequacy of funds for training teachers as well the general supply of teachers. Minority regions do not compare badly with the whole of China but the difference between urban and other figures is quite clear. Relative to other minority regions and the average for China, Xinjiang is better off on these measures. The ratio of minority teachers to all teachers is not available at the regional level but data for the whole of China show that minority teachers comprise 9.70 per cent of teaching staff at teacher training schools and 9.23 per cent at primary schools, with the figures going down to 3.56 per cent at kindergartens.

Data are collected each year on the condition of buildings in general secondary, vocational and primary schools. Table 3.3 shows the percentage of the floor space of primary schools which is described as dilapidated. Minority regions, especially Ningxia and Xinjiang, rate badly on these measures indicating a low commitment of resources to the maintenance of educational buildings. Responsibility for maintenance rests with local authorities and depends on the allocation of local funds, except in cases where eastern regions have provided resources and teachers to particular locations. Clearly minority education is suffering from inadequate resources in relation to infrastructure and along with this goes a lack of teaching and learning materials. Many parents complain about the cost of school fees and their inability to cover the cost of their children's books, etc. As pointed out earlier, many schools have taken up other activities to raise funds for buildings and salaries but this depends on the initiative of the school.

Table 3.3 Indicators of education, various regions, 1998

Region	*Minban* teachers %			Pupil-teacher ratio		Dilapidated buildings %
	Primary	Junior	Senior	Primary	Junior	Primary
Beijing	0.0	0.0	0.0	14.9	12.8	0.19
Shanghai	0.0	0.0	0.0	16.4	16.0	0.01
Inner Mongolia	24.0	5.9	0.1	19.9	15.1	2.49
Yunnan	9.6	0.5	0.0	25.0	16.8	1.19
Tibet	3.8	0.0	0.0	22.3	11.0	4.35
Qinghai	8.9	0.1	0.0	17.6	12.8	3.44
Ningxia	0.5	0.1	0.0	19.8	15.2	7.12
Xinjiang	0.3	0.3	0.3	20.3	14.2	4.94
Total China	13.8	2.14	0.06	23.4	17.6	1.09

Note: *Minban* teachers are village or rural teachers who do not have formal employment and who receive their salary from the village or township rather than the state or county government.

Source: Department of Development and Planning (1999, pp. 72-81).

CONCLUSION

China had no concepts of 'race' or 'ethnicity' throughout its history but *minzu* was borrowed from the Japanese in the early twentieth century and was tied up with the process of nation-state building. Nation-builders had two jobs: to redefine all notions related to 'ethnicity' and to adjust the 'facts' and make the signifier and signified fit. In other words, to identify minority nationalities to suit their concepts. It was a job for government officials and influential intelligentsia but most of them did not travel beyond their own provincial or state boundaries. Hence artificial nationality groups were created and boundaries were drawn that included very dissimilar groups.

The sense of Han superiority was long standing but the influence of

Western 'orientalism' in helping to form the perceptions of minorities cannot be underestimated. Even though the CPC has tried hard to adopt Marxist ethnic theories and adapt them to Chinese reality there is still a long way to go, in view of the deep-rootedness of the prejudice that prevails towards minorities. Harrell (1994, pp. 25-6) refers to this as the 'Confucian co-optation of the communist project'. He states that in the 'communist project' ... 'everything was supposed to be different: the center was progressive but not explicitly Han, and all *minzu* were equal now' but 'the ingrained prejudice and local negative evaluation of minorities' and continued adherence to a 'belief in the five stages of history' (which Chinese children still learn as an objective fact) thwarted the project. Both of these aspects were an integral part of Confucian philosophy and ideology.

Shaw (1989, p. 49), for example, demonstrates the continuation of these attitudes when he advocates 'the study of counter-effects and ... how [the] remaining social formations hampered the prosperity and development of the ethnic minorities' or, in other words, 'the problems of the current ethnic process and development, traditional culture and counter-measures'. This attitude of the 'cultural backwardness' of minorities is also exemplified in *Poverty and Development – A Study of China's Poor Areas* (Yan and Wang 1992, p. 36) where the authors attribute much of the poverty in minority areas to the fact that 'ethnic people are lagging behind the Han in both social and economic development'.

At the international level, major changes in the 1990s have led to heightened concern about instability based on ethnic conflicts and the desire for independence. The disintegration of socialist states and 'the violent release of pent up ethnic tensions in the Soviet Union and in Mongolia just across the border, deepened Chinese sensitivities to shifting political currents' (Pasternak and Salaff 1993, p. 24). The continuation of problems in Xinjiang and Tibet and the international attention paid to the Dalai Lama continue to cause the Chinese government a great deal of concern. For example, the meeting in Sydney in September 1996 between the Prime Minister of Australia, the Hon. John Howard, and the Dalai Lama led to threats of trade sanctions and serious consequences for Australia's relations with China (Skehan and Hutcheon 1996, p. 1). These and other events demonstrate the extreme sensitivity which is attached to issues of minorities in China.

Education policies are one means, along with policies on autonomy and self government, that the central government and the CPC have used to try to encourage human capital development, economic development and social cohesion. The emphasis on improving education in minority regions is commendable and significant gains have been made. But the gains are far from uniform and the particular attention focussed on Xinjiang is evident. The training of minority cadres has been given special attention and has largely been facilitated by the affirmative action strategies that have been used to increase minority access to tertiary education. These minority cadres have been used, in turn, in the definition process and the production of minority materials for the government.

But education also brings about an increase in communication and the dissemination of ideas, as well as an increase in awareness and mobility. The role of education in both promoting the movement of particular groups and the impacts for education of movement will be analysed in depth in the chapters on Inner Mongolia, Tibet, Xinjiang and Beijing. But first, the overall level of mobility of minorities will be considered in order to provide a backdrop for the individual case studies of Mongolian, Tibetan and Uyghur movement.

4. Overall minority movement

No profile exists on the overall patterns of minority mobility in China. For this reason data from the 1990 Census of Population were used to analyse the trends that occurred between 1985 and 1990. To the authors' knowledge, this is the first time analyses of these data have been carried out. The results provide a preliminary picture of the profile of minority movement but the data are constrained by a number of factors. First, the definition of a migrant in the census, as pointed out in Chapter 1, is limited and this means that only those who had changed their place of residence for more than 12 months or who had changed their place of permanent registration (*hukou*) were captured as migrants in the census. Second, the data are now 10 years old. Attempts were made to update the data with information from the 1995 intercensal one per cent sample census. While the data were collected by nationality, the size of some of the samples makes it questionable as to whether the data can be regarded as reliable and Chinese statisticians agreed with this perception.[1] Data are collected by provincial statistical bureaus but are generally not available to outside researchers, and no Chinese researchers have utilised these data sets to understand minority migration.

In spite of these difficulties an analysis of the 1990 census data is used here to present an overall picture of the scale, directions and composition of minority migration. The purpose is to provide a general background for the four subsequent chapters which present more detailed case-studies of mobility to and from Inner Mongolia, Tibet, Xinjiang and Beijing and the movement of Mongolians, Uyghurs and Tibetans, in particular. Without some general profile it would be impossible to understand the movement of minorities in context.

SCALE OF MINORITY MOVEMENT

The 1990 Population Census data show that minorities accounted for 6.45 per cent of all movement, intra-provincial and inter-provincial, as defined by the census, between July 1985 and July 1990. Table 4.1 shows that between

---

[1] Discussion between Fei Guo and State Statistical Bureau (1997).

1985 and 1990, a total of 11 298 669 Han Chinese moved across provincial boundaries compared to 586 711 minority people.[2] Minority moves accounted for 5.2 per cent of all inter-provincial flows, which is lower than their proportion (8.04 per cent) in the total population. On the other hand, the minorities' rate of intra-provincial movement (7.1 per cent of the total) was only slightly below their population proportion. Therefore, they had almost the same overall propensity to move within regions as the Han but the pattern varies greatly between regions.

Table 4.1 shows that some provinces and autonomous regions had a high level of internal minority movement. For example, Jilin had 10.2 per cent minority population but 18.2 per cent of intra-provincial movement was of minorities. Other provinces and regions that had high levels of minorities did not have correspondingly high levels of intra-regional movement by these people. For example, in Xinjiang, minorities comprised 62.4 per cent of the population but accounted for only 38.8 per cent of the internal movement. For Yunnan, 33.5 per cent of the population belonged to minorities but they accounted for only 25.2 per cent of intra-provincial movement. Guizhou had 34.7 per cent minority population who accounted for 25.7 per cent of internal movement. The reasons for these differences need much further investigation. In the following chapters we discuss intra-provincial migration within Inner Mongolia, Tibet and Xinjiang informed by our survey and regional case studies. The remainder of this chapter will focus on inter-provincial movement to examine the broad national trends and to see whether a greater intermixing of nationalities is taking place.

PATTERNS OF INTER-PROVINCIAL FLOWS

Sources

It has already been shown that minorities tend to be heavily concentrated in the north, west and south. Table 2.4 in Chapter 2 showed that in 1990, Guangxi was home to the largest number (16 577 766) of minority peoples. Table 4.2 was constructed to summarise out-migration, in-migration and net migration by province and it shows that Guangxi was the major source region of minority inter-provincial migrants between 1985 and 1990 — accounting for 21.7 per cent of all minority migrants. Yunnan and Guizhou were the second and third most important source regions in terms of numbers. These three regions are all in the south and the flows are strongly towards Guangdong.

---

[2] See Chapter 1 for definition of migrant according to the 1990 census.

Table 4.1 Total population and number of minority migrants, 1985-1990

Destination	Population Total	Intra-province movement Total	Intra-province movement Minorities No.	Intra-province movement %	Inter-province movement Total	Inter-province movement Minorities No.	Inter-province movement %	Total No.	Total Minorities No.	Total %
Beijing	10 819 414	83 978	2 938	3.5	681 714	29 763	4.4	765 692	32 701	4.3
Tianjin	8 785 427	35 239	525	1.5	245 458	10 286	4.2	280 697	10 811	3.9
Hebei	61 082 755	807 282	34 798	4.3	525 948	34 680	6.6	1 333 230	69 478	5.2
Shanxi	28 758 846	620 757	1 561	0.3	313 822	7 158	6.6	934 579	8 719	0.9
Inner Mongolia	21 456 518	570 937	11 327	20.5	261 611	22 624	8.6	832 548	139 951	16.8
Liaoning	39 459 694	877 190	153 668	17.5	548 301	51 756	9.4	1 425 491	205 424	14.1
Jilin	24 659 790	603 859	109 698	18.2	244 850	28 189	11.5	848 709	137 887	16.2
Heilongjiang	35 215 932	1 039 870	68 111	6.5	383 223	25 295	6.6	1 423 093	93 406	6.6
Shanghai	13 341 852	171 536	499	0.3	672 226	6 317	0.9	843 762	6 816	0.8
Jiangsu	67 056 812	1 182 969	2 072	0.2	798 271	23 162	2.9	1 981 240	25 234	1.3
Zhejiang	41 446 015	793 969	3 071	0.4	344 076	14 034	4.1	1 137 338	17 105	1.5
Anhui	56 181 005	863 000	6 493	0.8	344 891	10 033	2.9	1 207 891	16 526	1.4
Fujian	30 048 275	714 375	6 696	0.9	249 648	10 620	4.3	975 315	17 316	1.8
Jiangxi	37 710 177	725 899	2 186	0.3	233 648	3 924	1.7	959 547	6 110	0.6
Shandong	84 392 104	1 183 125	6 927	0.6	617 289	20 927	3.4	1 800 414	27 854	1.5
Henan	85 534 200	1 232 123	18 581	1.5	485 106	13 924	2.9	1 717 229	32 505	1.9
Hubei	53 970 501	1 077 686	33 145	3.1	442 450	13 874	3.1	1 520 136	47 019	3.1
Hunan	60 657 992	1 287 764	67 880	5.5	282 518	23 305	8.2	1 570 282	91 185	5.8
Guangdong	62 829 741	2 646 043	7 301	0.3	1 285 642	93 313	7.3	3 931 685	100 614	2.6
Guangxi	42 244 884	877 476	347 339	39.6	153 817	16 780	10.9	1 031 293	364 119	35.3
Hainan	6 558 076	140 855	12 956	9.2	152 467	12 429	8.2	293 322	25 385	8.7
Sichuan	107 218 310	2 333 155	65 250	2.8	484 583	31 096	6.4	2 817 738	96 346	3.4
Guizhou	32 391 051	460 307	118 446	25.7	195 279	14 845	7.6	655 586	133 291	20.3
Yunnan	36 972 587	726 844	183 407	25.2	259 715	16 973	6.5	986 559	200 380	20.3
Tibet	2 196 029	n.a.	n.a.	n.a.	n.a.	n.a.	n.a.	n.a.	n.a.	n.a.
Shaanxi	32 882 286	700 045	3 910	0.6	320 995	7 669	2.4	1 021 040	11 579	1.1
Gansu	22 371 085	445 453	30 432	6.8	203 557	10 611	5.2	649 010	41 043	6.3
Qinghai	4 456 952	149 187	44 637	29.9	117 574	9 819	8.4	266 761	54 456	20.4
Ningxia	4 655 445	121 416	30 835	25.4	93 333	6 792	7.3	214 749	37 627	17.5
Xinjiang	15 156 883	357 306	138 790	38.8	345 365	16 513	4.8	702 671	155 303	22.1
Total	1 130 510 638	22 828 938	1 619 479	7.1	11 298 669	586 711	5.2	34 127 607	2 206 190	6.5

Source: Data from State Population Census Office (1993, Volumes 1 and 4).

It is very important to understand the factors behind migration and to see whether minorities are being driven by similar factors to Han migrants. Column 4 in Table 4.2 shows the ratio of minorities to migrate out of each region which was the number of out-migrants (1985 - 90) to the total number of minority peoples in the region in 1990. This is obviously an approximation only as the number present in 1990 is the result of in-migration and out-migration during 1985-90. The table shows that minorities in Shanxi Province had the highest rate of out-migration, one in 27 migrated out. Shanxi only has a very small proportion of minorities in its population (0.3 per cent) and is located close to the northern cities of Beijing and Tianjin. The raw data show, however, that while there was considerable movement of minorities to Beijing and Tianjin the movement to Shanghai was equal to the combined movement to these two municipalities. Shanxi was followed by Shanghai and Zhejiang — both of which are not traditional areas of minorities, suggesting a high level of re-migration of people who had moved in earlier. Thus the regions with the highest rates of minority out-migration were areas of low minority density. Regions with the lowest propensity for long term minority out-migration, as defined in the census, were Xinjiang (1:770), Shaanxi (1:599) and Fujian (1:424). Xinjiang has a very high proportion of minorities but Shaanxi and Fujian have low proportions. Shaanxi, in the western region, is a very poor province while Fuijian on the coast is one of the most active regions in terms of opening-up and economic development.

This diversity serves to indicate that many factors are at work in driving people to migrate out of their region. While poverty is one important factor, many other factors, such as business and other contacts, past history of migration, whether a 'culture' of migration and chain migration exist, ethnicity, the influence of local officials and government policy, are all important. The announcement in February 2000 of the 'Remake the West Campaign', as part of the 10th Five Year Plan (2001 to 2005) with its emphasis on economic development for the western region will be important in the future in terms of its impact on migration.

From the data in Table 4.2, Figure 4.1 shows the percentage of total minority movement by origin and destination — to provide an overall picture of their movement. Areas of traditional minority settlement are losing people to regions of historically low minority density and there is a general spreading out of minorities. The source areas are clearly heavily concentrated in the north, south and southwest while destination areas are much more dispersed.

Table 4.2 Minority movement — number of out-migrants, ratio of out-migrants to total, number of in-migrants and net migration, 1985-90

Area/ province	Minority out-migrants		Ratio of out- migrants to total minorities	Minority in-migrants		Net migration of minorities number
	number	per cent		number	per cent	
North						
Beijing	6 700	1.0	1:62	37 500	5.8	30 800
Tianjin	3 100	0.5	1:65	31 200	4.9	28 100
Hebei	28 200	4.4	1:82	28 100	4.4	-100
Shanxi	3 100	0.5	1:27	4 600	0.7	1 500
Inner Mongolia	45 400	7.1	1:92	28 000	4.5	-17 400
Liaoning	37 900	5.9	1:163	54 400	8.5	16 500
Jilin	51 900	8.1	1:49	19 200	3.0	-32 700
Heilongjiang	43 700	6.8	1:46	34 700	5.4	-9 000
Total	220 000	34.3	1:81	237 700	37.0	17 700
East						
Shanghai	1 900	0.3	1:33	10 600	1.7	8 700
Jiangsu	2 400	0.4	1.64	18 500	2.9	16 100
Zhejiang	5 800	0.9	1:37	11 900	1.9	6 100
Anhui	2 400	0.4	1:135	8 300	1.3	5 900
Fujian	1 100	0.2	1:424	10 100	1.6	9 000
Jiangxi	2 000	0.3	1:51	4 600	0.7	2 600
Shandong	4 600	0.7	1:110	19 100	3.0	14 500
Henan	6 600	1.0	1:153	13 000	2.0	6 400
Hubei	13 000	2.0	1:165	32 800	5.1	19 800
Total	39 800	6.2	1:125	128 900	20.1	89 100
South						
Hunan	18 600	2.9	1:259	23 000	3.6	4 400
Guangdong	5 200	0.8	1:68	97 900	15.3	92 700
Guangxi	139 000	21.7	1:119	18 600	3.0	-120 400
Hainan	3 400	0.5	1:328	8 200	1.3	4 800
Total	166 200	25.9	1:137	147 700	23.0	-18 500
West						
Sichuan	33 900	5.3	1:144	41 700	6.5	7 800
Guizhou	63 000	9.8	1:178	10 000	1.6	-53 000
Yunnan	61 200	9.5	1:202	16 000	2.5	-45 200
Tibet	6 700	1.0	1:316	n.a.	n.a.	n.a.
Shaanxi	3 100	0.5	1:599	11 400	1.8	8 300
Gansu	16 800	2.6	1:132	8 500	1.3	-8 300
Qinghai	7 300	1.1	1:257	19 300	3.0	12 000
Ningxia	11 500	1.8	1:135	3 300	0.5	-8 200
Xinjiang	12 300	1.9	1:770	17 300	2.7	5 000
Total	215 800	33.6	1:220	127 500	19.9	-92 400
Total	641 800	100.0	1:143	641 800	100.0	

Source: Data from State Population Census Office (1993, Table 3–1) and one per cent sample, analysed by Fei Guo.

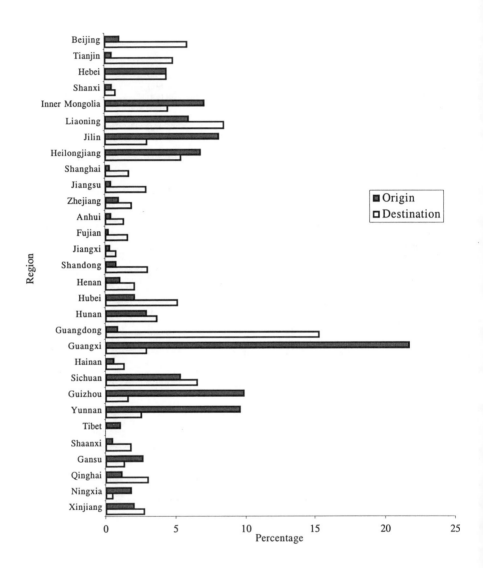

Source: State Population Census Office (1993, Volumes 1 and 4).

Figure 4.1 Origin and destination of minorities, 1985-90

Destinations

Figure 4.1 shows that the pattern of destinations for minorities is quite different from the pattern of sources. Column 5 in Table 4.2 gives the number of in-migrants per region. The regions receiving the highest proportions of in-migrants in 1985 - 90 were Guangdong (15.3 per cent of all minority inter-provincial migrants), Liaoning (8.5 per cent), Sichuan (6.5 per cent), Beijing (5.8 per cent), Heilongjiang (5.4 per cent), and Hubei (5.1 per cent). Guangdong has been shown to be an attractive destination for many Chinese, both Han and minorities, because of its high level of economic activity and contacts with the outside. Liaoning is a heavy industrial area on the coast to the north of Beijing.

Figures 4.2, 4.3 and 4.4 show the broad patterns in three regions — north, east/south and west. Three northern provinces which attracted recent high proportions of minorities were Liaoning, Jilin and Heilongjiang. Figure 4.2 compares the minority proportion of the region's population, the percentage of intra-provincial movement that was minorities and the percentage of inter-provincial in-movement that was minorities. Liaoning and Jilin had above average minority proportions in their populations, 15.6 per cent and 10.2 per cent, respectively, and Liaoning's intake of 9.4 per cent minorities was well below this existing composition. On the other hand, Jilin, Heilongjiang, Tianjin and · Beijing all attracted slightly higher proportions of minorities than were present in their existing populations. Figure 4.2 also includes the minority proportion of intra-provincial migration. Jilin stands out as having a very mobile minority population with minorities accounting for almost one fifth of the internal movement but one tenth of the population. Liaoning and Heilongjiang were both characterised by levels of internal minority mobility that were commensurate with their total population proportions. The overall pattern was one of minority movement being at least as great as Han movement.

The coastal provinces of Jiangsu, Zhejiang, Anhui, Fujian, Jiangxi, Shandong, and inland Henan and Hubei provinces, had low proportions of minorities but all attracted higher proportions of minorities in their intake. Table 4.2 shows that the numbers ranged from 4600 for Jiangxi to 97 900 for Guangdong. Guangdong has the most dramatic intake with over 7 per cent of inter-provincial migrants belonging to a minority group compared to 0.5 per cent of its population. Shanghai on the eastern seaboard had a low intake of minorities — 0.9 per cent of its permanent arrivals — but this was higher than its existing minority component.

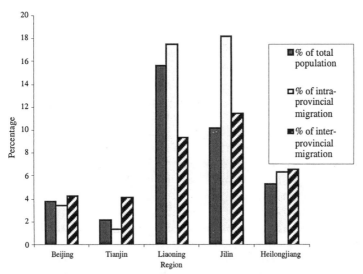

Source: Data from State Population Census Office (1993, Vols. 1 and 4), analysed by Fei Guo.

Figure 4.2 Percentage minority population and minority intra- and inter-provincial migration, Beijing, Tianjin, Liaoning, Jilin and Heilongjiang, 1985-90

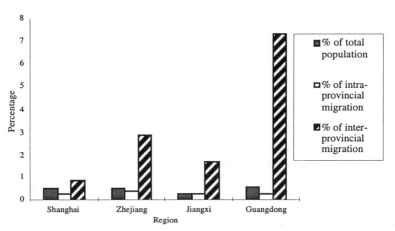

Source: Data from State Population Census Office (1993, Vols. 1 and 4), analysed by Fei Guo.

Figure 4.3 Percentage minority population and minority intra- and inter-provincial migration, Shanghai, Zhejiang, Jiangxi, Guangdong, 1985-90

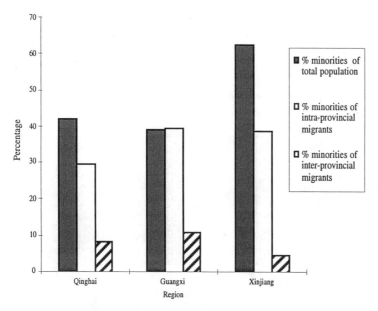

Source: Data from State Population Census Office (1993, Vols. 1 and 4), analysed by Fei Guo.

Figure 4.4 Percentage minority population and minority intra- and inter-provincial migration, Qinghai, Guangxi, Xinjiang, 1985-90

Figure 4.4 shows clearly that in the west and south, three regions with very high minority populations, Qinghai, Guangxi and Xinjiang, attracted considerably small proportions of minorities. The outstanding example is Xinjiang which contained 62.4 per cent minorities while only 4.8 per cent of the in-migration from other regions belonged to minorities. The remaining 95.2 per cent of the movement into Xinjiang was Han Chinese. Many Han Chinese have moved to this northwestern region as it is a huge area, it is sparsely populated, it has land available for agriculture, and rapidly growing populations are opening up opportunities for small business people (such as traders, shoe repairers, etc). Government policy, as we will see in Chapter 6, has also been driving migration of Han Chinese to this region for the last few decades. Within Xinjiang, the level of mobility among minorities was also lower than average. Qinghai and Guangxi had the same patterns though minority levels of intra-provincial mobility were relatively higher.

Figure 4.5, similar to Figure 2.1 in Chapter 2, shows the scale of flows of minorities within and between the three broad regions as depicted by Fan (1996). The size of the arrows indicates the relative magnitude of the flows and the percentage in brackets indicates the proportion of each flow that consists of minorities. The overall trend in Figure 2.1 was from the west to the east and centre and Figure 4.5 shows a similar pattern for minorities. By far the greatest number of minority moves were within the eastern region as was the case in Figure 2.1. Not surprisingly, given the pattern of past settlement, the western region had the highest proportion of minority moves and the lowest proportions were from the central and eastern regions to the western region.

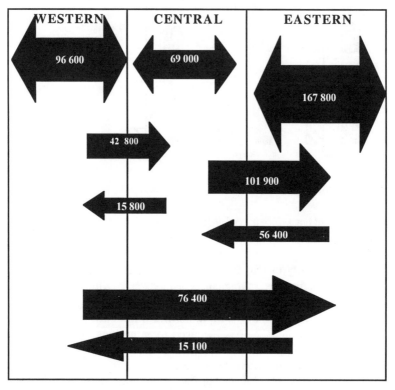

Source: Data from State Population Census Office (1993, Vols. 1 and 4), analysed by Fei Guo.

Figure 4.5 Minority inter-provincial migration by region, 1985-90

Net migration and the redistribution of minorities

There were, therefore, many minority peoples on the move between 1985 and 1990. As would be expected they mainly originated from traditional areas of high minority density in the north, west and south and they moved to a wide range of destinations. When out-migration and in-migration are summed the result is net migration. These figures were converted to a net migration rate and Figure 4.6 provides data equivalent to that in Figure 2.2 for total migration.

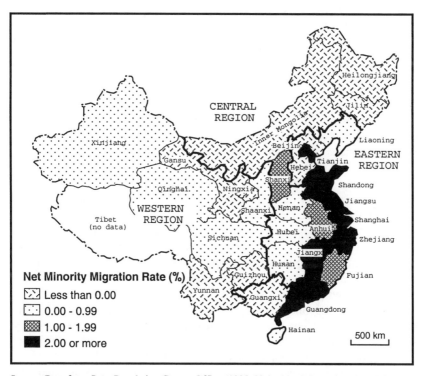

Source: Data from State Population Census Office (1993, Vols. 1 and 4), analysed by Fei Guo.

Figure 4.6 Rate of inter-provincial net migration of minorities, 1985-90

The map shows very clearly that Beijing and Tianjin and much of the east coast experienced net gains of 1 to 1.99 or 2 per cent or more. There is a central band running from Henan, Hubei and Hunan to Xinjiang that experienced net gains of 0 to 0.99 per cent. Beijing gained over 30 000 minority people in this period, just slightly more than Tianjin. The gains to the eastern area are slight in terms of numbers, though consistent. Guangdong with a net gain of 92 700 was clearly the most attractive destination. Guangxi was the biggest net loser. In the southwest, the pattern is mixed with Guizhou and Yunnan being major losers and Sichuan, Shaanxi, Qinghai and Xinjiang showing relatively small gains.

Comparison of minority and Han flows, 1985-90

It is possible to compare overall minority and Han inter-provincial movement
in terms of the percentages emanating from and arriving in each province.
This has been done in Figure 4.7 where the out-migration of Han and
minorities shows very different profiles. Sichuan is the source of the largest
proportion of Han out-migrants whereas Guangxi is the major source for
minorities. However, given the different distribution of minorities compared
to Han this comparison is not very meaningful.

The ratio of out-migrants to total minority population indicates
different patterns and various factors affect the rate of out-migration. In the
north, minorities were more likely to migrate out from Beijing, Tianjin,
Shanxi, Jilin and Heilongjiang than Han, while Han had higher rates of out-
migration than minorities from Hebei, Inner Mongolia and Liaoning. A
higher rate of minority out-migration from Shanxi is probably an addition to
the general trend described earlier in this chapter – that there is a clear
spreading out tendency of minorities from traditional high minority density
areas to lower ones. Shanxi is one of the lowest minority density provinces
with only 0.3 per cent minority population in its total population (Jiangsu
has 0.2 per cent and Shanghai and Jiangxi have 0.3 per cent), and it is not a
highly developed province. Conversely, a very low percentage of minorities
in a region's total population may not be very conducive to minority people
moving in and may serve as a barrier to minority in-migration. Reasonably
sized minority communities may be necessary to encourage significant further
in-migration by chain migration or some other effect.

The eastern seaboard contains a number of regions such as Shanghai,
Zhejiang, Jiangxi and Guangdong where minorities had much higher out-
migration rates than Han. The tendency for many minority migrants to move
back to their home town areas, after working for a period in industrial or
service employment on the coast, is evident. Very little is known, however,
about the return migration of minorities and detailed investigations are
required to understand what is happening.

For the western regions, the most startling figure is the high rate of
out-migration of Han between 1985 and 1990 from Tibet. There were 50 out-
migrants between 1985 and 1990 for every 100 Han resident in Tibet in July
1990. The same trend is obvious for Qinghai and Xinjiang though to a much
less marked extent. Many Han were located in Tibet as part of the military
presence and also to participate in government, education and infrastructure
projects. There is a high turnover of people in these projects and this is
manifest in these figures. The very low rates of out-migration of minorities
from all of these western regions is obvious from the figure.

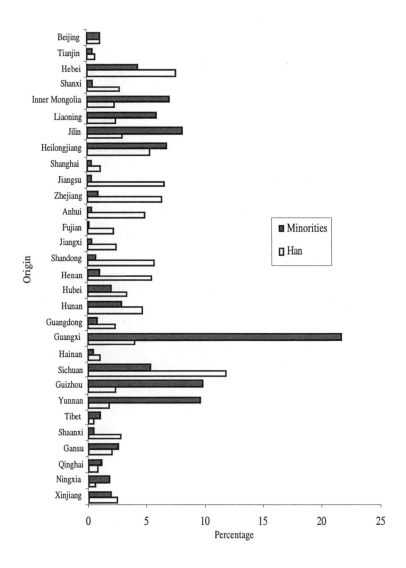

Source: Data from State Population Census Office (1993, Vols. 1 and 4), analysed by Fei Guo

Figure 4.7 Minority and Han out-migration by region, 1985-90

In Figure 4.8, the attractiveness of provinces to minorities and Han is compared. Guangdong was by the far the most popular destination for all ethnic groups but especially for minorities. On the whole, the northern areas drew reasonable proportions of all groups though Liaoning stands out as being a much more attractive destination for minorities than for Han. The high percentage of minorities in this province means that minority people have connections here already or feel more comfortable in an environment where there are other minorities. Shanghai, on the other hand, received a much greater proportion of Han migrants than minority migrants. In fact, the coastal seaboard was relatively more attractive to Han than to minority migrants — for reasons of distance, connections, familiarity, regulations, etc. In the south, Guangdong and Hainan attracted relatively more minorities than Han. It seems that after the initial people move, chain migration sets up between destinations and minority regions of origin — perhaps even more so than for Han. This phenomenon was investigated further through the surveys and case studies and is a subject of discussion in later chapters.

COMPOSITION OF INTER-PROVINCIAL MIGRATION

In order to better understand these patterns, the one per cent sample of the 1990 census was analysed. These data provide more insight into who moved and why between 1985 and 1990 but it must be borne in mind that the profile is only that of people defined as migrants by the census.

Age and sex

Table 4.3 provides data on inter-provincial movements, by age and sex. The most outstanding difference between the Han and minority migrants is the sex ratio. Han movement was 59.55 per cent male compared with 43.6 per cent male for minorities. The greater feminisation of minority movement is very interesting and we will try to understand this in later chapters. In both groups, migrants were concentrated in the 15 to 29 age brackets: 55.79 per cent of Han and 63.2 per cent of minorities. Particularly notable is the number of young minority women aged 15 to 19 when they moved, compared with the Han. This suggests less employment opportunities for minority women than for Han women in their region of origin. There was also a significant movement of 10 to 14 years old in both groups which is not easily understood. The role of education in accounting for this pattern needs further investigation.

Table 4.3 Inter-provincial migrants by age and sex, 1985-90 ('00)

Age	Han Chinese				Minorities			
	Male	Female	Total (no.)	Total (%)	Male	Female	Total (no.)	Total (%)
0-4	2 397	2 272	4 669	4.19	149	165	314	4.89
5-9	2 724	2 390	5 114	4.58	134	128	262	4.08
10-14	9 245	7 121	16 366	14.67	406	499	905	14.10
15-19	20 722	14 148	34 870	31.26	942	1 444	2 386	37.18
20-24	12 263	6 707	18 970	17.01	481	701	1 182	18.42
25-29	5 317	3 075	8 392	7.52	246	246	492	7.67
30-34	4 657	2 920	7 577	6.79	145	155	300	4.67
35-59	2 851	1 943	4 794	4.30	97	91	188	2.93
40-44	1 791	1 246	3 037	2.72	57	63	120	1.87
45-49	1 462	941	2 403	2.15	48	37	85	1.32
50-54	1 089	597	1 686	1.51	34	28	62	0.97
55-59	810	473	1 283	1.15	26	18	44	0.69
60-64	516	415	931	0.83	16	12	28	0.44
65-69	296	333	629	0.56	4	11	15	0.23
70-74	156	248	404	0.36	10	12	22	0.34
75+	136	292	428	0.38	3	10	13	0.20
Total no.	66 432	45 121	111 553	-	2 798	3 620	6 418	
Total per cent	59.55	40.45	-	100.0	43.60	56.40		100.0

Source: Data from 1990 Census of Population and Housing, one per cent sample, analysed by Fei Guo.

Level of education

Table 4.4 shows that minority inter-provincial flows contained higher proportions of people at the top and bottom levels of the educational spectrum. A higher proportion of minorities were illiterate or had only elementary schooling (43.9 per cent) than for Han (34.9 per cent) while a higher proportion of minorities had university education (12.7 per cent) compared to Han (9.2 per cent).

Occupation

Overall, 64.6 per cent of minority inter-provincial migrants were in the workforce compared with 69.7 per cent of Han migrants. The most notable difference in Table 4.5 is the high proportion (55.3 per cent) of agricultural workers among inter-provincial minority migrants, compared to 21.3 per cent for Han migrants. Conversely, only 22.3 per cent of minority migrants were industrial workers compared to 45.8 per cent of Han.

In all other occupational categories there was a higher proportion of Han than minorities, reflecting the limited opportunities that have been available for employment amongst minorities. The occupational profile

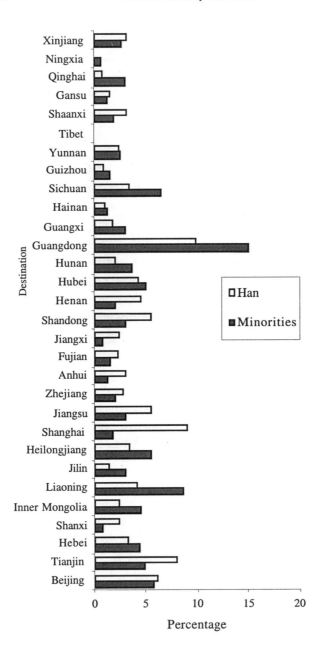

Source: Data from State Population Census Office (1993, Vols 1 and 4), analysed by Fei Guo

Figure 4.8 Minority and Han in-migration by region, 1985-90

Table 4.4 Education level of inter-provincial migrants, Han and minority, 1985-90

Ethnicity	Illiterate	Elementary	Junior high	Senior high	Tech. high	Tech. college	University	n.a.	Total
Han (no.)	9 326	29 598	40 219	13 049	4 338	3 806	10 303	914	111 553
Han (%)	8.4	26.5	36.0	11.7	3.9	3.4	9.2	0.9	100.0
Minorities (no.)	881	1 937	1 789	530	197	207	813	64	6 418
Minorities (%)	13.7	30.2	27.9	8.3	3.0	3.2	12.7	1.0	100.0
Total China (no.)	10 207	31 535	42 008	13 579	4 535	4 013	11 116	978	117 971

Source: Data from 1990 Census of Population and Housing, one per cent sample, analysed by Fei Guo.

Table 4.5 Labour force/occupational status of inter-provincial migrants, Han and minority, 1985-90

Ethnicity	Professionals	Cadres	Clerical	Sales	Service Workers	Agricultural	Industrial	Other	Total
Han (no.)	8 812	1 776	4 131	5 812	4 942	16 591	35 566	130	77 760
Han (%)	11.3	2.3	5.3	7.5	6.4	21.3	45.8	0.2	100.0
Minorities (no.)	310	69	140	251	155	2 292	925	3	4 145
Minorities (%)	7.5	1.7	3.4	6.1	3.7	55.3	22.3	0.1	100.0
Total China (no.)	9 122	1 845	4 271	6 063	5 097	18 883	36 491	133	81 905

Source: Data from 1990 Census of Population and Housing, one per cent sample, analysed by Fei Guo.

reflects the level of economic development in many minority regions, as described earlier.

Permanent registration (*hukou*)

Overall, approximately half of all inter-provincial migrants had moved without changing their household registration status (*hukou*). Table 4.6 shows that a slightly higher proportion of minorities who had moved across provincial boundaries had acquired local registration (*hukou*): 50.25 per cent had household registration in the destination compared to 46.41 per cent of Han migrants. These data suggest that minorities were perhaps slightly less likely to move without getting approval to transfer their *hukou* first.

Table 4.6 Hukou *status of inter-provincial migrants, Han and minorities, 1985-90*

Ethnicity	Local *hukou* registration		Non-local *hukou*		Total
	No.	%	No.	%	No.
Han	51 772	46.41	59 781	53.59	111 553
Minorities	3 225	50.25	3 193	49.75	6 418
Total	55 000	46.62	62 971	53.38	117 971

Source: 1990 Census of Population and Housing, one per cent sample, analysed by Fei Guo.

In summary, minority migration tended to be younger and more feminised than Han migration. Relatively more minority migrants were both poorly educated and well educated than for Han migrants. Minority migrants were predominantly from agricultural occupations and sectors while Han migrants were more evenly spread across occupational strata. This reflects the occupational structure of the two broad groups. Finally, minority migrants were slightly more likely to have gained local *hukou*, than Han, but this still only applied to half of all migrants captured by the census categories.

CONCLUSION

The picture provided by the 1990 census data is one of relatively similar rates of movement of Han and minorities within provinces but lower rates of minority movement across boundaries. The data on inter-provincial movement, the focus of this chapter, show that the largest stream of movement of minorities is from the southern provinces of Guangxi, Yunnan and Guizhou mostly towards Guangdong. In general, however, there is a dispersal of minorities from traditional areas of settlement in the north, west and south across most of China. Besides Guangdong province in the south, Liaoning, Beijing and Heilongjiang in the north and Sichuan and Hubei in the centre attracted the largest numbers of minority migrants. But in relative terms, the eastern seaboard experienced the greatest net gains, along with Beijing and Tianjin. In terms of numbers, Beijing ranked second with an overall net intake of 30 000 minority migrants between 1985 and 1990. Beijing, the subject of Chapter 8, was a major destination for minority migrants from Inner Mongolia, Liaoning, Jilin and Heilongjiang but also from as far afield as Guangxi, Guizhou and Yunnan. Its role as an administrative and education centre may explain part of this trend.

The comparisons between minority and Han mobility threw up a number of very interesting results from the census data. Minority migration tended to be more youthful and more feminised, with minority people largely coming from rural backgrounds. There was a bipolar pattern in terms of levels of education for minority migrants compared to Han migrants: more with low levels of education and a greater proportion of university-educated. Most minority migrants originated, as would be expected, from traditional minority areas but a significant proportion also came from non-traditional areas, suggesting re-migration or the movement of minority groups from already significantly dispersed areas. The destinations were more concentrated for minorities, indicating more reliance on chain migration.

When we looked at another measure, rate of out-migration, Shanxi, Shanghai and Zhejiang had the highest rates of minority out-migration. These are all areas of low minority numbers. The explanation for this phenomenon is not clear and needs to be explored. To a certain extent, it can be understood from the fact that although there is a clear tendency for minorities to move from high minority density areas to lower ones, they tend not to move to the very low minority density areas. It may require a reasonable proportion of minority people to allow them to form a community/ies so that they do not feel isolated when they move into the area. Does this relate to a lack of cultural affinity and feelings of isolation? Is there a tendency to migrate for a period and with a specific strategy? Is it part of some wider process of dispersing to spread minority industries, goods, etc? These and other issues will be addressed in the three case studies, that follow, on Mongolians, Tibetans and Uyghurs.

5. Inner Mongolia and Mongol movement[*]

BACKGROUND

The steppes of Inner Asia were the centre of Chinggis Khan's empire and a hinge of Asia. He and his descendants headed a strong army, blocked the eastern expansion of Europe, forced Russians to move the centre of their civilisation from Kiev to Moscow and opened the trade routes that meant a great deal to China and the world. Outer Mongolia became a republic in the early 1920s. When the Japanese were seeking to set up the so-called Greater Asia Co-Prosperity Sphere in the 1930s, Inner Mongolia was a front line for the CPC to fight against them. After 1945 it became a strong Liberation Army base in the civil war between Mao Zedong and Chiang Kai-Shek.

As one of largest and most important regions in China, Inner Mongolia has been the focus of much concern for the central government and it was set up as a role model for other nationality autonomous regions. The Inner Mongolian Autonomous Region was established on 1 May 1947. It covers most of the borderland with Russia and Mongolia. Within China it is adjacent to Heilongjiang, Jilin and Liaoning in the east, Gansu and Ningxia in the west, and Hebei, Shanxi and Shaanxi in the south. It is the third largest region in China and covers an area of 1 183 000 km^2. It is rich in minerals, coal and forest resources with vast expanses of pastoral steppes. Three quarters of the north and east are more than 1000 metres above sea level and comprise part of the Mongolian plateau. The plateau becomes arid to the northwest where it borders on the Gobi Desert. The Yin mountains divide this area from the fertile plains of the Yellow River to the south. The Yellow River flows south and then turns eastward and flows for 300 kilometres across Inner Mongolia.

The climate of Inner Mongolia is harsh, rainfall is irregular and floods and droughts are common. The pastoral economy predominates with regard to land coverage (75 per cent) and cultural identity. However 80 per cent of herders have now settled (Hurelbaatar 1996) and the remainder were expected to be settled by the year 2000. Though only 5 per cent of the land is

---

[*] This chapter has had particular input from Naran Bilik.

arable and only 3 per cent is actually cultivated an increasing area has been taken up by agriculture or semi-agriculture over the last 100 years. Much of the agriculture was first conducted by Han Chinese but many Mongolians have moved into this activity. These Mongolians have adopted the 'northern Chinese mode of farming and the Han manner of life' (Pasternak and Salaff 1993, p. 265).

The Mongolian language in China has three dialects: in the west (*oirad*), the northeast (*bargu-buriat*) and the centre (*Inner Mongolian*). The language is still in popular use among Mongolians at home and also in publishing, broadcasting and education. At the time of the 1990 census, Mongolians were enumerated at 4.8 million for the whole of China. This represents a significant increase from the figure of 1.4 million in 1953, around 2 million in 1964 and 3.4 million in 1982. The distribution of Mongolians is largely a legacy of the time when Mongolians spread across China, most of Asia, the Middle East and Eastern Europe, in the thirteenth century. Pockets of Mongolians were left behind after the defeat of the Mongolian empire. Outside of Inner Mongolia, Mongolians live mostly in Liaoning (587 311), Jilin (156 488) and Heilongjiang (139 077) in the northeast, Hebei province in the north and Xinjiang (138 021) in the west.

Population of the Inner Mongolian Autonomous Region

The composition of Inner Mongolia's population is the result of centuries of interactions and incursion from all directions. According to the 1990 census, there were 49 nationalities represented in the total population of 21 456 798. Han Chinese comprised 80.62 per cent and Mongolians 15.73 per cent. Table 5.1 shows the pattern of population growth in Inner Mongolia since 1947.

Table 5.1 Inner Mongolia's population, 1947 to 1990

Group	1947	1953	1964	1982	1990
Han (no.)	4 696 000	6 493 000	10 729 407	16 277 616	17 289 995
Han (%)	83.6	85.6	87.0	84.5	80.6
Mongol (no.)	832 000	985 000	1 384 455	2 489 378	3 379 738
Mongol (%)	14.8	13.0	11.2	12.9	15.7
Others (no.)	89 872	106 176	222 014	501 131	793 909
Others (%)	1.6	1.4	1.8	2.6	3.7
Total (no.)	5 617 000	7 584 000	12 334 138	19 274 282	21 457 000

Source: Hurelbaatar 1996, p. 7.

The Mongol-Han population ratio in Inner Mongolia is largely influenced by policies and events of particular periods and the movement of Han Chinese to Inner Mongolia has been well documented by Ma (1987) and Hurelbaatar (1996). This history goes back well over 1000 years and was propelled by a number of Chinese states wanting to settle this area. Then the imperial government lost control of almost all of modern Inner Mongolia when it was resettled by Mongol tribes immigrating from the north. The Mongolians established political and demographic dominance in Inner Mongolia in 1368 and this lasted till 1644. In 1579-82, the area with the current boundaries of Inner Mongolia had a population of around 1 790 000 and Mongolians comprised 60 per cent of the population (Hurelbaatar 1996, p. 4). After the end of Mongolian rule over China in 1636, many Han Chinese remained in Inner Mongolia, especially in the southwest around the Yellow River, and in the southeast.

The policy of the Manchus (Qing dynasty) from 1636 to 1911 was to limit Han migration and Han-Mongol contact. At the turn of the twentieth century, however, another migration stream came in the form of Russians moving eastwards from Siberia. They cut timber, built the railway from Moscow to Beijing and crushed Mongolian resistance to their immigration. Gradually more Russian settlers arrived and cities such as Harbin, Manzhouli and Hailar grew up along the railway line. A border dispute which developed in the early 1900s led to the arrival of Manchu forces and the Manchu rulers began to encourage the migration of Han Chinese to secure the frontier from the Russians. This policy of colonisation of borderland areas resulted in Han peasants pouring in. As a result, many Mongolians lost their pastoral land and were pushed into desolate areas. Tracts that were well watered were designated for agriculture and Mongolians lost their right to this land. Even those Mongolians who were sedentary were pushed back from the most fertile grasslands into desert areas. While the Mongolians were primarily pastoralists until the twentieth century, the long history of nomadic-sedentary interaction in Inner Mongolia means that 'the non-Han people in this area have never been exclusively pastoral nomads in their lifestyle' (Hurelbaatar 1996, p. 5). There were already Mongolians who were farmers but with the arrival of Han Chinese in much greater numbers many more Mongolians turned to a semi-pastoral/semi-agricultural or purely agricultural lifestyle. The Manchus also lifted their restrictions on Han-Mongol intermarriage and they allowed Mongolians to learn Chinese (Ma 1987, pp. 134-5).

Consequently, Inner Mongolia experienced a high rate of Han population growth from 1911. In 1912, there were 1.5 million Han Chinese but this figure increased to 3.7 million in 1937 (140 per cent increase or 5.6 per cent per year) and to 4.7 million in 1947 (26 per cent increase or 2.6 per cent per year). Civil war and agricultural disruption in central China led to the movement of impoverished, landless peasants from nearby northeastern provinces (the coastal regions of China south of Beijing) to Inner Mongolia. Initially the movement was mostly of single men, to build the railway, work on Russian cattle farms and trade, but by the 1940s more Han farming families had arrived and facilities such as Chinese schools had been established. Han converted more of the eastern pasture to farmland and by 1949, over two thirds of the population of eastern Inner Mongolia were farmers.

The size of the Mongolian population declined from 1.78 million in 1912 to 832 000 in 1947 (Hurelbaatar 1996, p. 7). In the 1940s, the infant mortality rate was almost 300 per thousand and average life expectancy was only 20 years (Ma 1987, p. 112). In fact the Mongolian population had been in decline from 1790. The reasons are thought to be that many men were celibate Buddhist monks or served in the Manchu court and so fertility was low but also that mortality rates were high due to poor sanitation and lack of health care. In 1947, Mongolians made up 14.81 per cent of Inner Mongolia's population but their proportion dropped to 11.22 per cent in 1964. The Mongol population increased by a total of 66 per cent (4.1 per cent per year) between 1947 and 1964 and by a total of 144 per cent or 9 per cent per year between 1964 and 1990. The higher rate of increase in the latter period is explained by higher birth rates and more people 'identifying' as Mongolian. After 1980, many Han people switched their identity to Mongolian for politico-economic and reproduction (being allowed to have more than one child) preferences. Second, there is a high percentage of Mongol-Han intermarriage (above 60 per cent) in cities and many children of these marriages are identified as Mongolian. These trends influenced the Mongolian population in terms of identities and numbers.

After the creation of the Inner Mongolian Autonomous Region in 1947, the Han population increased to 10 729 407 in 1964 (an increase of 126 per cent or 8 per cent per year) and to 17 289 995 in 1990 (an increase of 61 per cent or 3.6 per cent per year). The figures suggest a high rate of inward Han Chinese migration in the 1950s and early 1960s as well as a high birth rate. Many Han moved to rural areas of Inner Mongolia during the famine years after the Great Leap Forward (1960-1962) as Inner Mongolia was relatively better off than nearby provinces during this period. According to a former banner head interviewed in 1993, a staggering number of Han peasants came to the Khorchin steppe from the 1950s in a 'blind flow' to claim agricultural land, reducing the original 1 500 000km^2 of grassland to 100 000km^2 (Bilik 1996a). They settled in the wetter areas in the south and east and continuous pressure of encroachment by agricultural population led to three major changes in the borders between the Inner Mongolian pastoral Urad Middle banner and the adjacent Han agricultural areas after 1949. Ethnic conflict over land reached such an extent that the central government made special efforts to stop all spontaneous movement at this time (Pasternak and Salaff 1993, p. 15).

Population distribution

Inner Mongolia consists of 12 prefectures (leagues), 4 cities, 84 counties (banners), 15 county-level cities, and 16 districts under city administration. Even during the Qing dynasty the Mongolian concentrated places were called 'banners' and those where Han people clustered together were called 'xians' (counties). The same landscape exists nowadays: in cities and even in banner centres the Mongolians always have a small population and they are largely spread out in pastoral areas. Mongolians who have turned to agriculture or semi-agriculture often live interspersed with Han. The Han majority are largely concentrated in compact communities in agricultural areas and in metropolitan centres.

Socio-economic and cultural profile

The traditional basis of the Mongolian social system was kinship and the nuclear family and nomadic encampment were important social units. There was also the common descent group *obogh* (Jagchid and Hyer 1979, p. 245). Mongolians regard themselves as the offspring of the grey wolf and a yellowish-white deer and they worship heaven. They originally believed in Shamanism, the worship of natural phenomena, but the state religion became Lamaism, a sect of Mahayan Buddhism, after it spread into Mongolia in the thirteenth century. Herding and hunting are still the most common ways of life among older Mongolians but less than a third of Mongolians live entirely on herding. Due to the arid nature of much of the region, they move encampment and herds according to the seasonal cycle. They eat mutton and beef and drink the milk of cows and sheep. In order to cope with the dry and cold weather conditions, they dress in garments that are suitable for riding horses and that can also be used as quilts when camping out. Some still live in yurts that are built from lattice and felt. Many herders have now settled down, however, and they tend to occupy the more marginal pastoral lands with the better lands having been taken up by both Han and Mongolian agriculturalists. The retreat of the pastoralists has led to serious ecological damage of lands that are not only overstocked but which are unsuited to the grazing of animals.

Despite its rich resources, rural Inner Mongolia continues to be one of the poorest of China's regions. In 1989, rural per capita income was only 478 yuan compared to 602 yuan in rural China generally. Infrastructure is often poor and neglected. The abandonment of the commune system and the shift to family production has been welcomed in many areas. It means that the onus is now on local administrators and households to chart their own paths to economic improvement and social transformation and some areas are thriving and investing in the improvement of grasslands, roads, airports and other infrastucture while other areas are languishing.

Since the founding of the Inner Mongolian Autonomous Region there has been negotiation between state sovereignty and territorial integrity on the one hand and development and maintenance of Mongolian culture on the other. In the period from 1949 to the onset of the Cultural Revolution in 1966, Mongolian education and culture flourished in all areas. Mongolians were found in all regions of Inner Mongolia — in purely agricultural, semi-pastoral/semi-agricultural and purely pastoral areas, as well as in the cities and towns — not just in the dry steppe areas bordering on Outer Mongolia and the north and west. Mongolian cadres were recruited and trained by the CPC and they participated in the revolution.

The establishment of the Inner Mongolia Revolutionary Committee and the launching of a movement to 'cleanse the class ranks' (*qingli jieji duiwu*) in November 1967 marked the beginning of the full-scale Cultural Revolution in Inner Mongolia. In the spring of 1968, the movement began to be tinged with ethnicity as it was alleged that there was a 'New Inner Mongolian People's Revolutionary Party'. This was said to be a reincarnation of the 'old' Inner Mongolian People's Revolutionary Party which had been organised by the CPC itself and dissolved in 1947. This 'new' party was supposedly a 'counter-revolutionary' underground organisation of Mongolian separatists with close contacts with Outer Mongolia and the Soviet Union. As a consequence of this situation, the central government in Beijing partitioned Inner Mongolia in 1969. The region's three easternmost leagues became part of the provinces of Heilongjiang, Jilin and Liaoning, and its three western banners became part of Gansu and Ningxia. Inner Mongolia was reduced in size from almost 1.2 million square kilometres to slightly more than 0.4 million (Schoenhals 1993).

Many of the minority cadres had rejected their culture but during the revolution, minority cultural relics, symbols, institutions and buildings were attacked and damaged.

> Then, as the Cultural Revolution unfolded, they themselves came under attack. Their enthusiasm waned. They were accused of secretly reviving the 'Inner Mongolian Revolutionary Party', an outlawed nationalistic organization set up during the late 1940s. The balance struck between Han and Mongolians in the early 1950s shifted, and the rift between them widened. ... As Han cadres, eager to welcome Han settlers replaced

many Mongol cadres, the Mongolians could no longer contest Han in-migration. (Pasternak and Salaff 1993, p. 16)

On 20 April 1978, in a document issued by Hua Guofeng's Central Committee, it was finally acknowledged that the so-called New Inner Mongolian People's Party simply did not exist (Schoenhals 1993). The territory partitioned to neighbouring provinces in 1969 was returned on 1 July 1979. Following this, more autonomy was granted to Mongol leadership in the 1980s but the abuse and torture of loyal Mongol cadres during the Cultural Revolution meant that many were disillusioned. They either left Inner Mongolia for good or came to identify more closely with their own people rather than with the Han or central administration. The legacy of the Cultural Revolution can still be felt in parts of Inner Mongolia.

THE DEVELOPMENT OF EDUCATION FACILITIES

Participation and achievement

The role of Mongolian intellectuals in education became very important during the Qing dynasty (1644-1911). Mongolian writers and literary critics, such as Injanasi and Habo, heavily influenced Mongolian education by introducing and translating Chinese literature into Mongolian. A scholar and political activist, Guo Daofu (Merse), opened a school in 1910 in what is now Ewenki Autonomous Banner, and Manchu, Chinese, Mongolian, Russian and Japanese were taught at the school (Bilik 1998a). Despite a general setback during the Cultural Revolution, Mongolian education recovered dramatically after 1978. Mongolian culture, language and education underwent a revival and Mongolian schools were re-established in pastoral areas. As already outlined, Mongolians predominate in pastoral areas and their traditional livelihood still prevails in these areas.

Mongolians thus have a long history of valuing formal education. The enrolment ratio for primary schools in Inner Mongolia, that is the proportion enrolled out of the total eligible primary school-aged population, is 99.54 per cent, which is slightly above the national average. The drop-out rates of 0.29 per cent for boys and 0.15 per cent for girls, are much lower than the national average rates of 0.93 percent and 0.92 per cent, respectively. Enrolments at the secondary level are comparable with national rates except in specialised vocational high schools which we have already noted are not very common in outlying areas. Table 3.2 shows that the proportion of Mongolians with college education is slightly below the national average. The figures for Inner Mongolia show only 32.6 enrolments in higher education institutions per 10 000 inhabitants compared to 355.2 for Beijing (Department of Development and Planning 1999, p. 68) but this is more indicative of the level of provision of educational institutions than of actual participation rates. The relocation of people to gain a tertiary education is very common among Mongolians.

Curricula, teaching materials and staffing

Education takes places in a variety of mainstream and nationality institutions. In 1990, there were 153 ethnic kindergartens (out of a total of 630), 3027 ethnic primary schools (out of 14 634), 422 standard ethnic middle schools (out of 2058) and 37 ethnic professional schools (out of 347). In more than 30 specialised secondary schools (out of 81) and 10 universities and colleges (out of 19), courses and classes are taught in Mongolian. The enrolment of minority students at specialised secondary schools was 12 879 and at universities and colleges was 8576 in 1991. Of 17 997 teaching and assisting staff, 3293 were from minority groups (Buhe *et al.* 1991, pp. 743-9). Table 3.3 shows that the availability of resources for education facilities is quite scarce in Inner Mongolia. Around 2.0 to 3.0 per cent of all school space was dilapidated in 1998 but compared with other minority regions Inner Mongolia was not too badly off. Plate 5.1 shows one school in a northern *som* (village) which had been damaged and not repaired for a number of years. Meanwhile the children, some of whom are in Plate 5.2, were crammed into the remaining space.

In March 1980, the Inner Mongolian government approved recommendations contained in the *Inquiry Report on the Decision of Mongolian Basic Dialect, Standard Pronunciation and Phonetic Transcription* that resulted in the Chahar version of the central dialect being accepted as the accent for the Mongolian language. This was a significant step in language maintenance policy. The majority of Mongolians still use their own language, though some have lost it and switched to Chinese. In terms of social use and importance, the Mongolian language is no match for Chinese and English. Both reality and popular thinking hold that Mongolian is for local and family use while Chinese and English are used elsewhere. Many Han people, as well as some Mongolian cadres and educators, argue that the teaching of Mongolian should be replaced by Chinese in higher middle schools. These groups maintain that Chinese is a key medium of the state and has a dominant status in political promotion, economic betterment and other social achievements. Others argue for the continued maintenance of Mongolian in schools. The debate continues between the two groups of Mongolians.

Plate 5.1 Damaged primary school in northern Inner Mongolia, 1996 (Photo by R. Iredale)

Plate 5.2 Primary school children in Inner Mongolia, 1996 (Photo by R. Iredale)

[O]ne camp prefers that Mongolian be used only through the level of lower-middle school, while the Han language should step in at the level of higher-middle school. The other holds that Mongolian is an indispensable carrier of Mongolian culture and that it is against Marxist principles and state policies to 'mutilate' the Mongolian language. Besides, the latter add, Mongolian is a convenient medium for the Mongolians to communicate and express their emotions. (Bilik 1998b)

As pointed out already, national curricula are set by the state for most courses, while Mongolian and Han Chinese curricula for some courses are decided by the regional government. The Inner Mongolian Autonomous Region government decides on language policies, teaching materials, etc. It is a constant process to ensure the availability of teaching and learning materials in Mongolian. Textbooks used in Mongolian teaching are translations of standard Chinese textbooks and each year publishers print 350 varieties and 6 500 000 copies of Mongolian textbooks and teaching materials.

In the early 1980s, Hohhot (capital of Inner Mongolia) had three Mongolian schools with over 2000 students in total. Since the mid-1980s, however, the process of economic reform has led to a decline in Mongolian culture and language. Many parents now see little benefit in sending their children to Mongolian schools and opt for a Chinese education for their children, hoping that this will lead to a brighter economic future. Consequently children with little education in Mongolian language and culture, whose families migrate to urban areas when they are young, are losing their connection with their past heritage. In 1996, only one Mongolian school (shown in Plate 5.3) remained in Hohhot — with 662 local students (out of a total Mongolian population in Hohhot of 110 800) and 442 students from grassland and rural areas.

The school operates in Mongolian and with Han Chinese taught after the first few years. Some students (especially from the grasslands) often do not speak Han Chinese and they have some difficulty at first. Fees are set by the government and paid by parents, though some students are subsidised. Students from outside of Hohhot are encouraged to enrol in order 'to strengthen the Mongolian culture and language in the school', according to the school principal (Interview in Hohhot, July 1996). However, there was a distinct impression that the survival of the school was at stake and recruiting students from outside of Hohhot was seen as one way of ensuring the continued viability of the school.

The school plays an important role in acting as a reservoir of Mongolian culture and language teaching and learning. Many of the outside students come from rural areas where the Mongolian language has already

Plate 5.3 Mongolian nationality school, Hohhot, 1996 (Photo by R. Iredale)

disappeared and the school teaches the children who in turn return home and encourage the revival of their language and culture. This ethnic school program with its boarding facilities increases opportunities for peer group activities and ethnic experiences. Thus the school is operating to strengthen and sometimes revive Mongolian culture, though its overall impact is small. Once their schooling is over a significant proportion of the students at this Mongolian school stay on in Hohhot for employment or higher education. Those who acquire degrees in ranching science or veterinary science then often return to the grasslands and in this way the life of the family is not interrupted and the children and family benefit from better education. Education for these people is seen as a crucial way to bring economic and social development to outlying minority areas.

At the tertiary level, the Inner Mongolia Normal (Teachers') University in Hohhot is regarded as a 'Mongolian language island'. Almost half of the students are Mongolian and much of the teaching is conducted in Mongolian. A Mongolian Anthropology and Cultural Change Unit was established in 1994 in the university. The Inner Mongolian Academy of Social Sciences also promotes Mongolian history, language, literature and culture. The government of Inner Mongolia is behind all of these developments and has wide policies on Mongolian education. New resource materials, such as films, books and radio and TV programs, are constantly being produced in Mongolian.

The recent emphasis that has been placed on Mongolian education has resulted in 48 per cent of Mongolian students who complete high school going on to tertiary education. This is higher than for any other group and is indicative of the fact that education is seen as an important tool for raising the economic status of Mongolians, including the pastoralists. Those who return to grassland areas are an important resource for raising productivity and setting up new enterprises and networks, and families perceive that time spent in cities encourages growth and personal development. This is a very positive approach to migration and where it is seen as a means of assisting economic advancement in rural areas.

Table 3.3 showed a relatively high rate of *minban* teachers, 24 per cent of all teachers in primary schools in Inner Mongolia. Inner Mongolia and also had the highest rate of such teachers (5.9 per cent) in junior high schools. This is generally seen as indicating a poor level of resourcing as these teachers are not well trained or paid. For Inner Mongolia it indicates that a considerable amount of primary schooling, in particular, in predominantly Mongolian areas is being conducted by Mongolian *minban* teachers but as fewer speak Mongolian this will change. The pattern of ethnic schooling has already become dissipated and this trend is likely to continue.

PATTERNS OF MIGRATION IN THE 1980s AND 1990s

Migration to and from Inner Mongolia

Large numbers of Han people moved into Inner Mongolia during different periods in line with central government policies and in response to natural events. However, after the open-door policy many Han moved out of Inner Mongolia back to their home towns or they moved elsewhere for higher education. In-migration is still continuing, however, and within this flow Han in-migrants outnumber minorities by about ten to one. Figure 5.1 shows the number and origin of Han and minority migrants (as defined in the 1990 census) from 1985-90. The 28 000 minority in-migrants originated from a much narrower range of provinces than the 269 400 Han in-migrants. They came mainly from the neighbouring provinces of Liaoning, Jilin, Heilongjiang and Hebei whereas Han originated from these and other northern regions as well as from east coast provinces and from Sichuan, Shaanxi and Gansu in the inland.

Figure 5.2 shows that minority out-migrants left Inner Mongolia mainly for northern areas, including Beijing, but small numbers also went to Shandong, Henan, Hunan and Ningxia. Han also left largely for northern

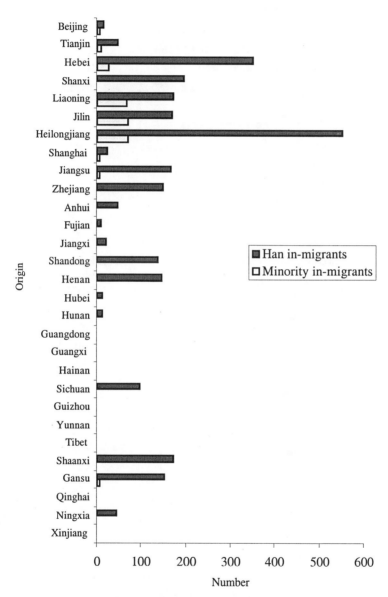

Source: State Population Census Office (1993, Vols. 1 and 4).

Figure 5.1 Minority and Han in-migration to Inner Mongolia, 1985-90

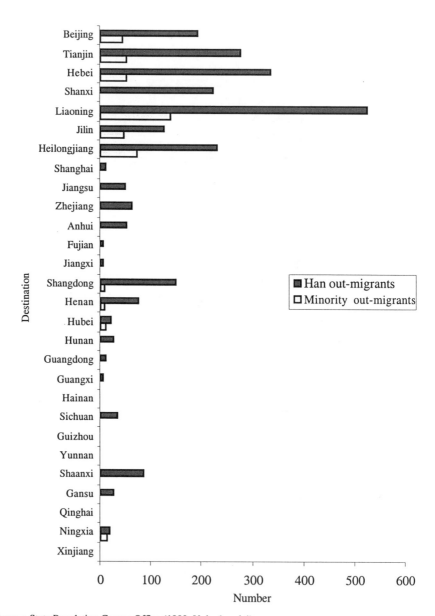

Source: State Population Census Office (1993, Vols. 1 and 4).

Figure 5.2 Minority and Han out-migration from Inner Mongolia, 1985-90

regions but with some out-migration to other provinces, especially Shandong and Shaanxi.

Figures 5.3 and 5.4 show the origin and destination of Mongolians who moved between 1985 and 1990 and who were captured in the 1990 census. The figures show that Inner Mongolia was the source of almost 60 per cent of Mongolian movement but only 22 per cent of Mongolians came into Inner Mongolia. The most popular destination for the 53 900 Mongolians who moved across provinces was Liaoning (25 per cent), with Beijing ranking fifth — 4000 moved to Beijing to study or serve as teachers and in other professional occupations. The revival of Mongolian culture and language together with the preferential policies adopted again by the central government have boosted many minority cultural aspects, including language, and opened up opportunities for Mongolians in education and other professional fields. Inner Mongolia is now suffering from a 'brain-drain' as more talented people go out rather than come in. In banners such as *lang qi* ('the blue banner'), no graduate students have come back here to work for years though many have gone out to study in universities and colleges.

Movement within Inner Mongolia

During the predominantly nomadic period, mobility was more important than settlement, the aim being to gain control of pastures and populations. But after 1949, Mongolians were encouraged to become more sedentary and consequently bound, to some extent, by the household registration system. In the 1950s to 1970s, there were two ways for Mongolians to move to cities. One was through worker recruitment by factories while the other was admittance into colleges and universities. In the period of the planned economy, up till 1978, large proportions of workers were recruited for urban construction and many Mongolians went to cities and towns for this reason. The following case studies provide a couple of vignettes of how this occurred for some.

After the herdsmen settled down and their life became more settled and rhythmic, they began sending their children to large cities to receive university education. According to the 1990 census, 20 per cent of university graduates remain in cities after graduation. Some become cadres in government agencies or the communist party organisations, others work in radio stations, news agencies, TV stations, publishing houses, or become teachers in colleges and universities. They are increasingly working in private enterprises or setting up their own small businesses with the help of relatives. The number of urban Mongolians rose from 136 964 in 1981 to 179 400 in 1982, an increase of 42 436 people in one year. Much of the increase in the size of the Mongolian population actually came from

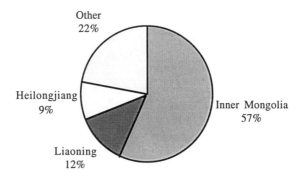

Source: State Population Census Office (1993, Vols. 1 and 4).

Figure 5.3 Origin of Mongolians, 1985-90

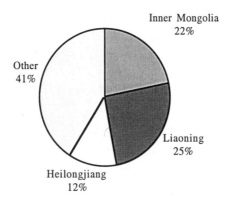

Source: State Population Census Office (1993, Vols. 1 and 4).

Figure 5.4 Destination of Mongolians, 1985-90

CASE ONE

In the 1970s, a Mongolian and Ewenki mixed couple suffered in the Cultural Revolution, especially during the 'Unearthing of the Inner Mongolian Revolutionary Party Movement'. [1] Two of their relatives (nephew and niece) from a rural town went to work in Hohhot as state-employed workers. Since the couple had been tortured and wronged by the 'Gang of Four' they had the right to have their sons and daughter signed up in factories or state-run units. The two sons and one daughter were still teenagers so they asked their relatives to fill in and work in a chemical fabric work plant and a lock-making industry, respectively. The registration rule of *hukou* was tight for people who wanted to settle in cities in China, but after a considerable campaign, the couple succeeded in getting their two relatives registered as permanent Hohhotian citizens.

During the 1980s, China's doors became more open and allowed more population movement from rural areas to metropolitans. The two relatives, who by then had already established themselves in Hohhot as full time workers, asked one of their sisters to come and work in a private restaurant. Then the next year, they again asked their younger brother to come and work in another restaurant. They were all equally hard-working and had firmly established themselves. They, however, cannot get registered as permanent Hohhotian residents nor find themselves a full time job.

CASE TWO

Again in the 1970s, a retired 'revolutionary old couple', senior cadres who had worked and contributed to the state for more than 40 years, asked a daughter of their close relatives to come from the rural countryside to help them with house duties. The girl, Gowa, worked well for the old couple and she eventually married a local Han peasant and got registration as a full Hohhotian citizen. In doing this, the couple mobilised many of their social contacts and 'old comrade network'.

'identity-shift' or Han identifying as Mongolian. This was in response to an administrative decision of the government.

In general, intra-provincial migration has come to be seen as a means of development for Inner Mongolia. 'It's time to put down the lasso and take up the rod' is a common saying and social and ethnic modernisation is a very important part of the government of Inner Mongolia's policy. The challenge is how to do this and retain Mongolian culture and language within the context of economic reform and the 'sinification' of Inner Mongolia. Constant encroachment of agricultural areas into pastoral zones is putting increased pressure on fragile environments. The semi-agricultural zones are home to around one million Mongolians but the migration rate out of these areas is high due to both increased pressure on the land and the inability of many families to make an adequate living (Plate 5.4). Some are moving to cities and towns while others are moving into the remaining pastoral regions.

Plate 5.4 Environmental damage to pastoral region, 1997 (Photo by R. Iredale)

---

[1] *Wa xinneirendang yundong*, 1968-1969, a notorious purge, launched by the central government, aimed at stopping Mongolian separatist movement, had a death toll of 16 662, according to official figures (Tumen and Zhu 1995).

CONTEMPORARY MINORITY MIGRATION TO AND WITHIN INNER MONGOLIA

To the authors' knowledge, no recent research has been undertaken into current internal migration within Inner Mongolia. The following section is largely based on data from the *Sample Survey of Ethnic Minority Migration*. The focus is on patterns and issues of minority migration to and within Inner Mongolia. In total, 282 migrant households consisting of 133 minority households and 149 Han Chinese households were interviewed, and for purposes of comparison, a non-migrant sample of 139 Mongolian households were interviewed. The size of the sample necessarily means that the findings are indicative only. The survey was undertaken in early 1998 in Hohhot (capital of Inner Mongolia). The interviews were conducted by a team of local researchers who were trained and supervised by the research team. The minority migrant sample consisted mostly of Mongolians (96.2 per cent), with very small percentages from other ethnicities. A small percentage of minority migrant (3.9 per cent) and non-migrant (5.9 per cent) households stated that their first language was Han Chinese though they still identified themselves as Mongolian.

Social-demographic characteristics of the sample

Both the minority and the Han migrant groups were unevenly distributed by sex: 68.4 per cent were males in the minority sample and 66.2 per cent in the Han Chinese sample. The non-migrant sample also consisted of 66.2 per cent males. These proportions may be more an indication of the sampling procedure rather than patterns. The minority migrant sample had 72.4 per cent aged 20-39 compared with 64.3 per cent for the Han Chinese. The proportion of never married was highest (38.8 per cent) in the minority migrant group compared with 28.2 per cent in the Han Chinese migrant sample. The non-migrant sample of Mongolians was both slightly older and more settled in that 83.7 per cent were married. The size of the migrant households was similar across the two groups except that there was a higher proportion of minority households with more than three people. This can be explained by the larger number of children in minority rural families. The non-migrant Mongolian households mostly consisted of three to four people.

 The minority groups were generally better educated than the Han Chinese sample. The minority migrant sample had 46.6 per cent with university or professional school level education and the non-migrant minority sample had 53.3 per cent in these categories. This exceptionally high level of education is partly a reflection of the sample selected for the study. A much lower proportion of Han Chinese migrants (8.7 per cent) had these levels of education and one quarter had only primary schooling or none at all. Current employment status shows that 83.9 per cent of Han Chinese migrants were employed compared with 48.9 per cent of minority migrants and 81.2 per cent of minority non-migrants. This again indicates a high rate of selection of student minority migrant households. Work training was much more common among the non-migrant group indicating that Hohhot offers much better opportunities in this regard.

Migration process of the sample

Most of the migrant sample were born in Inner Mongolia: 96.1 per cent of minority migrants and 85.0 per cent of Han Chinese migrants. A small number of Han Chinese were born in Gansu (10.3 per cent), Hebei (3.4 per cent) and other provinces. All minority migrants had moved to Hohhot directly from their source and the pattern for the Han Chinese sample was similar. Minority migrants had moved mainly from rural villages (47 per cent), small towns and larger centres while Han Chinese movement was more from villages (63.8 per cent) and less from towns or cities. About a quarter of minority migrants had *hukou* elsewhere, while 61.2 per cent had permanent registration and 14.0 per cent had temporary registration in Hohhot. The pattern was much the same for Han Chinese migrants except that slightly more had permanent registration in Hohhot. It is obvious that *hukou* is not confining people to their place of registration and that many migrants had generally been able to get a Hohhot *hukou*.

In both migrant sub-groups, about four fifths had sought advice from other people about moving and about three quarters had received positive support. The Han Chinese sample had slightly less knowledge about work opportunities, with 41.2 per cent saying they had no knowledge compared with 32.3 per cent of minority migrants. Relatives were an important source of information for both groups as well as the media/public information being a significant source for minority migrants.

The number of people moving alone was high among the minority sample (50 per cent), followed by 40.9 per cent moving with their immediate family. Among the Han Chinese, 39.7 per cent moved alone and 56.2 per cent moved with their immediate family. Four fifths of minority migrants had left family members behind while less than half the Han Chinese migrant sample had left family member/s behind. Han tended to move together while for Mongolians movement appeared more complicated and fragmented. Similarly, more minority migrants had family members moving elsewhere indicating a wider pattern of dispersal than for the Han Chinese where 64.4 per cent did not have family members moving elsewhere.

Employment and income of the sample

The livelihoods of migrants before they moved varied by nationality and sex. Minority males were more heavily concentrated in agriculture and semi-agriculture and in government offices. Minority females were spread more across all areas. On the other hand, 70.5 per cent of Han Chinese males and 60.6 per cent of Han Chinese females were from agricultural backgrounds reinforcing the importance of Han movement out of villages. Low income and the desire for a modern lifestyle were the most common reasons for moving, though there was variation by sex and nationality. Long term movement was the aim of significant proportions of all sub-groups but most notably minority and Han females. This probably reflects the smaller range of job possibilities for women in rural areas, other than in farming and herding. It may also reflect marriage migration or escaping from family controls. The movement of minorities for education purposes is reflected by the fact that 27.5 per cent of both males and females gave this as their aim of moving. They had come from other parts of Inner Mongolia to enrol in the wide range of educational institutions available in Hohhot.

Family income before migration was heavily concentrated in the nil or low income brackets. This was especially among Han Chinese where 80.3 per cent of males and 77.9 per cent of females said they had no income prior to moving and all Han interviewed earned less than 400 yuan per month before moving, to Hohhot. Among minority migrants, smaller proportions earned no income before migrating though 88 per cent of males and 96 per cent of females earned less than 400 yuan per month. The improvement in family income as a result of migration was very noticeable for all groups. Han Chinese migrants, in terms of their family income, did better than minority migrants. Only 28.6 per cent of Han males and 26.0 per cent of Han females were members of households where monthly income was less than 400 yuan after migration. In comparison, 35.6 per cent of minority males and 31.7 per cent of minority females were in households with less than 400 yuan per month after migration. At the upper end, all migrant sub-groups had households that earned more than 2000 yuan per month after migration whereas only a few minority females were in such households before migration. A comparison of incomes after migration and non-migrant incomes shows that migrants had begun to match the incomes of non-migrants.

Patterns of employment after moving varied considerably. The service and business sectors were the most common areas of employment for all four sub-groups. The differences are that minority migrants were generally employed in a wider range of occupations which is not surprising given their generally higher level of education. Among the Han Chinese, a sizeable proportion of both males and females were labourers. A proportion of each group were professionals though this proportion is much smaller than for the non-migrant sample. By comparison, the non-migrant sample contained higher proportions of professional/ technical workers, managers, clerks (among the males) and service workers (among the females). The numbers are not large enough to be representative but overall figures for Hohhot show that by comparison migrants occupy less skilled jobs.

The two migrant sub-groups contained around 45 per cent who were self employed compared with the non-migrant sample where only 14.8 per cent were in this category. Almost one quarter of minority migrants had not had a job since arriving while 61.6 per cent had had one or two. Changing jobs is a common feature of migrants though it is less marked among the Han Chinese migrants. The non-migrants, as would be expected, had been in their current jobs for much longer. More than three quarters of all migrants had received assistance in locating a job, mostly from relatives and friends. The government and media were a slightly more important source of information for minority migrants. Getting a job was not an easy matter for most people and only 15 out of 133 minority migrants and 26 out of 149 Han Chinese migrants reported that they had had no problems. The rest had a range of problems, the most important of which were their lack of work experience and not enough opportunities. Language and cultural problems were significant for both groups, though more for minority than for Han Chinese migrants. This suggests that workplaces are not bilingual and language is a common barrier to employment. These factors accounted for a number of people going into their own businesses. Finding work was also difficult for non-migrants but they reported fewer problems and obviously had better employment networks than migrants.

Social/personal aspects of migration

In terms of standard of living, a sightly higher proportion of minority migrants than Han Chinese migrants reported being at an economic level which was above the basic level. Han migrants generally reported a less satisfactory economic level with a much higher percentage (39.3 per cent) feeling that they were living below the basic economic level. For the majority of migrants movement had led to an improvement in their economic situation but there had been a deterioration for 32.6 per cent of minority and 29.4 per cent of Han Chinese migrants. Obviously money is not the only factor influencing their perceptions as incomes were generally higher than before moving. A quarter of Han Chinese migrants considered themselves richer than average, compared with 38.6 per cent of minority migrants and 41.6 per cent of non-migrants. The savings rate in China is about one third of annual income and the need to save has obviously been well inculcated: 48.6 per cent of Han said that they could save compared with slightly smaller proportions of the minority samples.

There was very little private home ownership among either sub-group. Half the minority migrant sample and 61.9 per cent of the Han Chinese migrant sample were renters and only a small proportion of each group had access to public housing. Three quarters of the minority sample had been resident here for more than one year compared with 83.8 per cent of the Han Chinese sample. The minority sample had a larger percentage that did not know how long they had been here or they were unwilling to say. Two fifths of the minority migrant group intended to stay for a long time and a further 48.1 per cent said they were not sure how long they would be staying. The important point is that only 7.5 per cent intended to stay for a short time, so it is safe to say that most movements were fairly permanent. The Han Chinese sample had similar long term intentions.

One of the major benefits of moving to Hohhot was clearly an improvement in health status. Good health status was reported by 61.7 per cent of minority and 85.8 per cent of Han Chinese migrants and for 60.9 per cent and 71.8 per cent, respectively, their health had improved since they moved. The health of minority non-migrants was better than that of minority migrants but not as good as that of Han Chinese migrants. Only a quarter of non-migrants felt that their health would improve if they moved. Hohhot clearly has a range of health facilities to which people are able to gain access. Even migrants without *hukou* appear to be able to get reasonable health and medical services.

Migration and education

Education features high on the agenda for Mongolians. Mongolians' history of having once ruled China and the perception of them as a strong group that has to be well catered for in order to avert further trouble, have ensured that considerable resources have been channelled in their direction. The overall statistics show that the level of education among Mongolians is similar to or better than the average for China. But the data for minority migrants to Hohhot show a significant problem: only two thirds of migrant families with school age children had their children enrolled in school compared with 98.1 per cent of Han Chinese migrant families. This indicates that either lack of *hukou* among Mongolians is stopping their children enrolling in school or other reasons exist. The children may be needed in family businesses or school fees may be too high. Even among minority non-migrants there was a sizeable proportion (17.7 per cent) whose children were not attending school. This suggests that a range of explanations may be at work.

As has been discussed, preferred type of schooling is an indicator of ethnic identity and signifies concern about the maintenance of culture, language and history. Of those who attended school, the majority (75 per cent) of minority migrants' children attended a nationality school though most would prefer a nationality class in a Han Chinese school. Almost a fifth of minority migrants' children attended a Han Chinese school. The pattern was similar for minority non-migrants with more people preferring a nationality class in a Han school though this clearly was not always available. The benefits of a bilingual education are obviously recognised by many Mongol parents. Most Han Chinese children attended a Han school but small proportions had children who attended a nationality school.

The high level of satisfaction with schooling that was indicated by minority migrants, compared with non-migrants, is most likely an indication of better school facilities in Hohhot compared with other parts of Inner Mongolia. The two most common problems with schooling for migrant households were the cost and the fact that their children could not attend school because of lack of *hukou*. The latter was not a major problem for Han Chinese families for whom the overwhelming problem was the cost of schooling. On the other hand, the non-migrant minority group reported very few problems with schooling, the major problem being the absence of an adequate number of nationality classes in Han schools. This reinforces the clear preference of most minority families for an educational setting for their children which is reflective of their nationality but incorporated in an institutional setting which is Han Chinese. Half to three quarters of all groups preferred their children to attend a nationality university, the highest percentage being 72.5 per cent for Han Chinese migrant families. Changing nationality is not uncommon in Inner Mongolia due to the high rate of intermarriage and the perceived advantages (especially in terms of access to university) for minority children. These data suggest that perhaps a strong motivation for moving to Hohhot is to enable children to access tertiary educational facilities that would have been out of their reach elsewhere.

About half of all minority parents wanted their children to learn both Chinese and their nationality language and a only few wanted their children to learn their own nationality or the local language only. The second preferred option was for their own nationality language and a foreign language (preferably English). Few Han households were interested in their children learning Mongolian and half were happy with Chinese only. The majority of the remainder were interested in a foreign language as well.

This picture is fairly typical of the language hierarchy that has developed in Inner Mongolia. English or some other foreign language (for international dealings) is at the top, Chinese is second and is the means for political promotion and economic procurement and Mongolian is at the bottom (Bilik 1998b, p. 73). Mongolian is mostly used locally, at home and at Mongolian functions. The language situation is complex and reflects the confrontation between rationalism, economic betterment and individualism, on the one hand, and politics, history, emotions, and ethnicity on the other. It also has much to do with the linguistic hierarchy that is in turn related to power relations.

> Mandarin stands at the pinnacle of a metalinguistics hierarchy which mirrors the vertical basis of power in China today. State language policies have established official minority languages and Chinese 'dialects' under the arching umbrella of the Chinese state; yet their domain is strictly constrained through prescriptive standardization. (Dwyer 1998, p. 80)

There is a risk of oversimplification when dealing with the language landscape in Inner Mongolia if not enough attention is paid to the distribution of Mongolian speakers. Mongolians who live in cities where the use of Mongolian is limited invariably put forward problems in continuing to emphasise the value of teaching the language. At the same time, much theorisation and symbolisation of Mongolian teaching and speaking is going on in metropolitan areas. On the other hand, the Mongolian language is very much alive in pastoral areas and these people are fighting not only for their language but also for other indicators of the cultural identity. The situation is compounded by ethnic pride versus practical gains. Daniels outlines the situation with regard to attempts at reviving Mongol culture.

> ... [W]e immediately come upon several contradictions that face the policy makers. First, should such programs be compulsory or voluntary? For some or for all Mongolians? And so forth. If they are voluntary, then one cannot accuse the government of forcing Mongolians to remain Mongol and forego the countrywide advantages of a Han education (more on this supposed advantage in a moment). This is an important question for governments already painted in the west as 'totalitarian'. Voluntary programs also guarantee a certain amount of enthusiasm for the project. But learning a second language, especially from a totally separate language family (Mongol is Uro-Altaic, Han is Sino-Tibetan) and in a difficult and totally different orthography, is not a project to be taken lightly and not to be done in a few weeks. So how does one guarantee some commitment to carry through such programs in more than a token manner? Moreover, many Chinese of both the Han and minority nationalities perceive a Han education at a 'good' (usually central Chinese) university to be of more value for individual career advancement than a degree from a small university in an autonomous region. As much as we might like to, we cannot entirely banish such individualistic venal concerns in a socialist society, and such concerns are not dispensed with

> by listing Mongol alumni from educational institutions in Inner Mongolia who have succeeded 'outside' in central China. Conversely, making education in the Mongol language compulsory for all Mongolians, including those who have lost the language and been 'Sinified', might be seen by the very critical as a means of 'ghettoizing' the Mongolians to (perhaps) a second-rate education or perhaps to a good career only in their own autonomous region. (Daniels 1984, pp. 19-20)

The principal of Tumed Left-Wing Banner Mongolian School explained this dilemma very convincingly (Interview 1996). The school was established in the early 1980s under the support of Inner Mongolian leaders from the area. The Tumed Mongolians started to lose their language last century and they saw this as a drawback for gaining a better position in the political hierarchy. Under a 'closed-door-Mongolian-teaching' program, Mongolian was the only permitted communicative medium on the school campus. Pupils were sent out to the pastoral areas to learn from herdsmen on a regular basis. After a few years, however, optimism dampened. The enrolment rate slumped dramatically and the dropout rate was high. They had expected that the school would redress what they had lost, at least symbolically, but the school became an enclave.

> The graduates from the school, with only moderate knowledge of Chinese, if they fail to pass examinations and go to the few Mongolian middle schools in Hohhot, would be crippled or 'wasted' (as the local Mongolians would tell me) upon return to their original community where few know any Mongolian. Besides, the biggest concern the Mongolians have is that there are too few opportunities for academic advancement or social promotion for Mongolian monolinguals in the Autonomous Region, let alone the whole of China. In the face of such difficulties and allegations from outspoken local Mongolians that 'crimes' were committed against the Mongolians, the regional government, with the support from the school authorities, is now considering adopting a 'two way' voluntary system, ie. to run both Mongolian and Chinese courses tailored to the pupils' own will. Those who want to major in Mongolian will be given supplementary Chinese courses and vice versa for those who want to in Chinese. This plan has been severely criticized by some old Mongolian intellectuals and cadres, who supported the establishment of the school and invested a lot of emotional capital. (Bilik 1998a, pp. 71-2)

The continuation of this debate can be expected for some time but the most likely outcome is that the emphasis on teaching Mongolian will continue to decline, especially with the passing away of old Mongolians and increased economic opening up. While the role of the Mongolian language is emphasised by authorities as part of ethnic integration and cultural maintenance, the reality is already quite different. The major language has come to be Chinese just as many of the Mongolian facilities are actually run by Han rather than Mongolians. In a region where Mongolians comprise only 15 per cent of the population 'it is impossible for Mongolians to enjoy their autonomous rights' (Borchigud 1994, p. 298).

The reasons given by both male and female non-migrant minorities for not moving stressed enough income and work and 'wanting to stay with their nationality group. However, Hohhot is clearly not seen by most people as a desirable place for their children to live and the majority of people would prefer their children to move elsewhere after graduation. This sentiment was strongest among the Han Chinese migrants (98.1 per cent) but both minority migrants and non-migrants had four fifths who wanted their children to move elsewhere. Hohhot can only accommodate Mongolian speakers in state-run work units (*danwei*), such as the publishing house, TV stations, printing factory, etc., and thus many young people go out of the region to receive further training and education. After graduation they have to go elsewhere to find employment. The attraction of other parts of China for people with education and skills is a strong force and is creating a deficit of skilled personnel in outer areas such as Inner Mongolia.

Relationship of sampled population to local community

In response to questions about the nature and quality of social life and forms of interaction with others, television was the most popular form of entertainment. The data show that overall minorities engaged in a wider range of activities and were more likely to read, play games and visit relatives and friends than Han Chinese. Singing and dancing were more common activities among minority migrants than minority non-migrants though interestingly Han Chinese reported participating in these activities as well. This reflects the long period of interaction between nationality groups in Inner Mongolia. Migrant sub-groups had similar levels of contact with relatives while minority non-migrants spent a great deal of time in this way. The availability of a wide family network was clearly an important element for minorities staying in Hohhot for a long time.

The mixing of nationalities is a long-standing feature of Inner Mongolian society and this is reflected in the fact that 98.5 per cent of minority migrants and 94.1 per cent of minority non-migrants interacted with a range of nationalities. On the other hand, 30.5 per cent of Han Chinese migrants still mixed with Han Chinese only, reflecting the fact that they had moved to Hohhot from predominantly Han agricultural areas. Han don't learn Mongolian and so they are limited in who they mix with. In recent years, the rate of Mongol-Han intermarriage in large cities such as Hohhot has reached 60 per cent of all marriages. As would be expected, cultural transmission has been a two-way process. Most Mongolians have adopted the Han Chinese way of living while many Han people have developed Mongolian tastes such as drinking milk tea and preferring mutton over pork.

The situation of Inner Mongolia is unique among the minority regions being investigated here. There has been minority-Han interaction over a long period of time and Han have settled here as a result of a range of policies — for construction, for defence, etc — as well as a result of spontaneous migration from other regions. One factor differentiating the Mongolians from other minorities, for the Han Chinese, is their power in the past and the high regard in which they have traditionally been held. This factor was grasped by Mao Zedong when he referred to them as the 'sons and grandsons of Chinggis Khan' (Khan 1994, p. 266). Mao had a wider aim than simple reassurance as to their status and identity, however. He evoked a 'kinship bond' as an 'ethnic tie'. Mongolians continue to emphasise this aspect and to use this 'fictive biological ancestry, and its symbolic value as an identity marker' (Khan 1994, p. 277). According to Hobsbawn (1983, pp. 4-5), an invention of traditions occurs when a 'rapid transformation of society weakens or destroys the social patterns for which "old" traditions had been designed' or, in short, 'when there are sufficiently large and rapid changes on the demand or supply side'. The continued threat of assimilation by the Han, especially during the Cultural Revolution, led to a revival of ethnic identity among Mongolians and this is demonstrated in the research into migration. Political events, such as the 'unearthing' of the New Inner Mongolian Revolutionary Party during the Cultural Revolution, together with their minority status, have helped to unite them to ensure that they look after their kinfolk.

Minorities are not the only ones reviving old traditions or folk customs. Many Han, in the face of increasing pressure from outside since China's opening up, have also revived many old traditions. In the face of both opening-up and assimilationist tendencies in Inner Mongolia, many Mongolians are particularly eager to renew their culture and language. This is evident in the discussion and debate about ethnic education in general, and language policy in particular, in Inner Mongolia. Pressure to retain Mongolian schools and the Mongolian language in Hohhot schools is a microcosm of what is occurring in the region. A language hierarchy has developed over time and is being exaggerated with businesses booming and spreading from metropolitan cities into remote areas (Bilik 1998a, p. 73). Mongolian is receding into the home in urban areas though it is still prevalent as the language of discourse in some primarily Mongolian pastoral regions.

CONCLUSION

The desire for education, better incomes, greater job opportunities and a more modern lifestyle are all important factors in explaining both minority and Han movement into Hohhot. The survey data shows that minority movement appears to be for a wider range of motives than Han migration, which is mostly for moving out of agriculture into small businesses. Most movement seems to be permanent but some minority movement appears to be a strategy for acquiring skills and expertise for reinvestment in the home region. Some minorities also attend the cadre school, a training place for minority party officials, and then become administrators throughout the region. Interestingly, there is no University of Nationalities in Inner Mongolia and minority students must move to Beijing or elsewhere for training in one of these institutions.

The quality of life in Hohhot appears to be a considerable improvement over village and township life elsewhere and once word of this travels back to the source it acts as a further inducement for more people to move. Thus, as in the rest of China, people are voting with their feet. The relaxation of *hukou* means that people are no longer bound to one place but are relatively free to move and change their *hukou* or get temporary *hukou*. Nevertheless, we found that the lack of urban *hukou*, together with the high cost of schooling, are preventing some children from gaining access to education. This is especially the case for minority children in migrant and non-migrant households. The need to earn income for the household, under the household responsibility system, is also a factor in keeping children out of school.

Interviews reinforced the observation that generally migration is seen as a good thing by both individuals and officials and academics and as a positive force for aiding economic development. For many, Hohhot is a stepping stone to elsewhere and is the start of a process that may end up as either inter-provincial or international migration. Some go abroad, while others go to the coastal special economic zones to make money or to Beijing, Shanghai and other metropolitan areas for study and work. Many educated Mongolians are converting their human capital into economic gains outside of Inner Mongolia.

For Mongolians, the most important useable social resource for migration to Hohhot is the kinship network or 'cultural capital'. Most Mongolian cadres in Hohhot come from rural areas and their ties with the hometown are still strong enough to motivate them to help relatives to achieve economic betterment through migration. The 'negotiated boundaries' (Barth 1969) that have been formed around those of Mongolian identity overcome urban-rural divisions. In a place such as Hohhot, kinship ties still have very strong meaning and they serve to both bring people to Hohhot and then keep them from moving on elsewhere. Amongst Mongolians we found that the role of education and education policy in the maintenance of ethnic identity is disputed. Older Mongolians still see Mongolian language education as a vital tool for cultural maintenance while many younger Mongolians see their future as being dependent upon their capacity to speak and interact with Han Chinese. The rural-urban divide is also a significant factor in the language and cultural maintenance debate.

The relationship between Mongolians and Han in Inner Mongolia, irrespective of whether they are migrants or not, is largely decided by politics. When the central government's ethnic policy is good the relationship between minorities and Han tends to be quite smooth but when the policy turns 'sour', as in the Cultural Revolution, the society is divided along nationality lines. Inner Mongolia is one of the poorest parts of China and competition between Han and Mongolians for scarce farming and pastoral land has led to increased pressure on the environment. How this is negotiated in the future will play a major role in avoiding out-migration from ecologically damaged areas.

6.   Tibet and the movement of Tibetans[*]

BACKGROUND

Tibet Autonomous Region (TAR), with an area of 1.2 million square kilometres, covers 12.5 per cent of the area of the People's Republic of China but it is home to only 0.002 per cent (2.2 million) of the PRC's population. Tibetans actually live in an area of about 3.8 million sq. km. or about fifteen times the size of the United Kingdom and half the size of the United States. The history of Tibet in the early 20th century is one of Tibet being a 'pawn in the power struggles of Great Britain, Russia, and Imperial China' (Grunfeld 1996, p. 34). China and Russia were forced out of the region and Great Britain, by means of the 'blatantly illegal' Simla Convention, made Tibet into a British protectorate in 1914 with the prime aim of providing a buffer state on the northern border of India. Britain retained its 'protector' role until 1933 when:

> [t]he Nanking government saw in the 13th Dalai Lama's death the opportunity to send a 'condolence' mission to Lhasa. When the mission returned to China two 'liaison' officers with a wireless transmitter remained in Lhasa. ... The Chinese had regained a foothold in Tibet ... (Spence 1993, p. 312)

The period between when the British pulled out and 1949 was one of ongoing negotiations between the 14th Dalai Lama, the British, the United States and the nationalist leader Chiang Kai-Shek. The latter wanted Tibet as part of China, stressing that they were all 'of the same race' (Spence 1993, p. 313). The disintegration of Nationalist China and victory by the Communists eventually led in 1950 to the arrival of communist forces. On 24 November 1950 the East Tibetan Autonomous Region, headed by Tian Bao and encompassing a population of 70 000 (80 per cent Tibetan and 20 per cent Han and Yi), was established. The TAR as it stands now was formed in 1965.

The landscape of Tibet is predominantly a plateau averaging 3600

---

[*] This chapter has had particular input from Wang Su, drawing on work by Wang Shuxin and Zhang Tianlu.

metres above sea level that is surrounded by mountains. While Tibetans have learned to live with the rarefied air and strong winds many newcomers find these conditions difficult. Lhasa is situated in a valley where the annual temperature range is from 10 to 24 degrees centigrade. There are four broad regions in Tibet: the central area, or province of U, with the capital of Lhasa; the province of Tsang to the southwest and centering on the second largest town, Shigatse; Kham in the east (some of it is in Sichuan) and Ngari in the far west. Amdo, which is also part of the Tibetan plateau, is now in Qinghai.

Population of Tibet

Censuses were held in Tibet from 653 AD onwards but they were all highly inaccurate. It is generally agreed, however, that the population was declining over time due to the spread of disease, the practice of polyandry, the large mostly celibate clergy and the natural environment (Grunfeld 1996). The population was estimated to have been close to three million in the early 1950s or four million if all ethnic Tibetans are included. Within the TAR, there has been a growth in population numbers from 1.89 million in 1982 (94.4 per cent ethnic Tibetans) to 2.196 million (95.5 per cent Tibetans) in 1990. According to Zhang (1997, p. 6), the latter figure is reliable 'as every resident in Tibet was directly interviewed and registered'. The census was conducted in full with the exception of three items that were omitted. They all related to migration and were left out for reasons of sensitivity. By 1993, it was estimated that the total population in Tibet had risen to 2.32 million (Zhang 1997). The ethnic composition of Tibet is the most homogeneous for any area in China.

Table 6.1 Ethnic composition of Tibet and neighbouring provinces, 1990 ('000)

Area	Tibetans		Other minorities		Han		Total Pop'n
	No.	%	No.	%	No.	%	No.
Tibet	2 096.7	95.5	18.5	0.8	80.8	3.7	2 196.0
Qinghai	718.3	49.2	210.4	14.4	531.5	36.4	1 460.2
Gansu	332.4	42.0	57.3	7.2	402.4	50.8	792.1
Sichuan	1 037.2	60.3	228.5	13.3	545.4	26.4	1 720.1
Yunnan	104.4	33.1	159.7	50.7	50.9	18.1	315.0
Total	4 289.0	66.2	674.1	10.4	1 520.0	23.5	6 483.1

Source: Zhang (1997, p.14).

Table 6.1 shows that in 1990, 95.5 per cent of the population were Tibetans and the next most heavily Tibetan region, Sichuan, consists of 60.3 per cent Tibetans. Han Chinese comprise 3.68 per cent of Tibet's population and other minorities constitute the remaining 0.84 per cent. Tibet is predominantly rural and only 11.5 per cent of the population are urban (Plates 6.1 and 6.2). There are two cities, Lhasa with 139 800 and Shigatse with 30 200. There are 30 towns with a total population of 82 900, or 2700 on average for each town. The population of Lhasa Prefecture grew by 2.3 per cent per annum between 1982 and 1990. Only one other region in Tibet, Ngari Prefecture which grew by 2.62 per cent per annum, surpassed this. According to Zhang (1997, p. 17), the ethnic composition of Lhasa changed greatly between 1949 and 1990 and Lhasa now has residents from 31 ethnic groups: Tibetans rank first with 69 per cent of the total, Han comprise 28.9 per cent and Hui comprise 1.7 per cent. The remainder includes Mongolian, Uyghur, Miao, Yi, Zhuang, Bouyei, Korean, Manchu, Dong, Yao, Bai, Tujia, Kazak, Thai, Lim Gaoshan, Shui, Dingxiang, Naxi, Jingpo, Tu, Qiang, Sala, Gelo, Pumi, Menpa and Lopa residents.

Plate 6.1 Tibetan village and landscape in Lhasa Valley, 1995 (Photo by R. Iredale)

Plate 6.2 Lhasa, 1995 (Photo by R. Iredale)

Number and distribution of Tibetans

The number of Tibetans in China totalled 4.59 million at the time of the 1990 census. The figure had increased from 3.87 million in 1982 representing an average annual growth rate of 2.15 per cent. Of this 4.59 million, 45.8 per cent (2.1 million) live in the region, which is currently the TAR. The remainder are scattered mainly throughout 10 Tibetan autonomous prefectures and two autonomous counties in Qinghai, Sichuan, Gansu and Yunnan. Table 6.2 shows that from 1982 to 1990, the Tibetan population living in Tibet and the four provinces in the Tibet-Qinghai Plateau area increased by 18.43 per cent. The Tibetan populations in Qinghai and Gansu experienced rates of total increase of over 20 per cent. The Tibetan population in Tibet increased by 17.36 per cent from 1982 to 1990 or 2.17 per cent per year.

Socio-economic profile

The Tibetan economy before 1952 consisted mainly of rural activities. The Lhasa valley was the most important agricultural area as the altitude is lowest but agriculture also occurred in other smaller valleys. The rest of Tibet was taken up by herding or was left unoccupied. The proportions

Table 6.2 Population ('000) and distribution of Tibetans, PRC, 1982 and 1990

Province or region	1982		1990		Growth rate
	No.	%	No.	%	%
Tibet	1 786.5	46.12	2 096.7	45.65	17.36
Sichuan	922.0	23.8	1 087.8	23.68	17.98
Qinghai	753.9	19.46	912.2	19.86	20.99
Gansu	304.6	7.84	367.0	7.99	20.49
Yunnan	95.9	2.47	111.3	2.42	16.06
Total	3 862.9	99.71	4 575.0	99.61	18.43
Rest of China	11.1	0.29	18.1	0.39	63.06

Source: Zhang (1997, pp. 12-3).

engaged in agriculture and herding are open to dispute. According to the original Chinese version, three quarters of the workforce were engaged in herding and one quarter in agriculture. A later Chinese government breakdown in 1959 was of only 20 per cent herdsmen or nomads, 60 per cent serfs, 15 per cent clergy and 5 per cent nobility (Grunfeld 1996, p. 14). Other scholars also argue that the contemporary independent nomadic lifestyle is a comparatively late development in Tibetan society, emerging only after the establishment of substantial agricultural communities (Upton 1996, p. 99). For example, Stein (1972) claims that the majority of Tibetans were agriculturalists or at the very most, they were semi-nomadic, living primarily in sedentary communities and raising stock as a secondary occupation when time, money and ecology allowed. Nevertheless, the image of Tibetans as nomadic herders is still strong in the minds of both Tibetans and the Chinese nation generally.

On balance it appears that the majority of people lived in a 'feudal' type of system where most land belonged to landlords. The term 'feudal' is used here as it is the adjective which most closely describes Tibetan society (Grunfeld 1996, p. 9). Serfs or *mi ser* ('yellow person') were tied to their masters and paid taxes and *ulag* (corvée labour) in exchange for the right to work the land. Ownership of land was in the hands of three groups: the monasteries, the lay nobility and the Lhasa government. The first two controlled well over 50 per cent of Tibet's land area. There was no modern industry in Tibet before 1952 though there were small cottage industries (carpet making, shoes, cooking implements). There was a very low level of urbanisation and Buddhist temples accounted for one half of the people living in towns and cities.

From 1951, the central government assumed responsibility for the management of Tibet and the most crucial development in the early years was the construction of two highways, Qinghai-Tibet and Sichuan-Tibet, which linked Tibet with other provinces. These were the first roads in Tibet's history and they not only brought down the price of most goods but also enabled Tibet's trade to be with the rest of China rather than the south. These two highways were completed in 1954 but there was little change in the social or economic structure of Tibet until after 1959. During the 1950s, Han officials and professionals were sent from all over China and Tibetan nationality officials and professionals were assigned to Tibet from Sichuan, Gansu, Qinghai and Yunnan to aid development. Attempts were made to 'reduce the use of *ulag* and to strip local Tibetan officials of the power to tax their subjects and to hold their own courts' (Grunfeld 1996, p. 122). The arrival of Chinese troops in 1959 led to the Dalai Lama's flight and the social structure of Tibet began to change. According to the statistics there were 36 700 Han in Tibet in 1964 (Dojiecaidan and Jiangchunluobu 1995, p. 586). Land was redistributed to the peasants and herders (35 *mu* or a little less than six acres per peasant) and between 1965 and 1975 administration was put in their hands, under peoples' communes. The socialisation of agriculture skipped the 'cooperative' stage that occurred in the rest of China and went straight from private landlord ownership to communes. Efforts were made to settle nomads down and to convert grasslands areas to wheat production.

The TAR was founded in 1965 and in order to help 'develop' Tibet many more officials, scientific and technical personnel, medical doctors, teachers and other skilled people were transferred to Tibet from the rest of China. Changes began to occur slowly but in 1966, the Cultural Revolution spread quickly to Lhasa and only four days after the Red Guards had rallied in Beijing, they had reached Lhasa (Grunfeld 1996, p. 183). Damage and destruction was widespread even though Zhou Enlai immediately ordered the Red Guards out of Tibet — owing to it being a region with special status.

> Attacks were not only against the Tibetans but also the Chinese leadership which had shaped the moderating policies in Tibet — treating it as a 'special case' and 'backward', thereby precluding dramatic and sudden revolutionary change. It was an attack on the policy of working with the Tibetan elites and allowing them to maintain their feudal positions in the midst of a socialist state. (Grunfeld 1996, p. 186)

In 1969 the fighting and destruction stopped. China then became concerned about the growing Indo-Soviet friendship and its borders with these nations, and with the emergence of an independent Bangladesh (aided by India). The Chinese considered it essential that minority peoples in Tibet and other areas not be alienated from Beijing and that they remain loyal to the PRC. Policies to restore traditional Tibetan culture that had been destroyed in the Cultural Revolution were put in place. These included the 'four basic freedoms' (to practice religion, trade, lend money with interest and keep servants). While the more moderate policies improved the situation, in September 1976 the local newspaper, (*Renmin Ribao,* September, p. 6), called on Han living in the TAR to 'strictly abide by the Party's nationalities policy, respect the habits and customs of the minority nationalities and learn their language ... [for Han–Tibetan unity is an] indispensable condition for making further efforts to build a Socialist New Tibet'.

The death of Mao Zedong and the political resurrection of Deng Xiaoping heralded in economic reforms as well as the admission of 'errors' in past policies towards minorities. Western travellers were allowed to visit Tibet from 1975 and American government officials arrived from 1977. Tian Bao, the Sichuan-born Tibetan who had formerly been head of the East TAR, was elected chair of the TAR in 1979. He became the first ethnic Tibetan in a major leadership position since March 1959. Other changes occurred which amounted to an easing of central government control over the local areas and the break up of communes into smaller production teams after 1979. In May 1980, a high level delegation, consisting of Hu Yaobang (General Secretary of the CPC), Wan Li (a Politburo member and Vice-Premier), Yang Jingren (Chair, State Nationalities Affairs Commission) and Ngawang Jigme arrived in Lhasa on an inspection tour of Tibet. They reported that the economic situation was so bad that dramatic reforms were required. They called for authentic regional autonomy, exemption from state purchases of grain, subsidies, flexible economic planning, a 'revived and developed' Tibetan culture, education and science and a commitment to two thirds ethnic Tibetan cadres within two to three years.

As a consequence, by 1984 communes were abandoned and there was no mention of the household responsibility system which was introduced in the rest of China. The household responsibility system requires peasants to deliver a percentage of their output to the state in return for the use of the land but in Tibet, each household assumed control of its own land and outputs in a 'do-as-you-like' policy (Grunfeld 1996, p. 215). After the introduction of economic reform and the opening up of Tibet, collective and individual businesses became the main producing units. Markets, not government, regulated the producing, consuming and exchanging of goods and the price of labour. Residents' committees were set up to manage education, culture and health facilities, and schools were made totally free — the only place in China where this occurs. The next section will trace the impact of socio-economic change on education.

THE DEVELOPMENT OF EDUCATIONAL FACILITIES

Participation and achievement

Prior to 1951, there were only two formal schools in Tibet, one for the clergy and one for the laity. Monasteries and private individuals ran schools but they only catered for a small percentage of the population. The emphasis was on learning to recite the scriptures rather than learning to read and write. The first modern school was set up in Tibet in 1951 and by 1990 there were 2556 such schools (Zhang 1997). Growth has not been consistent or steady, however, according to data provided by the Tibetan Education and Science Committee (Baomingzhi 1997). The number of primary schools (for children age 6 to 12) rose slowly from 1959 to 1970 but from the early 1970s there was a very rapid increase till 1976. This coincided with increased Chinese emphasis on the expansion of basic education facilities and with reconstruction after the Cultural Revolution. From then, however, there was no increase in the number of schools till 1980 and then a dramatic decline set in. The number of primary enrolments rose from 1969 to 1978 but after that the number declined quickly. These trends are depicted in Figure 6.1.

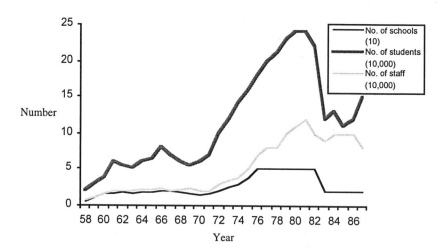

Source: Baomingzhi (1997, p. 283).

Figure 6.1 Changes in primary schools in Tibet, 1959-1987

The explanation for the dramatic decline in primary schools after 1978 is fourfold: rapid expansion meant the emergence of a large number of poor facilities and after 1980 the emphasis was placed on quality rather than quantity and poorer schools were closed down; the household system for operating land meant that many parents withdrew their children from education after 1984 so that they could work on the farm or in herding; the more open policy on religion meant that many children joined temples to study religion; and the central government's policy after the 1980s became to encourage other provinces in China to fund education facilities for Tibetan children outside of Tibetan areas.

Figure 6.2 shows that the number of middle schools (12 to 15 years olds) barely changed between 1959 and 1973 but from 1974 the number increased to 1979 and then also began to decline. After a temporary decline in the number of middle school students between 1979 and 1982 the number of students rose steadily till 1987. On the other hand, the increase in college (second professional school) student enrolments occurred in two major phases: the first between 1959 and 1964 and the second between 1973 and 1980. The variability in the number of schools, enrolments and teachers indicates significant policy shifts as well as decisions made by families as to the economic costs and benefits of education.

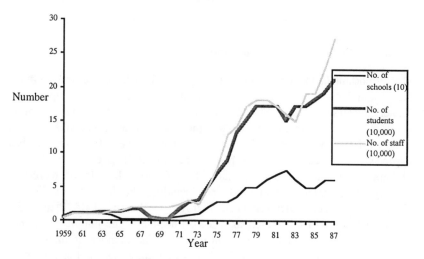

Source: Baomingzhi (1997, p. 283).

Figure 6.2 Changes in middle schools in Tibet, 1959-1987

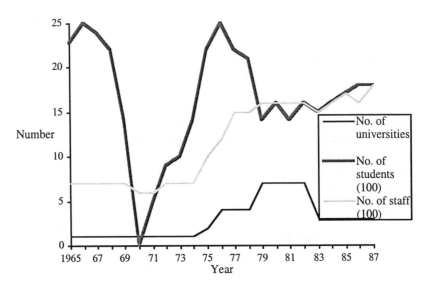

Source: Baomingzhi (1997, p. 283).

Figure 6.3 Changes in higher education in Tibet, 1965-1987

One important factor for all education facilities in China was the Cultural Revolution between 1966 and 1976. This is most evident in the figures for higher education in Tibet. Figure 6.3 shows that only one higher education institute existed in Tibet until 1974 and there was a drop in enrolments from 2500 in 1966 to zero in 1970. By 1976, the number of institutions had expanded to four and enrolments had returned to the level of 1966. Serious attempts were made in the second half of the Cultural Revolution to restore the higher education system of Tibet, including the Institute of Tibetan Traditional Medicine that had been destroyed in the first half (Plate 6.3). Between 1976 and 1982, there was a second decline in the number of higher education enrolments, followed by an increase. The number of institutions has remained about the same, indicating greater emphasis on the policy of sending people out for higher education.

As a consequence of this sequence of events and the earlier socio-cultural system, minorities in Tibet still have a particularly low level of education. Tibetans have the second lowest level (only higher than the Monba people). Table 6.3 shows some improvement since 1982 but by 1990 only 18.6 per cent of the Tibetan population in Tibet had primary level schooling and extremely low percentages had higher levels of education.

Plate 6.3 Bare hill which was formally the site of the Institute of Tibetan Medicine, 1995 (Photo by R. Iredale)

Table 6.3 Educational attainments of minorities in Tibet compared with rest of China, 1982 and 1990 (%)

Region	1982			1990		
Ethnic Group	University	Senior/ Junior middle school	Primary school	University	Senior/ Junior middle school	Primary school
Tibet						
Tibetans	0.16	2.72	15.68	0.29	3.70	18.52
Monba	0.25	1.85	6.50	0.53	3.58	14.07
Lopa	0.35	1.71	10.50	0.45	4.33	19.98
Han	5.50	46.00	32.60	7.57	63.47	19.91
Hui	3.60	31.00	35.00	2.28	28.59	31.16
China						
Tibetans	0.20	4.33	16.52	0.44	6.62	19.40
Kazaks	0.40	18.30	38.70	1.20	23.50	43.90
Koreans	1.98	49.05	28.48	4.32	54.65	23.29
Total	0.42	4.82	16.33	0.57	5.97	18.60

Source: Zhang (1997, p. 104).

More recent data indicate a better situation in 1997 in relation to the primary school enrolment rate. According to the *Essential Statistics of Education in China 1998*, the net enrolment rate of primary school age children in Tibet was 81.25 per cent and 92.10 per cent in Qinghai (Department of Development and Planning 1999, pp. 72-73). These figures indicate below universal education but nevertheless a significant improvement over previous times. However, female children in Tibet have a net enrolment rate in primary school of 76.56 per cent, well below the Qinghai female rate of 90.97 per cent and the total China female rate of 98.86 per cent. Table 6.4 shows the number and range of institutions at the secondary school level and above in Tibet.

Table 6.4 Basic statistics of secondary and higher education in Tibet, 1997

Type of Institution	No. of institutes	Undergraduate students		
		No. of graduates	No. admitted	Total enrolment
Regular Higher Education	4	857	717	3 200
Comprehensive University	1	240	234	1 305
Institution of Agriculture	1	239	120	527
Institutions of Medicine and Pharmacy	1	25	24	124
Institutions of Nationalities	1	353	339	1 244
Special Secondary Schools	16	1 483	1 552	5 730
Secondary Technical Schools	11	741	821	3 157
Other Secondary Technical Schools	1	85	39	260
Secondary Industrial Schools	1	113	0	282
Teacher Training Schools	5	742	731	2 573
Secondary Agricultural Schools	1	60	159	533
Secondary Health Schools	2	150	195	571
Secondary Finance and Economics Schools	3	167	315	898
Secondary Politics and Law Schools	1	36	79	315
Secondary Physical Culture Schools	1	57	22	105
Secondary Art Schools	1	23	12	97
Total	51	5 371	5 359	26 280

Source: Department of Planning and Construction (1998, pp. 116-214).

In total there were 51 such institutions in 1997 with an enrolment of 26 280. Figures for graduates and new students admitted in 1997 show virtually no change, which indicates that there has not been a growth in the secondary and tertiary education population in Tibet in recent years. As pointed out earlier, the growth, according to Zhang, is in the number of students leaving Tibet for secondary and higher education.

Curricula, teaching materials and staffing

It has been shown that the Tibetan school system emerged with the input of considerable resources from outside of Tibet but in the 1980s this was reduced. There was an expansion in Tibetan language education and in the 1990s, Tibetan language schools became important. They not only taught Tibetan language and literacy but they also started to play an important role in socialising students to a common Tibetan identity, though in reality there are many different identities. Schools, especially those with boarding facilities, began bringing together children with different languages and cultures from herding and agricultural areas. Upton (1996, p. 112) argues that educators and educational institutions have had an important mediating effect on Tibetan culture and society in the 1990s and in this way 'Tibetan educators are participating in the formation of a new "imagined community" (see Anderson 1991)'. The classificatory system used by the Chinese led to the Zang or Tibetans being grouped together as one ethnic group or nationality. The notion of a unified Tibetan identity is both promoted and reinforced, not only by Tibetan educators, but also by a nationally approved, standardized Tibetan-language curriculum' (Upton 1996, p. 119). This curriculum has been standardized through the production of the *Five Provinces and Regions Jointly Published Teaching Materials,* which is used in Tibet, Qinghai, Gansu, Sichuan and Yunnan. Originally this was a straight translation of the Han version but it is now being made more culturally relevant by Tibetan educators.

The traditional school system, where schools are attached to monasteries, still functions though to a much lesser extent than previously. The relationship between the secular and religious education systems is distant and educators in secular schools are cautious. Any overemphasis on Tibetan culture may bring accusations of 'split-ism' or a desire for independence, according to Upton (1996, p. 118), and this makes educators wary about close contacts with monasteries.

The relative shortage of well trained teachers in Tibet is a legacy of past times and is partly responsible for the policy of exporting students to other provinces. The proportion of *minban* teachers is very high in primary schools (31.33 per cent), the highest in China, but at the junior and senior middle schools there are none. The availability of vocational high schools is low and the pupil teacher ratio at these was 85 to 1 in 1998 (Department of Development and Planning 1999, p. 79). Fewer good students are going into teaching and as in the rest of China the teaching profession is experiencing losses as some people opt to leave and go into business.

The decentralisation of education has been particularly damaging for education in Tibet. The withdrawal of funds means that many schools have become more heavily reliant on fees and contributions from local business people. Families often require children for farming and herding let alone having the money to pay fees. Upton's fieldwork shows (1996, p. 114) that as a result schools 'are increasingly becoming dependent on local businessmen not only for extra equipment and expenses, but also for their survival'. Given that they are contributing to schools these new businessmen are also wanting to have more say in the direction of education. Their mobility through other Tibetan areas and the rest of China means that they not only understand the diversity of Tibetan culture but they 'are also poised to introduce new concepts and new ideas from other areas into the modernization of that culture' (Upton 1996, p. 116). The negotiations between educators/intellectuals and businessmen is about the future course of Tibetan culture and the relative importance of tradition and modernity. Who will be the major spokespersons, the educators or the businessmen, is not yet clear.

PATTERNS OF MIGRATION IN THE 1980s AND 1990s

Movement in and out of Tibet

In the 1960s and 1970s net migration was into Tibet and much of the migration was of Han Chinese moving to fill government positions in Lhasa (Ma 1997). On the whole these people stayed for three to eight years and then returned to other parts of China. From 1971 to 1975, organisations and factories in Tibet recruited a large number of Han workers from the rest of China, many of whom were relatives or children of people already working and residing there. After 1976, many Han students who graduated from inland universities, demobilised soldiers, and school graduates also came to Tibet voluntarily. The number of Han increased to 112 600 in 1978 (Dojiecaidan and Jaïngchunluobu 1995, p. 587). From 1964 to 1978, it is estimated that there were 5600 in-migrants per year but only a few out-migrants, mainly young people going to universities in other provinces.

Table 6.5 shows that in 1981, there was a marked change and a significant net loss of 30 567 occurred. By 1980, when the number of Tibetan officials had increased, the central government implemented a new policy of 'mainly Tibetans will manage Tibet'. As a consequence, large

Table 6.5 Migration in and out of Tibet, 1981 to 1992

Year	In-migration	Out-migration	Net-migration
1981	2 252	32 819	-30 567
1982	1 800	20 900	-19 100
1983	6 356	7 706	-1 350
1984	4 958	12 357	7 399
1985	5 194	7 021	-1 827
1986	4 156	7 821	-3 665
1987	11 436	6 166	5 270
1988	7 916	7 795	121
1989	6 760	12 064	-5 304
1990	4 860	13 425	-8 565
1991	3 818	6 101	-2 283
1992	4 702	7 684	-2 082

Source: Dojiecaidan and Jiangchunluobu (1995, p. 588).

numbers of Han officials started returning to their original provinces under the government's arrangements. Thus, from 1981 to 1985, 80 803 persons moved out of Tibet to other provinces whereas in the same period there were only 20 560 in-migrants. Some Tibetans, mostly peasants, workers, businessmen, lamas and teachers, returned from living abroad (mainly India and Nepal) but they were small in numbers. The changes in government economic policy led to increased contact between Tibet and other provinces but it is estimated that only small numbers came from other provinces to do business, set up factories and to work on construction projects. Out-migration, mostly of Han Chinese, continued throughout the 1980s as shown in the 1990 census data (Figure 6.4) and it far outweighed in-migration. Minority out-migration to Shangai was the largest stream. Only 1984, 1987 and 1988 manifested net gains to Tibet.

It is estimated that there were 130 000 temporary migrants in Tibet in 1992 and 20 000 of these had come from other provinces (Yu 1999, p. 208). Deng Xiaoping's trip to the south of China in 1992 had significant consequences not only for the southern provinces but for all provinces. He directed the southern provinces to develop more quickly. As a consequence, coastal areas made changes in their industrial structure and in doing this some factories that needed more labourers were transferred to inland provinces.

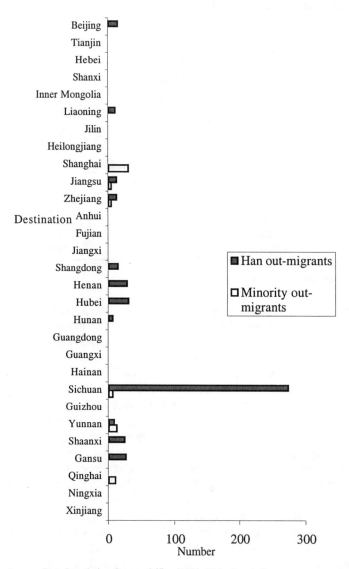

Source: State Population Census Office (1993, Vols. 1 and 4).

Figure 6.4 Minority and Han out-migration from Tibet, 1985-90

At first, the changes taking place in the east and inland provinces had no influence on Tibet because of its distance but gradually, with jobs in the big cities becoming more difficult to find, floating migrants began looking for new opportunities. Tibet became a new destination for some of these migrants, just as had occurred in Xinjiang in the 1980s. It is estimated that there were about 10 000 people a day moving in and out of Tibet in 1997 (Wang 1998c). These in-migrants were mostly Han Chinese though minorities comprised 25 per cent. Lhasa has dominated Tibet as the destination for migrants: 40-60 per cent of migrants come to Lhasa each year while smaller numbers go to other cities, such as Shigatse and Lizhi.

The movement of ethnic Tibetans is small by comparison. Figure 6.5 shows that the census captured 6000 Tibetans who moved out of Tibet from 1985 to 1990 and 10 800 who migrated out of Sichuan. The destinations are shown in Figure 6.6 but Tibet is missing as there are no data available. The major destination in the figure was Qinghai (12 200) which is part of the Tibetan plateau area and is very similar to Tibet in landscape and culture. Shanghai, on the opposite side of the country, was next and received 3000 Tibetans while only 300 Tibetans went to Beijing between 1985 and 1990. Tibetan out-migrants to the east generally have a higher level education. For example, of those migrating to Beijing, 74.4 per cent had at least 15 years of education and 24.5 per cent had middle school education (9-12 years). Among them, 8.9 per cent were students, 7.8 per cent were professionals, 58.9 per cent were working in official units and 23.5 per cent were engaged in other businesses and jobs. More than half, 52.6 per cent, had Beijing *hukou*, that is, have become Beijing citizens, 34.7 per cent had been settled in Beijing for more than 10 years and only 31.4 per cent had been in Beijing for 1-3 years.

The Tibetan population living outside of Tibet and the four provinces in Table 6.1, the traditional area of Tibet, increased by 63.06 per cent, from 11 100 to 18 100, between 1982 and 1990. The regions with high growth rates were Guizhou, Shandong, Hebei, Anhui, Shanghai, Hunan, Fujian, Heilongjiang, Ningxia, Jilin, Hubei, Liaoning, Jiangxi, Zhejiang and Tianjin. The provinces with low growth rates were Xinjiang, Shaanxi and Guangxi. This demonstrates some spreading out of Tibetans. According to Zhang (1997, p. 13), the rapid growth in the Tibetan population outside of the five major areas of Tibet and the Tibet-Qinghai Plateau is 'attributable to an increasing number of Tibetan students being sent to study in junior and senior middle schools and special classes attached to schools run by [and located in] these provinces'.

From the 1950s, schools, colleges and universities in Beijing and Shaanxi trained Tibetan students in Tibet. After 1984, however, the central government encouraged 16 provinces and cities, including Beijing, Lanzhou

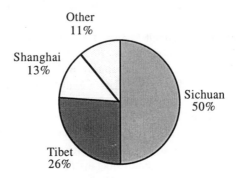

Source: State Population Census Office (1993, Vols. 1 and 4).

Figure 6.5 Source of Tibetans, 1985-1990

Source: State Population Census Office (1993, Vols. 1 and 4).

Figure 6.6 Destination of Tibetans, 1985-1990 (excluding Tibet)

in Gansu Province, Tianjin, Shanghai, Anhui, Liaoning, Sichuan and Yunnan to open up special classes for Tibetan students or establish Tibetan schools (Beijing, Tianjin and Chengdu) to admit Tibetan primary school graduates. The main reason given for this change of policy was that many

Han Chinese could not tolerate either the problems associated with living at a high altitude or the cultural differences that they faced in Tibet. Therefore, provinces had difficulty recruiting people to go to Tibet. Another reason was that the cost of building a high quality school in Tibet was much higher than in other parts of China.

There are now 10 000 Tibetan students in primary and secondary schools outside of Tibetan areas, as well as Tibetan students in colleges and universities elsewhere (Zhang 1997, p. 103). Most of them will return to Tibetan areas after graduation from university or vocational school. Therefore, much of the current out-migration of Tibetans from traditional areas of living is largely education driven and is expected to be temporary. According to Zhang (1997, pp. 13-4), this phenomenon will 'contribute to a transition of the Tibetan population from a closed society to an open society and will help improve the educational quality of the Tibetan population and promote the socioeconomic development of the areas inhabited by the Tibetans'. This is clearly the central government's aim.

The following section is based on two main data sources. The Sample Survey of Ethnic Minority Migration in 1997 has been supplemented by findings from a larger survey conducted by the research team for the University of Michigan in 1996. The latter survey encompassed 136 000 temporary migrants, 3685 (25.26 per cent) of whom were minority migrants, who were found in Lhasa. Of the total migrants, 14.78 per cent were Tibetans followed by Hui (mainly from Gansu, Qinghai and Ningxia). Other minorities included Sala, Baoan, Dongxiang, Uyghur, Bai, Dai, Tujia and Menba (Wang 1998c, p. 3).

CONTEMPORARY MINORITY MIGRATION TO AND WITHIN TIBET

A survey of 299 households in Lhasa was undertaken for the present study in 1997 by a team of Tibetan interviewers led by Professor Zhang Tianlu. The questionnaire used in Tibet was reduced to one page as the perception of the interviewers, which had been gained from prior experience by the interviewing team, was that interviewees would be unwilling to provide more than basic information. As a result the analysis for Tibet is much less detailed than for Inner Mongolia, Xinjiang and Beijing. Nevertheless, given the absence of previous work of this kind it was felt that it was valuable to proceed with analyses of these data. The sample consisted of 162 minority migrants (54.2 per cent) and 137 Han Chinese migrants (45.8 per cent). The minority sample consisted mostly of Tibetans but there were 27 people belonging to other minorities.

Socio-demographic characteristics of the sample

The minority group in the sample was fairly evenly distributed by sex whereas the Han Chinese sample was more heavily male. Other data show that 62.5 per cent of all in-migrants to Lhasa were male and the sex ratio among migrants was 166.8 compared with 106.3 among total Lhasa citizens (Cheng 1999, p. 6). More Han Chinese men than women go to Tibet as most go for building and business, which are regarded as male jobs. Generally they do not intend to remain permanently so they leave the women and children behind.

The minority sample consisted of a very high percentage of young people (80.2 per cent less than 30) whereas the Han Chinese sample had 49.6 per cent less than 30 and more people in the 30 to 50 age range. The University of Michigan survey found that people aged 20-34 comprised 70.2 per cent of all migrants, with the 20-24 age group being the peak followed by the 15-19 age group. There are three main reasons for this profile. First, most people cannot cope with the altitude of Tibet but young people have the least difficulty. Second, there is no railway in Tibet and the long journey by car or bus is better suited to young people. Third, the industrial and service sectors are growing most rapidly and they need young migrants with better education and skills.

There was a higher percentage of unmarried people amongst the minority migrants than among the Han Chinese. The minority group was made up of two thirds who had never married whereas two thirds of the Han Chinese in the sample were married. This is largely because of the age difference between the two groups and indicates an older, more stable Han Chinese population that has had time to accumulate money and skills before moving to Lhasa.

The educational profile of the two migrant groups shows that 42.6 per cent of minorities had only primary schooling while 43.8 per cent had no schooling and were illiterate or quasi-illiterate. On the other hand, the Han Chinese were better off in terms of human capital resources though they still predominantly had only junior middle school (51.8 per cent) or primary school (27.0 per cent) education. Only 5.1 per cent of the Han Chinese sample were illiterate. The difference is predominantly due to the better level of educational service provision outside of Tibet. In China as a whole, 80 per cent of children complete primary school and junior middle school and even in relatively less developed areas most children receive primary school education. As we have seen the education level in Tibet is lower than in other provinces and almost 69.4 per cent of Tibetans aged above 15 are illiterate (Zhang *et al.* 1998, p. 278). The relatively higher education levels of both Han and minority migrants, compared with people in Tibet generally, means that migrants bring new skills and knowledge to Tibet as well as being in a good position to take the better jobs.

Migration process of the sample

Four fifths of minority migrants in the Sample Survey had moved to Lhasa from other parts of Tibet and one fifth had come from outside Tibet. Most came from nearby areas, especially from adjacent counties, such as Linzhou, Dweilongdeqing, Qushui, Nimudazi, and Muozugongca. Other sources were Shigatse and Shannan, both of which are linked to Lhasa by convenient traffic roads (Wang 1998c, p. 2). Lhasa citizens are mostly Tibetan and Lhasa is the biggest city and religious centre for Tibetans. It holds a great attraction for all Tibetans but only those living in nearby areas are able to come easily. All Han Chinese migrants in both surveys were from outside of Tibet. One third originated in Sichuan and the remainder came from a wide range of provinces with the most important being Zhejiang, Qinghai, Hubei, Hunan and Fujian. Most had relatives or friends in Tibet before they came, indicating the importance of chain migration (Wang 1998c).

Plate 6.4 Entrance to the Potala, Lhasa (Photo by R. Iredale)

There is a fair degree of stability among the migrants: almost three-quarters of the minority sample had been in Lhasa for more than three years compared with 51.1 per cent of the Han Chinese sample. It appears that most minority migrants coming from other parts of Tibet want to stay permanently. Most

Han migrants stay for a period of perhaps five or six years and then go back taking with them the money that they have accumulated. The cost and

Plate 6.5 The Jokhang Market, Lhasa (Photo by R. Iredale)

difficulty of getting to Tibet is a factor in the length of stay. In terms of housing, 61.1 per cent of minority migrants lived in rented accommodation compared with 96.4 per cent of Han Chinese. A few minority people owned a house while others shared with other minority people.

Previous research has shown that many factors influence migration and an important one among them is the availability of networks that can provide assistance and information. The Sample Survey showed that 99.3 per cent of minority migrants and 89.6 per cent of Han migrants had received some help in their move. Types of assistance for moving for minorities ranged from the provision of accommodation, food and money to the supply of information. According to Sun (1996, p. 6), Tibetans are very hospitable and have the tradition of helping each other. Zhang (Tibetan language) is the common language of the whole of Tibet so settling down in Lhasa is easy for Tibetans. For Han Chinese, 90 per cent received information that was of assistance in helping them to migrate but very few received concrete help by way of housing, food or money. Han in-migrants tended to settle in the same streets and similar jobs as earlier Han in-migrants from the same province or village. For example, Han from Sichuan tended to congregate near building sites or vegetable farms while sites near hotels, such as the Gaoyuan Hotel (Plateau Hotel), the Linxia Hotel (Near Ningxia Province Hotel) and the

Jiaotong Hotel (Traffic Office Hotel), had become residential locations for migrants from Gansu, Qinghai, and Ningxia provinces. The latter were mostly engaged in transporting (Wang 1998c, p. 2). They helped each other in many ways, including borrowing household items and sending things back to their hometown area.

Employment and income of the sample

Before migration the occupational profile of the two groups was reasonably similar though there was a higher percentage of agricultural/herding workers (79.0 per cent) among minorities than among Han (64.2 per cent). Many farmers/herders/fishers in parts of China suffer from lack of land and very low incomes and they see outlying areas such as Tibet as having both land and a small population. These frontier areas, with opportunities for farming and other activities, have always attracted migrants from more heavily populated areas and the government now has policies for encouraging people to move to these areas, rather than the resettlement schemes of earlier periods. Of the Han Chinese migrants, almost three-quarters (73.7 per cent) migrated to Tibet for commercial reasons while only 37 per cent of minority migrants came for this reason. On the other hand, almost a quarter of minorities (23.5 per cent) came to work in restaurants and 17.3 per cent came to work as domestics or family nurses.

> The state has the development of a commodity economy as a priority, and since late 1992 has offered financial incentives for entrepreneurs, with tax relief, to set up secondary industry through classifying central Tibet as one of the 70 or 80 special economic zones in China. In 1992 there was again a policy debate within China on the western regions, between those who advocate training of local people as the key stage in economic development, and those who see the first step as bringing in outsiders from more developed areas to promote rapid economic change. If Tibetans cannot or will not take up this role, then Han and other peoples will be encouraged to move into the region.

> Local people may well maintain their dominance in local border trade, but Han may well acquire a more dominant position in service industries which will be more dependent on exchanges with lowland China. (Clarke 1994, p. 248)

Lhasa is clearly providing job and business opportunities for temporary migrants but there is a clear differentiation between the employment and industry profiles of minorities and Han Chinese. This pattern of segmentation is more extreme than in other parts of China and is largely a response to the lack of business experience and interest amongst Tibetans as compared with Han Chinese who have explicitly come for this purpose. After migration, 75 per cent of the Han Chinese in the sample were in business. They appeared to use their contacts in other parts of China to establish commercial enterprises in Tibet. Thus Han migration to Tibet is now a strategy for earning money for use in other regions. Such people are unlikely to be committed to the region and antagonism may be directed towards them by Tibetans. Others had brought their vegetable growing skills to this harsh environment and were making a better living than before. Altitude sickness is a common problem among Han Chinese in Tibet and only the hardy are able to remain. Of the 162 minority people in the Sample Survey, 37 per cent were occupied in business after they moved to Lhasa. This group tended to be young (between 20 and 39) and with low levels of education. Many of them had begun businesses that traded in Tibetan culture — selling Tibetan artefacts and medicines to tourists, and as tourist guides. Tibetans living in Lhasa also provided employment to other members of their own ethnic group and 25.9 per cent of minority migrants worked in the service sector in restaurants etc and 16.7 per cent worked as family nurses. The balance worked in agriculture and labouring.

Family nurses tended to be young (under 29) unmarried females who migrated alone to Lhasa, leaving their families behind in farming areas. Many Tibetan families in Lhasa hire family nurses to care for babies and the elderly and it is important that they are of the same ethnicity and speak Tibetan. Family nurses had low levels of education — 64.3 per cent were illiterate and only 32.15 per cent had attended primary school. For them, Lhasa not only provided new experiences but for 96 per cent monthly earnings rose from less than 50 yuan in their hometown to 150 yuan. Although these earnings seem low compared with other migrants, nurses live in the employer's house and therefore have no living expenses. In addition, they may receive presents or gifts, such as clothing or personal items, from their employer. Their earnings are clear pocket money. This avenue of employment provides an important opening for many young rural women in China's cities, including Lhasa. The young women build up a strong network to support each other and help locate employment for new arrivals. Some use the family nurse job as a springboard and after some years of nursing and gaining local knowledge, they find other jobs or get married. Most of them do not wish to go back to the rural areas.

Social/personal aspects of migration

Movement to Lhasa resulted in a considerable improvement in income for many in the minority sample. Nobody was worse off as a result of the move. All minority migrants earned below the Lhasa average before migration and about third earned more than this after moving. Before migration, 57.1 per cent earned less than 50 yuan per month but after moving to Lhasa their incomes were considerably higher plus many were provided with food and accommodation. A small proportion of minorities was still farming/herding or working as labourers, after moving to Lhasa. Therefore, for minorities there was some improvement in income levels as a result of the move but for many the move seemed to be strongly associated with the desire for a better life style and wider opportunities.

The figures show that, on average, minority incomes were lower than Han Chinese incomes both before and after moving. For Han Chinese, 65 per cent earned more than the average for Lhasa after moving. The improved economic circumstances of most people who have moved to Lhasa is probably the reason why they are relatively settled and do not keep moving from one place to another. Given the distance from elsewhere, Han who move to Lhasa are committed to staying a reasonable time to accumulate the amount of money they need before they return home. In this case, Tibet provides a place for migrants to make money fairly quickly, as there are plenty of opportunities for business and service activities. The proportion of people engaged in businesses in Lhasa is 0.83 per cent which is well below the national average of 3.01 per cent while the proportion engaged in service provision is also well below the average at a low 0.70 per cent (Zhang 1997, p. 90).

Migration and education

It is clear from the above discussion that Tibetans have been disadvantaged in the past by their lack of education and there is still room for a great deal of improvement. Level of education is often a significant factor in migration selectivity but within Tibet there is little evidence of this being the case. Many young Tibetans appear to be moving to Lhasa in spite of their low level of education, to find jobs in the service sector. Those who have slightly higher levels of education and even those who have a university degree find opportunities in the tourist industry where they can earn higher incomes.

The major correlation between education and migration is occurring in the sending out of young people to other provinces for education. In 1997, the government of TAR assigned 7000 Tibetan pupils to 108 classes in other-province schools. After finishing school these students either go on to universities or jobs in various parts of China or come back home. It is anticipated that the departure of these people and their subsequent return will bring new ideas and skills to Tibet. This is urgently needed as only 29.7 per cent of professionals have senior middle school education and as many as 38.93 per cent have only primary education. By comparison, 71.2 per cent of professionals have senior middle school education in China as a whole (Sun 1994, p. 97). The departure of skilled Tibetans, as we saw with skilled

Mongolians, is an issue. Once people have a university degree or other skills they often look for better opportunities elsewhere. The general shortage of skilled personnel was met in the past by sending Han Chinese and others to Tibet from elsewhere to fill positions as officials, professionals and teachers. This policy failed in many instances as most people could not adapt to the altitude and the cultural landscape, despite the favourable conditions and high salary they were offered. Some people are still sent but it is now on a rotating method and people only stay for short periods. Local organisations in Tibet also use this method and, for example, Tibet University invites professors from elsewhere to work in Tibet for a one year period (Yu 1999, p. 250).

Relationship of the migrant population to the local community

Most Han migrants to Tibet from outside are temporary. They come from all over China and bring their own customs as well as their business practices and acumen. They also bring capital for establishing factories and other enterprises. In this way, temporary migration is leading to increased economic activity. There are also official projects and since 1994 there have been 62 such projects supported by other provinces or the central government, including public facilities and infrastructures projects and cultural and medical facilities. These projects all require labourers and materials that in turn stimulate more employment and migration. Most Han migrants do not settle permanently in Tibet and while they interact with the local community they do not become part of it. On their return home they take knowledge and information about Tibet which in time leads to further migration.

Minority migrants to Lhasa are likely to stay and integrate into the wider community without a great deal of difficulty. There are plenty of opportunities open to them and it does not appear that they are marginalised to the extent that migrants without *hukou* are marginalised in other cities.

Tourism is the other important influence on the development of Tibet's culture and economy. Tourism brought 20 225 foreign visitors in 1992 (Dojiecaidan and Jiangchunluobu 1995, p. 589) and the numbers have increased since then. Tourism is opening the society up to many new ideas and businesses are growing up to service the needs of the tourist industry. This is a particularly important factor in terms of bringing about changes to traditional attitudes and practices. These developments have changed the landscape of Lhasa. Before 1980, most of the necessities for daily living were brought from other provinces but now cities are all encouraging people to do business.

CONCLUSION

A number of migration streams likely to have an impact on the identity of Tibetans have been described here. The increased movement of Han Chinese into Tibet to set up businesses and for construction and other jobs is the most significant in terms of numbers. Most of these people are coming for a specific period and with the aim of making money. This is being 'encouraged' or at least permitted by the Chinese authorities just as it is in much of China. In Tibet it has the express purpose of speeding up the process of economic reform. The nature of this stream is such that local Tibetans are likely to feel ambivalent towards the incomers.

The movement into Lhasa of largely young single minority people, many of whom take up employment in businesses and restaurants, means a move away from the traditional life styles and cultures of their agricultural or herding background. As they engage in the money economy that is emerging and the growing tourist industry, often using their 'Tibetan-ness' as a factor, they are undergoing various changes. The Tibetan business community is raising its status and increasing its influence. As a consequence, tension has emerged between them and educators, who are highly respected and who up till now have been the major 'representatives of the future of a modern Tibetan society' (Upton 1996, p. 113-14). This and other tensions described by Upton are bound to become important in the future as Tibet opens up more to the global economy, especially the tourist industry.

Economic development has increased and a growing number of Han have been allowed to migrate into Tibet. Grunfeld (1996, p. 243) contends that the Chinese have abandoned 'serious efforts to Tibetanize the TAR' and have de-emphasised 'linguistic, cultural, and religious tolerance'. However, the negotiation of Tibetan identity is continuing and it is occurring in close juxtaposition with the education system. Tibetan culture is not uniform and unchanging, however, and the many pressures on Tibet (tourism, economic change, migration, etc) are leading to a significant reframing of Tibetan identity. As Upton states, in 'the polemic discussions of Tibetan experience in the twentieth century, the main actors are typically seen as the "Chinese Government" and the "Tibetan people" and the absence of the role of Tibetan cadres is very noticeable'. She maintains (1996, p. 121) that Tibetans (cadres, educators and businesspeople) are playing a crucial role in the continual transformation of their culture within China. Discussions about Tibetan identity among these people have for the last ten years or so involved the emergence of a discourse of cultural critique.

> Within Tibetan intellectual circles, discussions of Tibetan culture and tradition as a hindrance to development are circulating and that criticism takes many forms (see Thul bstan 1993; Basang 1991). (Upton 1996, p. 120)

Through education, Tibetan language and literacy will be maintained and improved and in this way Tibetan culture will also be altered. But economic pressures on families in Tibet mean that education is not an option for all children. Teaching is also becoming a less attractive option and teachers are leaving the profession for business activities. Tension within the educational profession will continue to grow as will debates about Tibetan-language based education versus Han Chinese-based education.

The stream of Tibetan students going out of Tibet to study in other parts of China may be even more significant in its impact. Many Tibetan parents see this as an ideal way for their children to gain a better education so that they can acquire a secure job, such as one in the government. In this respect they are no different to the majority of parents who are prepared to sacrifice close contact with their children for the sake of their children's future. Sending students elsewhere to study has been used as a policy tool in other countries — often as a way of minimising the impact of the source region. Australian Aboriginal history, as well as the history of schooling of American Indians in the United States and Canada, all contain this policy. In these instances the policy often led to a major identity shift for students but they did not give up their ethnic identity. The impact of the policies on the families and communities in the regions of origin depended on the amount of contact maintained and whether they eventually returned home.

7.   Xinjiang and Uyghur movement[*]

BACKGROUND

Xinjiang was established as a province of China in 1902 and designated the Xinjiang Uyghur Autonomous Region in October 1950. By 1990 the province had been sub-divided into self governing areas, districts, cities, counties and smaller administration areas, in effect mirroring the structure to be found in most other provinces. It is notable for its officially designated nationality areas such as the 42 nationality villages. Autonomous status theoretically gives the designated area authority over certain aspects of its governance as discussed earlier.

In terms of its physical geography, Xinjiang is normally associated with desert but it is crossed by three mountain ranges and two basins. Towns and cities mark the site of oases punctuating the Silk Road that ran from Xian, central China, through Xinjiang to the west. Xinjiang contains valuable mineral and oil deposits and is important in terms of heavy industrial production (Leiberthal 1995). The central government has invested heavily in modern infrastructure and one significant example of this has been the construction of a highway through central Xinjiang. The highway crosses the Talimakan desert and provides access to oil rich areas.

Population of Xinjiang

Xinjiang itself is one of the largest provinces in China in terms of total area but one of the smallest in terms of population. It is notable for being one of only two regions in which the non-Han population out-numbers the Han. The 1990 Census enumerated a total of 15 156 883 people in Xinjiang, 5 695 409 or 36.6 per cent of whom were Han Chinese and 47.5 per cent of whom were Uyghur. Other significant minorities in demographic terms were the Kazaks and Hui. Ethnically, the region is very diverse with 48 of China's 55 recognised minority populations present. These populations range in size from nationalities such as the Naxi and Shui with only one representative to

---

[*] This chapter has had significant input from Caroline Hoy.

the large nationalities identified in Table 7.1. Table 7.1 shows the patterns of population growth in Xinjiang since 1949.

Table 7.1 Composition of Xinjiang's population, 1949-1990

Ethnic group	1949	1964	1982	1986	1990
Uyghurs (no.)	3 291 145	3 991 577	5 955 947	6 431 015	7 194 675
Uyghurs (%)	76.0	54.9	45.5	46.5	47.5
Han (no.)	291 021	2 321 216	5 286 532	5 386 312	5 695 626
Han (%)	6.7	31.9	40.4	38.9	37.6
Kazaks (no.)	443 655	489 261	903 335	1 010 543	1 106 989
Kazaks (%)	10.2	6.7	6.9	7.3	7.3
Hui (no.)	122 501	264 017	570 789	611 816	681 527
Hui (%)	2.8	3.6	4.4	4.4	4.5
Others (no.)	185 078	203 996	365 030	396 713	476 961
Others (%)	4.3	2.8	2.8	2.9	3.2
Total (no.)	4 333 400	7 270 067	13 081 633	13 836 399	15 155 778

Source: Mackerras (1994, p. 253).

The most significant demographic change since the founding of the PRC has been the increase in the Han population. In 1949 only 6.7 per cent of the province's population was Han Chinese but by 1990 this figure had reached 37.6 per cent. In-migration of Han, rather than natural increase, has largely been responsible for this growth. In the main, this has been government sponsored and aimed at increasing border strength (Lary 1999). The migration of Han from other parts of China to Xinjiang has been the subject of criticisms relating to the motivation for this migration and its consequent socio-economic impact on the minorities in terms of integration and exclusion, provincial governance and the distribution of facilities and opportunities.

State sponsored migration to Xinjiang has been taking place at least since the reign of the Qianlong Emperor (1736-95). Historically, such migration was deemed a punishment and this system of banishment has been reinterpreted in the People's Republic of China. Lary (1999) quotes the example of over 100 000 individuals sent to Xinjiang with the dual purpose of punishment for their crimes and the development of the province. To these must be added those banished for political 'crimes'.

Number and distribution of Uyghurs

The Uyghurs are the second largest Muslim nationality in China, after the Hui. Table 2.5 in Chapter 2 shows that according to the 1990 census there were 7 214 431 Uyghurs in China, of whom 98.6 per cent were registered as based in Xinjiang province. The Uyghurs are a Turkic-speaking people, remote descendants of nomads whose kingdom extended over modern northwest China some 1200 years ago. The population converted to Islam and adapted the Arabic script for its own written language. In 1958, this script was replaced by a 'new' script (based on a modified Latin alphabet) as part of China's language reform program. But the 'new' script was seen as a Han imposition and in 1978 the 'old' script reappeared and was then authorised for use in 1980 for the Uyghur and Kazak languages (Dillon 1995, p. 5).

The widespread use of the term Uyghur, however, is a modern convention that dates to the 1930s. Gladney (1990) argues that prior to this the people now called the Uyghur were not a discrete population. Uyghurs identified with an oasis rather than with a Uyghur nation (Dillon 1995, p. 4). In fact, the population is more diverse than the name suggests. In effect, the Uyghur nationality, along with some other nationalities (for example, Hui, Yi), are an artificial construct of the state as seen in Chapter 3 (Gladney 1990, Hoy 1996).

Minorities in Xinjiang are not evenly distributed across the province. Distinct population concentrations can be identified and these are reflected in area and district names such as the Yanqi Hui Autonomous County, based in Bayingguoleng prefecture. Significantly, nearly two thirds of the non-Han population is found in the southern half of the province, away from the more developed regions of the north. Some 82 per cent of this southern-based population is Uyghur. Of the five prefectures that make up southern Xinjiang, in all but one, Bayingguoleng, over 90 per cent of the population are members of the Uyghur nationality (Yuan 1990, Hoy 1996). Half the Hui population are located in two prefectures in the north of the province: Changqi and Yili (Yuan 1990).

Rural and urban residence statistics provide further indication of the differing distribution of the population by nationality. Urban and rural residence is shown in Table 7.2 for four nationalities. The Han are the most urbanised population with 3 328 626 (58.4 per cent) of the Han population living in cities or towns. This residential pattern is a reflection of the organisation of past in-migration schemes that directed Han in-migrants to urban centres or gave migrants urban residency permits (Hoy 1996). Han also came to work in concentrated irrigated agricultural projects. In Xinjiang, 32.0 per cent came to work in concentrated irrigated farming projects. The next most urbanised are the Hui and 32.0 per cent of the Hui live in urban areas.

The Hui have adopted a wide variety of economic niches throughout the history of China and are amongst the most urbanised of the minority groups (Gladney 1998, p. 37). By contrast, the Uyghur are very rural with 84.5 per cent living in the counties of Xinjiang and a mere 8.5 per cent living in cities and 7.0 per cent living in towns. The Kazaks display a distribution pattern very similar to that of the Uyghurs. The effect, in Xinjiang, is to separate different nationalities, by geographical location (urban or rural), and therefore by opportunities for economic and social interaction and access to facilities and infrastructure, such as schools and hospitals (Hoy 1996).

Table 7.2 Urban and rural residence of selected minorities, Xinjiang, 1990 census

Nationality	City	Town	Counties	Total Population
Uyghur	608 996	501 925	6 080 924	7 194 675
Hui	167 467	50 722	464 723	681 527
Kazak	73 962	80 475	951 834	1 106 989
Han	2 768 749	559 877	2 366 783	5 695 626

Source: State Population Census Office (1993, Volume 1, pp. 320-66).

Socio-economic profile

Uyghurs were traditionally herders and traders and it is believed that they migrated around the Tarim Basin and to Western Asia. Though they were restricted in their movement after 1949 their occupational structure remained heavily centred on agricultural and herding activities up till the early 1980s. Table 7.3 shows that in 1982 Uyghurs were heavily concentrated in animal husbandry, even more so than the Kazaks, while only a small proportion were engaged in other activities such as skilled technical work and factory and production work. On the whole, their occupational structure was not very different to that of all minorities in China at that time.

Table 7.4 shows the occupational structure of Xinjiang using figures from the 1990 census. The first thing to notice is the expansion in the number of occupations, reflecting major changes that have occurred in China since the initiation of reform. For example, there is a separate category for those engaged in geological surveying and prospecting, reflecting the importance attached to the search for mineral resources in Xinjiang and elsewhere. There are also separate categories for those employed in various kinds of financial institutions and real estate, public utilities, residential and advisory services. Table 7.4 also contains reference to individuals engaged in government and party work indicating a greater degree of 'openness'.

Table 7.3 Occupational structure of Uyghurs and Kazaks, 1982 (%)

Occupation	Uyghur	Kazak	All minorities
Skilled technical	4.2	11.2	4.0
Administration	0.7	2.0	1.0
Office & related	1.0	2.0	1.0
Commercial workers	1.5	1.2	1.2
Service workers	1.5	1.5	1.2
Farming, forestry, fishing and animal husbandry	84.0	74.5	84.0
Factory, production and transport workers	7.0	7.5	7.5
Others	-	-	-
Total	100.0	100.0	100.0

Source: Gladney (1996, p. 32).

While agriculture remains the single most important occupation for Han Chinese (41 per cent) in this province, the majority of Han are not engaged in agriculture. Han Chinese are more diversely occupied compared to the Uyghur, Kazak and other minority populations. Han dominate areas such as administration and the skilled technical areas of employment. A substantial number of Han are employed in the industrial sector as well as in commerce, catering, the supply of goods and materials as well as in educational, cultural and broadcasting activities. This employment structure is perhaps to be expected at this juncture and is consistent with the domination by the Han of urban areas and minorities of rural areas.

Additionally, many Han were recorded as involved with the national government or provincial government, party and social security sectors. In fact 59 per cent of the total population of employees in this sector were Han Chinese, who are thus over-represented in demographic terms in one of the most important areas of society. Han Chinese also dominate the geological surveying and prospecting occupations where they make up 88 per cent of employees. This dominance is repeated in the real estate market where 70.4 per cent of those employed are Han, and in the hygiene and health arena where they form 66 per cent of employees. Finally, 85.2 per cent of personnel engaged in scientific research and services are Han. The picture is of a divided society in which Han dominate the skilled employment market and minorities the agricultural.

Table 7.4 Occupational structure of Xinjiang, 1990 (%)

Occupation	Uyghur	Kazak	All other minorities	Han
Farming, forestry, fishing and animal husbandry	85.31	82.57	69.83	41.00
Industry	4.39	3.21	9.47	24.20
Geological surveying and prospecting	0.04	0.03	0.22	0.70
Construction	0.61	0.22	1.57	7.15
Transport and communications	0.82	0.75	2.55	4.98
Commerce, catering, supply storage and marketing of goods	2.83	2.25	5.69	6.57
Real estate, public utilities, residential and advisory services	0.46	0.20	1.13	1.85
Hygiene, health and social welfare	0.62	1.08	1.25	2.15
Education, cultural and broadcasting activities	2.71	5.87	4.00	5.12
Scientific research and services	0.05	0.06	0.22	0.61
Finance and insurance	0.26	0.42	0.50	0.78
National, government, party and social security organisations	1.88	3.32	3.59	4.85
Other	0.01	0.00	0.01	0.03
Total	100.00	100.00	100.00	100.00

Source: State Population Census Office, Xinjiang (1992, pp. 510-17).

Plate 7.1 Outdoor eating, market place in Turpan, 1997 (Photo by R. Iredale)

THE DEVELOPMENT OF EDUCATION FACILITIES

Participation and achievement

Xinjiang enrolment figures from the 1990 census have been converted to percentages to show the spread of students, by nationality, across the five levels of education. What is clear from Table 7.5 is that at the highest level, college and university, relatively equal proportions of Han and Uyghur students were enrolled but Kazaks and other minorities had much lower proportions of their total student enrolled population at this level. This says something about the overall human resource development of the various populations. Han also had higher proportions enrolled at the technical college and technical school levels than all minority groups as well as at high and junior high school levels. Conversely, Uyghurs, Kazaks and other minorities were all over-represented at the lowest level, primary schools. This profile indicates a continuation of better education for Han compared to minorities and therefore continued disadvantage in terms of minority access to higher levels of employment.

Table 7.5 School and college enrolments in Xinjiang by nationality, 1990 (%)

Nationality	College/ uni.	Tech. college	Tech. school	High school	Junior high	Primary school	Total
Han	0.87	2.31	3.38	14.82	26.29	52.32	100.00
Uyghur	0.85	0.60	1.78	4.38	13.43	78.96	100.00
Kazak	0.73	0.90	2.54	6.34	17.05	72.43	100.00
Other minorities	0.51	0.95	1.90	6.37	16.17	74.11	100.00
Total	0.82	1.33	2.49	8.81	19.02	67.53	100.00

Source: State Population Census Office, Xinjiang (1992, Vol. 1, pp. 500-3).

The above figures do not indicate rates of participation in education but rather how those who are enrolled are distributed. Figures on participation in education for Xinjiang (but not by nationality) show that Xinjiang lags slightly behind the national average for school enrolments. In 1998 there were 2 326 765 school age children (6 to 18) in Xinjiang and 2272 701 of these were enrolled in school (Department of Development and Planning 1999, pp. 72-3). The participation rate was 97.68 per cent for Xinjiang compared to the average for China of 98.93 per cent. A slightly higher proportion of girls than boys was enrolled in schools in Xinjiang. Schools include the whole range from primary through vocational and junior high to senior high. Xinjiang has above average enrolments per 10 000 inhabitants in the region in primary, general junior and senior, and specialised secondary schools, but well below average in vocational schools (Department of Development and Planning 1999, pp. 68-89). As pointed out earlier, these figures do not take account of the age structure of the population but are the best available. The net primary enrolment rate of 97.73 per cent for Xinjiang was only slightly below the national average of 98.86 per cent in 1998, but the drop out rates for primary and junior secondary school were lower than the national average indicating higher retention rates.

At the post-school level, the enrolment rate was 57.40 per 10 000 inhabitants for Xinjiang in 1998 compared to 50.44 for China as a whole (Department of Development and Planning 1999, p. 68). There are 18 regular higher education institutions in Xinjiang, out of a total of 1020 for China. They consist of vocational, comprehensive, science and technology, agriculture, medicine and pharmacy, teachers, finance and economics and art institutions (Department of Planning and Construction 1998, pp. 116-43). Interestingly there are no nationalities or language and literature institutions in Xinjiang.

Chapter 3 showed that both Xinjiang and Inner Mongolia appeared to be doing relatively well in terms of education with average, or just above average, percentages of their population achieving a college education. On the other hand, Tibet and Yunnan's populations face a far harder struggle to achieve tertiary level education. Table 7.6 shows the percentage of Han, Uyghur, Kazak and other national minorities in Xinjiang, who had obtained a college degree.

Table 7.6 Selected nationalities with a college degree, Xinjiang, 1990 (%)

Nationality	%
Xinjiang	0.65
Han	1.00
Uyghur	0.43
Kazak	0.49
Other minorities	0.48

Source: State Population Census Office, Xinjiang (1992, Volume 1, p. 496).

A higher percentage of the Han population in Xinjiang had achieved a degree than for all other groups, and this percentage is higher than that for the country as a whole. However, it must be recognised that we are examining very small percentages and a situation such as this where one per cent of a sub-group of the provincial population lays claim to a college degree is indicative of under-financing of the education opportunity structure. Education is very important, however, as it provides access to higher level jobs and decision-making roles.

Curricula, teaching materials and staffing

As pointed out in Chapter 3, national curricula are set by the state for most courses. However, regional governments can decide on language policies. For Uyghur children, their schooling may be in Uyghur and they start learning Chinese in third grade of primary school, for two hours per week. The absence of teaching materials in minority languages, as well as the shortage of minority teachers, continues to be a major hurdle to be overcome in much of Xinjiang. Table 3.3 in Chapter 3 shows that unlike some other regions with high minority populations, Xinjiang has a low proportion of *minban* teachers. This is generally seen as good as *minban* teachers are poorly trained and poorly paid but on the other hand it may indicate a low rate of participation of minority teachers. Xinjiang compares well with China as a whole and with other minority regions on pupil-teacher ratios. Xinjiang rates badly, though, on the state of its schools with almost 5 per cent of primary schools classed as dilapidated. This indicates a low commitment by local authorities to maintenance of school buildings and the inability of many parents to pay school fees.

Several new initiatives have begun recently in Xinjiang to try to get more minority students into mainstream tertiary institutions. One is the streaming of minority students into special accelerated science classes in middle schools from 1995. For example, in Turpan, students are selected (by testing) from nationality schools to participate in science classes conducted in Han Chinese at the No. 1 Nationality School in Turpan. According to the Principal of the No. 1 Nationality School in Turpan, these children are selected as the science education in other Uyghur schools 'is not up to standard'. First year students are taught mathematics, and physics and chemistry are added in later years. The children have limited Chinese at the commencement of middle school but their Chinese improves markedly. In all, they receive three years of junior middle schooling and three years of senior middle schooling. At the end of the six years it is anticipated by the principal that both their Chinese language, as well as their science knowledge, will be sufficient to enable them to gain access to mainstream tertiary institutions.

PATTERNS OF MIGRATION IN THE 1980s AND 1990s

Migration to and from Xinjiang

Table 7.7 locates migration to and from Xinjiang in the wider context of migration in China as a whole. It summarises some of the data in Table 2.2 and allows Xinjiang's macro patterns of migration to be compared with those of other selected provinces. Overall 702 671 migrants, as defined in the census, were recorded for Xinjiang province in 1990 and of these 341 718 or 48.7 per cent originated outside of Xinjiang (inter-provincial migrants). In a ranking of provinces in terms of total mobility, as shown in Chapter 4, Xinjiang is placed eighteenth and is therefore a minor player numerically. In terms of the type and explanations for migration, however, Xinjiang is of significance and merits further attention. Additionally, it is a province whose population can be demonstrated to have increased through net migration by some 64 000 people between 1985 and 1990.

Xinjiang is unusual in terms of its migration pattern as, unlike in many other provinces, inter- and intra-province migration numbers are almost equal. Xinjiang's proportion (48.7 per cent) of inter-provincial migrants is well above the average for the whole country (32.5 per cent). Beijing and Shanghai had higher proportions but on the whole provinces, especially those on the periphery, had low rates. As seen in Table 4.2, Xinjiang has the fourth highest net migration rate after Beijing, Shanghai and Guangdong.

Table 7.7 Comparative migration to Xinjiang, 1990

Province	Total registered migrants ('000)	Inter-provincial migrants (%)	Net migration ('000)
Beijing	766	88.9	541
Shanghai	844	79.5	533
Hebei	1 333	39.1	-125
Jilin	849	27.9	-118
Jiangsu	1 981	40.0	171
Hubei	1 520	28.4	85
Guangdong	3 932	32.1	1 007
Sichuan	2 818	16.8	-846
Gansu	649	30.7	-82
Xinjiang	703	48.7	64
China	34 128	32.5	0.0

Source: Hoy (1996, p. 131).

Part of the explanation for these trends undoubtedly lies in the history of migration to Xinjiang since 1949. In the early 1950s, a 'detailed plan was made by the state to relocate a large number of, mainly young, to Xinjiang' (Ren and Yuan 1999, p. 5). In the 1950s, planned in-migrants were mostly soldiers who were later assisted to find and bring wives from the east. In the 1960s, peasants and labourers were assisted to move from Jiangsu, Hubei, Hunan and Anhui. There was often return migration by these people who found living conditions difficult, especially in the 1960s when construction projects were halted and other events led to disruption. However, 'the state quickly controlled the emigration trend by means of strong political pressure' (Ren and Yuan 1999, p. 6). In the 1980s, when income differentials widened between the east and west, a second wave of planned in-migrants began returning east, taking with them information about economic and social conditions in Xinjiang.

Planned in-migration was supplemented by a smaller stream of spontaneous in-migration in the 1950s and 1960s, but since 1978, spontaneous in-migrants have outnumbered planned in-migrants. Spontaneous in-migration expanded in the 1980s and has grown even more in the 1990s. In the five years from 1985 to 1990, the number of inter-provincial in-migrants was 345 365 and from 1990 to 1995 it was one million (Ren and Yuan 1999). It is still growing as people are strongly attracted to the *Bing Tuan* (Production and Construction Corps) areas along the second Europe–Asia railway corridor and the irrigated cotton and petroleum mining areas of Korla, Aksu and Kashi. Most spontaneous migrants have come from more developed provinces such as Jiangsu and Zhejiang and they have tended to remain in Xinjiang permanently because they migrated with 'specific goals for living and business' (Ren and Yuan 1999, p. 6).

The 1990 census shows that 95 per cent of in-migrants between 1985 and 1990 were Han, moving mostly from Sichuan, Henan, Zhejiang, Jiangsu and Gansu. Figure 7.1 provides a picture of in-migrants to Xinjiang in this period. One survey based in the Tacheng region of northern Xinjiang shows that 87 per cent of the migrant population had originated from Sichuan, Zhejiang and Jiangsu (Feng 1993). Anecdotal evidence suggests that these migrants are especially associated with the food business and vehicle repair. Solinger (1999) also notes the presence of a colony of migrants from Jiangsu. The approximately 17 000 minority in-migrants came largely from Ningxia (39.3 per cent) and Gansu (35.8 per cent), and Hui accounted for 82.1 per cent of minority in-migrants. These are both provinces with large Hui populations.

The 1990 census data show that low ratios of both Han and minority in-migrants had obtained local *hukou* in Xinjiang: 13.0 per cent of Han and 19.1 per cent of minority migrants. The education levels varied quite considerably with minority migrants having much lower levels on the whole. Whereas minority migrants were mostly formerly in agriculture related occupations (47.8 per cent) followed by labouring (26.5 per cent), Han in-migrants tended to be labourers (56.0 per cent) followed by agricultural workers (18.8 per cent). Both groups had around 14 to 15 per cent who had been commercial/shop workers/traders before migration. The goals of in-migrants were business and employment (40 per cent), visiting relatives (30 per cent) and training and marriage (20 per cent) but in fact some of the latter groups came indirectly for employment (Ren *et al.* 1998). Significant male/female differentials exist and not unexpectedly the most obvious of these is the domination of marriage migration by women. Additionally, more women than men were to be found engaged in 'associational' migration which is presumably the result of job allocations and transfers on behalf of husbands and fathers. Men dominate migration routes connected with employment or business, and education and training are probably the only reasons cited almost equally by men and women (7.3 per cent and 6.3 per cent respectively). The balance, however, is still in favour of men.

The single highest proportion of out-migrants from Xinjiang province captured in the 1990 census was to Sichuan province to the south of Xinjiang, as shown in Figure 7.2. This was a totally Han Chinese stream. Other popular destination provinces for Han were Shandong, Jiangsu, Henan and Shanghai suggesting high rates of return migration. Large numbers of Han also migrated to provinces geographically closer to Xinjiang, such as Shaanxi and Gansu. Of all those who left Xinjiang between 1985 and 1990, 7625 (mostly Han) headed for Beijing; the majority to Beijing city proper rather than the surrounding suburbs and counties. Of these out-migrants to Beijing, 55.1 per cent were from cities within Xinjiang, 18.6 per cent from towns and the remainder from the countryside (State Population Census Office, Xinjiang 1992). While few people crossed the border into Qinghai and Ningxia (2 per cent in total), an interesting exchange of migrants appears to have taken place between Xinjiang, Sichuan, Jiangsu and other eastern seaboard provinces. Figure 7.1 shows quite a different destination pattern for minorities. While Sichuan was the foremost destination for Han (35 600), followed by many coastal provinces, Shaanxi attracted the largest number of minority out-migrants (3500 or 28.46 per cent) followed by Gansu, Qinghai and Ningxia. Beijing, Tianjin, Shandong and Henan were destinations for relatively smaller numbers of minority out-migrants from Xinjiang.

Uyghur inter-provincial migration that was captured in the 1990 census is shown in Figures 7.3 and 7.4. In total, the 1990 census recorded that 7300 Uyghurs moved inter-provincially between 1985 and 1990. On the basis of these data, Uyghurs were ninth in terms of level of mobility of minority groups. It must be reiterated that these data are from the one per cent

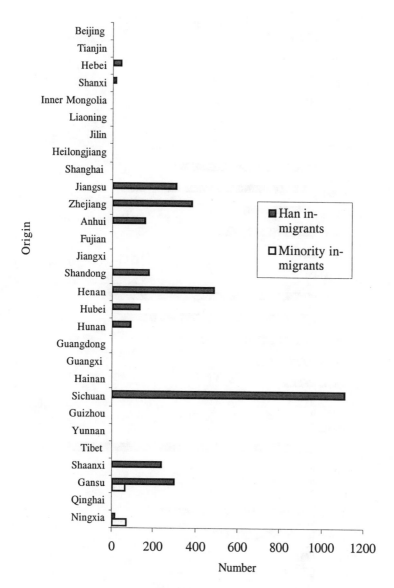

Source: State Population Census Office (1993, Vols. 1 and 4).

Figure 7.1 Minority and Han movement to Xinjiang, 1985-90

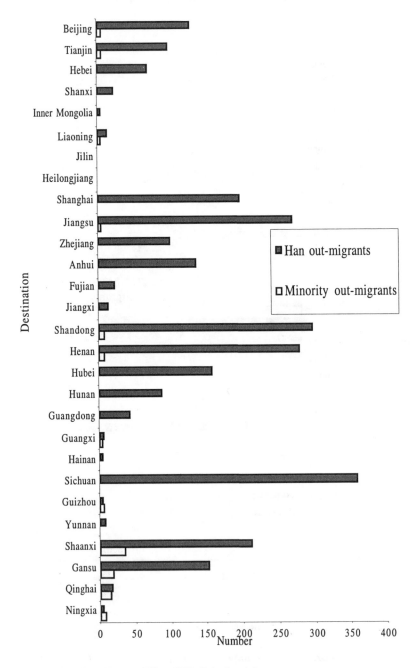

Source: State Population Census Office (1993, Vols. 1 and 4).

Figure 7.2 Minority and Han movement from Xinjiang, 1985-90

sample data analysis and the numbers may not be totally reliable or represent the real picture. Nevertheless, they do show movement trends. The major origin of Uyghurs (4600) was Xinjiang, as would be expected. Beijing was the second major source (2500) indicating a high level of re-migration of Uyghurs who had moved to Beijing at some earlier stage.

The major destination for Uyghurs (5500) was Shaanxi which accounted for 5500 or 75.3 per cent of Uyghur arrivals. Shaanxi is one of the most developed provinces in China's northwest region and may function as a regional social and cultural centre for migrants from surrounding regions. It is mid-way between Xinjiang and the coast and therefore the distance of travel is not too great. Shaanxi's population of around 33 million puts it in the low to middle range in terms of population size and minorities only comprise 4.5 per cent of its population. Its 'receptiveness' to in-migrants may be a significant factor in the number of Uyghurs who moved there or other factors may be at work. Smaller numbers of Uyghurs went to Liaoning, Henan and Shandong. The latter two have very low minority proportions in their populations, as was shown in Table 2.4. Beijing gained only 100 Uyghur migrants as defined in the 1990 census between 1985 and 1990. This figure shows the narrowness of the census definition and reflects more the lack of granting of *hukou* to unofficial migrants, particularly Uyghurs.

Overall, these data indicate a spreading out from traditional areas into new areas with low minority populations. The reasons for this trend are apparently very diverse. The reasons for migrating to Beijing were articulated in a 1994 survey by Hoy to include marriage, to see something of the outside world or to be with relatives, children, parents or friends. Others went to work or seek work, attracted by the economic opportunities offered by Beijing. One couple had retired in Xinjiang but realising that they still needed to pay for their children's weddings they migrated to Beijing and took over a restaurant in order to generate sufficient income to ensure the future nuptials of their children. One woman originated from a mountainous region of Xinjiang in which men were able to find full employment but there was little work for women. Another accompanied her husband to Beijing in search of her husband's children by a prior marriage. Another sought medical care, of a quality she felt was unobtainable in Xinjiang, for her son. Migration across significant geographical areas in order to get good medical care has become more common in China recently, as local access to medical services has become more problematic in the reform area.

Hoy's 1997 survey revealed a different side to migration explanations. The desire to find further educational opportunities dominated the list of explanations. Despite this wish only 1.2 per cent described themselves as students. It is possible that some may have been preparing

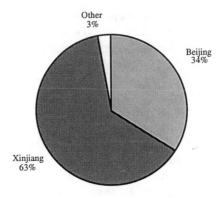

Source: State Population Census Office (1993, Volumes 1 and 4).

Figure 7.3 Origins of Uyghurs, 1985-90

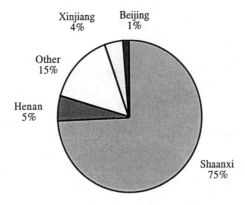

Source: State Population Census Office (1993, Volumes 1 and 4).

Figure 7.4 Destinations of Uyghurs, 1985-90

themselves, financially, for school later on through employment while it is also possible that some of them interpret education to mean training through work or apprenticeships and not formal schooling. What is clear is that while many want to undertake some form of education, most are unable to do so.

We will return to this subject later in Chapter 8 where the difficulties parents face when trying to get their children into Beijing schools will be discussed.

Movement within Xinjiang

Mobility was a common feature of Xinjiang life before liberation, especially around the Tarim Basin and with Western Asia. However, between the 1950s and 1960s, because of the establishment of people's communes, the strict control exercised over household registration and the tight economic system, people could no longer move where they wanted. Also because of the communes, people could not get access to land outside their communes. The commune structure was disbanded in 1976 and since then people have been able to move around more freely again. Tsui (1999) describes this as the first phase of migration since 1949. In the late 1970s, the rural Uyghur population began a new search for migration. Some moved to the coast and to cities such as Beijing, Shanghai, Guangdong, etc., but most moved out for a short time to earn some money when they were not busy with farming. They came back when the farming season started again. Three types of work were mainly done by temporary rural migrants in towns: construction and repair of houses and mosques, self employment in small businesses in bazaars, and gardeners in public gardens.

The second stage of migration began in 1986 when governments at different levels no longer strictly controlled migration and some even encouraged movement to towns and other cities outside of Xinjiang to overcome problems of 'overpopulation' (Tsui 1999). Some migrants set up restaurants, sold goods and worked on construction sites (mostly for a short time only before moving on to something else). Of the 360 912 intra-provincial migrants captured by the 1990 census in Xinjiang, 29 per cent originated in cities, 28 per cent in towns and 48 per in rural areas. In contrast, destinations were predominantly urban. Over half of all intra-provincial migrants moved between or to cities within Xinjiang, 23 per cent between or to towns and the remaining 23 per cent between or to rural areas. Of those from an urban area, 86 per cent moved to another urban location. Of those with a rural origin 71 per cent moved to an urban destination (Hoy 1996). Thus the lure of the urban was strong.

The overall sex ratio for these migrants was 119 (119 men to 100 women) indicating that more men than women migrated within Xinjiang between 1985 and 1990. However, the sex ratio declined progressively down the urban hierarchy. City migrants exhibited a very high sex ratio of 135, town migrants a lower ratio of 119 and rural migrants a ratio of 108. However, 69 per cent of all women moved to cities compared to 67 per cent of men. These figures imply that women were less likely to be migrants compared to men at this stage but they were slightly more likely to migrate to urban areas than men.

The third stage of migration began in 1992, according to Tsui. The magnitude of migration has become much greater and while there is some movement to cities outside of Xinjiang, there is much more intra-provincial migration to towns and cities in Xinjiang. Tsui maintains that the age structure has changed and whereas in the early and mid-1980s, many migrants were middle aged there are now more young, educated people, including college graduates, moving to cities and towns. Many are not satisfied with the lack of recreation and activities in towns and villages. There is increased diversity in the jobs that they are taking up and many have become engaged in the recreation and tourist industries, as entertainers, waiters, hostesses, etc. A survey by Tsui (1999) in Urumqi of 15 middle to large hotels found that young Uyghur women had jobs as dancers and singers, in karaoke bars, etc. Many were college graduates and had very limited training in these jobs. Tsui attributes this partly to the fact that tertiary graduates often could not find jobs that used their knowledge and skills when they returned home to their rural areas. The lack of economic development in their region of origin often means moving elsewhere to find employment but the employment they find may not necessarily be appropriate to their training.

The following section is based primarily on data from the Sample Survey of Ethnic Minority Migration and covers migration over the last two periods. The focus is patterns and issues of minority migration to and within Xinjiang and draws both on the sample survey and Tsui's anthropological in depth investigations carried out in Urumqi and other parts of Xinjiang.

CONTEMPORARY MINORITY MIGRATION TO AND WITHIN XINJIANG

The Xinjiang survey for the present study was undertaken in 1998 in Urumqi (capital of Xinjiang). The interviews were conducted by local researchers, led by Professor Tsui. In total, 318 migrant households consisting of 168 minority households and 150 Han Chinese households were interviewed and 192 non-migrant households consisting of 104 minority households and 88 Han Chinese. The non-migrant sample was included, as pointed out earlier, to enable comparative analysis. Unlike the Beijing survey, the size of the sample prohibits regression analysis as the cells are too small. The minority samples consisted of 96.4 per cent Uyghurs with very small percentages from other ethnicities. A small proportion of the minority interviewees stated that their first language was Han Chinese, and another 1.8 per cent claimed bilingualism. A small and equal proportion of each group (4 per cent) said that they had changed their nationality in the past indicating that these respondents had sufficient grounds (commonly called 'genetic'), whether Han or non-Han, to convince the authorities that they were eligible for re-classification.

Social-demographic characteristics of the sample

Both Uyghur and Han Chinese migrant groups were unevenly distributed by sex: 86.9 per cent males in the minority sample and 69.3 per cent in the Han Chinese sample. Both Han and minority migrants tended to be young with 69 per cent of the minority group and 77 per cent of the Han under age 40. The background section of this chapter demonstrated more males than females in the past amongst internal migrants in Xinjiang and 1990 census data show that the inflow to Xinjiang in 1985 to 1990 was around 60 per cent male for both Han and minority in-migrants. Therefore the sample is not a true reflection of the sex ratio.

Within the sample, there was a larger married proportion among the Han Chinese (73.2 per cent) than among the minorities (60.4 per cent) reflecting a greater tendency for family migration among the Han. The proportions of never married were about the same (24 to 27 per cent). The Uyghur sample had higher proportions of both widowed and separated/divorced. The relatively high numbers of divorced respondents aligns with findings from elsewhere which point to a more complex arrangement of relationships among Uyghurs than among Han. While divorce may be more common re-marriage is also frequent and Uyghurs are more likely to have multiple, serial relationships. The non-migrant sample was more evenly balanced in terms of sex and was spread across a wider age range. This is most noticeable for the Han Chinese non-migrant sample where 46 per cent were 40 and over compared with the Han migrant group where 22.8 per cent were 40 and over.

Migrants based in minority households tended to live in larger households than those of Han origin: 49.9 per cent of minority respondents lived in a household consisting of five or more people compared with 14 per cent of Han respondents. This pattern held true for the non-migrant households where the percentage of 'larger' households, ie. five people or more, in the minority sample rose to 62.0 per cent. The percentage of larger households also rose in the Han non-migrant population, from 14 per cent to 17 per cent. Most households, both Uyghur and Han Chinese, consisted of one or two generations of close relatives.

The minority migrant sample consisted of a larger proportion (50.3 per cent) with primary education or little/no schooling compared to the Han Chinese migrant sample (31.4 per cent). Migrants had lower levels of education, in general, than non-migrants. Among minority and Han Chinese non-migrants, 13 per cent had university level education and 22 to 28 per cent had professional school education. There is little difference in the level of work training between all four groups. Approximately half of each group had no work training while the remainder had one year or more. The exception was among the minority migrant group where 23.2 per cent said that they had more than three years work training. A fifth of the minority migrant sample were looking for work compared to smaller percentages amongst the other three groups.

Migration process of the sample

All minority migrants were born in Xinjiang and their movement had been intra-provincial or they had migrated outside of Xinjiang and back again. In contrast, only 10.2 per cent of the Han Chinese migrants were born in Xinjiang. The rest were born in Jiangsu (18.4 per cent), Sichuan (15.6 per cent), Henan (12.2 per cent), Gansu (10.2 per cent) and elsewhere. The importance of these four provinces for providing Han migrants to Xinjiang was discussed earlier. An examination of location prior to moving shows that 42.4 per cent of both migrant samples were living in villages before they moved to Urumqi. Slightly more minority migrants than Han Chinese had moved from a city to Urumqi. The balance came from small and large towns. About one third of minority migrants had household registration elsewhere, while 32.7 per cent had permanent registration and 35.8 per cent had temporary registration in Urumqi. Fewer Han Chinese migrants had permanent registration elsewhere (20 per cent) or here (20.7 per cent), and many more (59.3 per cent) had temporary registration in Urumqi. These proportions indicate that *hukou* is no longer working to tie people to the place of their household registration but that temporary *hukou* seemed to have been more readily available for Han than for minority migrants.

Around one third of each group did not seek friends or family members' attitudes to their movement. Of those who did, there is not much difference between the responses received by the two groups except that the Han Chinese received slightly more support for their move than minorities. About two thirds of the total sample had some knowledge about work opportunities prior to moving. Minorities were slightly more inclined to move without such knowledge as the availability of nationality networks probably provides some form of safety net, as information about employment opportunities was usually supplied by relatives and friends. Most migrants moved alone or with their immediate family. Han Chinese were more inclined to move with non-relatives and other, non-related individuals than minority respondents. Families are often split by migration and 96.4 per cent of minorities and 71.3 per cent of Han Chinese had left at least one family member behind when they migrated. The families of the migrant sample seem to be very mobile with 83.3 per cent of minorities and 77.3 per cent of Han Chinese having members of their families who had moved to other places besides Urumqi.

The actual process of moving was rather more difficult to identify. People were asked to list all the places in which they had lived. The majority could only identify their current and previous locations. Twenty minority respondents and fifteen Han Chinese respondents indicated that they had moved more than twice. Most minority respondents had moved within Xinjiang province only, indicating a high level of intra-regional movement, but four of the twenty respondents also recorded a move to Beijing. In contrast, the Han Chinese had moved over a much wider area initially but most of their recent moves had been within Xinjiang.

Employment and income of the sample

The livelihoods of migrants before they moved were spread across the whole spectrum of agricultural, semi-agricultural, business, government/other office and other (including students). More minority migrants were employed in offices than Han Chinese but this is a reflection of the sample not the overall pattern in Xinjiang. Migration is always selective and within Xinjiang we could expect minority migrants to move to fill government and other positions. More Han Chinese were agriculturalists and businesspeople which again is a reflection of their pattern of movement. Low income was the most common reason given for moving though the desire to experience 'modern life' was important among minorities, especially females. The other significant reason that some female minority migrants gave for their mobility was the existence of family problems in the place of origin. For these respondents, migration may be a means of avoiding family control and/or conflict as well as a means of acquiring additional resources to support their families at home. When asked about aims of moving, all four sub-groups focussed on getting work. Minority women were less likely to emphasise access to long term work and this group had a much wider spread of aims, including marriage, education and other. Moving for education was more common among minority migrants than among Han migrants.

The occupations of migrants after moving showed heavy concentrations in the business and service sectors, with high proportions of female minority migrants also moving into professional and technical occupations. Amongst minority migrant males business proved to be the most popular type of employment. The non-migrant sample was heavily involved in government, management and other office work, which is not surprising given that the interviews were conducted in a large city. Common occupations among the non-migrant population included professionals/ technicians, managers, clerks, business people and service workers. Service work was much less common among the non-migrants than migrants and labouring was more common amongst migrants. Migration was not always concomitant with a change in employment. For example, some minority males were still peasants/herders after migration.

Of those who were employed, the Han Chinese migrants had the highest rate of employers or self-employed (67.4 per cent). In contrast most people in the other population groups were employees. The number of jobs held by migrants since arriving was very small on the whole: most people had only had one or two jobs since arriving in Urumqi. Most migrants had received assistance with finding a job from relatives and friends. This suggests that the informal migration networks work strongly and that most people had contacts who could help them locate jobs. As would be expected, the migrant sample demonstrated shorter periods of employment and they used a wider range of agencies and mechanisms for locating work. Despite this, difficulties in finding work were experienced by the majority of people. The minority sample reported more difficulties than the Han Chinese migrant sample and for the former the major problems included lack of experience, and linguistic and cultural problems. Han Chinese migrants reported fewer problems but 'language' and 'not enough work training' were identified as problems. It is interesting that both the minority and Han sample cited linguistic hindrances to getting jobs. This suggests that workplaces are not bi- or multi-lingual and that language is an important selection factor. Finding work is difficult for many people in Xinjiang and the non-migrant sample reported significant problems as well. Fewer Han migrants reported problems with finding employment. This is possibly because many migrated under job transfer and assignment programs, thus avoiding the problems associated with the job market experienced by others.

Questions concerning the level of family income before migration showed that many respondents experienced relatively low levels of income at this point in time: less than 400 yuan per month. Additionally, a sizeable component stated that they had no income. Some of these, however, were students who moved to find office work in Urumqi. Family incomes after moving showed an overall improvement for all migrant households. More families were in receipt of incomes of 400 yuan and above per month. Han Chinese migrants, in terms of their family income, did rather better than minority migrants. Prior to migration no Han individual belonged to a family with an income of 2000 yuan per month or more. After migration 18.2 per cent of male and 14.3 per cent of female Han Chinese respondents were members of families that enjoyed an income in this highest of brackets. In comparison, only 2.1 per cent of male minority migrants and no female minority migrants reported that their family income was at such a level. A comparison of the migrant family income and single income after migration and non-migrant family and single incomes shows that migrants have almost matched the incomes of non-migrants.

Social/personal aspects of migration of the sample

Overall, relocation on the part of the migrant sample led to an improvement in their economic situation: 65 per cent of minorities and 78 per cent of Han Chinese felt their position had improved after migration compared with their pre-migration situation. The rest reported either no change or a deterioration in their economic situation. Only 4.3 per cent of Han said that their situation had deteriorated. A small, but significant percentage (10 per cent) of the minority migrant population felt that their economic situation had declined and 31.8 per cent of minority migrants felt that they could only classify themselves as poor or very poor. Thus life for many remains a struggle and these figures serve as a reminder that migration is not always consistent with an improvement in every aspect of life. A comparison across the sample showed that migrants seemed to be slightly better off than non-migrants — at least smaller proportions reported living below the basic level. There was no information from migrants about savings levels but among non-migrants a higher proportion of Han Chinese than minorities were able to save, which is probably a function of the differing distributions of wages between the non-migrant populations.

Higher proportions of Han Chinese migrants were living in rented (56.7 per cent) and private (13.0 per cent) accommodation than minorities, where 40 per cent inhabited public housing. This reflects the fact that many Han Chinese in the sample had moved independently to Xinjiang and did not have work unit provided public housing. More than two thirds of the two groups had been resident in Urumqi for more than one year, though on average the Han Chinese were relatively newer arrivals. There was considerable uncertainty as to the length of intended residence among both groups but a higher proportion of minorities (35.2 per cent) than Han Chinese (26.7 per cent) intended to stay for a long time.

The economic consequences of migration are often crucial but they are not the total story and wider social repercussions, such as maintenance of contact with family, the nature and quality of social life, forms of entertainment and contact with others are all important. The health of individuals is often closely related to their current situation: dissatisfaction with migration, for example, could manifest itself in health problems, and we

Plate 7.2 Temporary housing of migrants on outskirts of Urumqi, 1997 (Photo by R. Iredale)

Plate 7.3 Bread seller in temporary migrant village, Urumqi, 1997 (Photo by R. Iredale)

were anxious therefore to identify any patterns related to the health of the individual respondents. The health status of most migrants had improved considerably after migration. This may be a function of increased income which has resulted in improvements in nutrition and living conditions and indicates satisfaction with the outcome of their migration.

Among minority migrants, a quarter of minority males gave satisfaction with their income as their major reason for not moving, followed by the assertion that they liked the locals and would be afraid to leave. Reasons given by minority females for not migrating included the belief that they had sufficient work, enough income and they too liked the local population. Few minorities gave lack of permission to move as the reason for not moving compared with the Han Chinese where 19.5 per cent of males and 13.3 per cent of females gave this as their reason. Enough income and work were also predominant reasons amongst the Han population for not moving.

Migration and education

The issue of access to education for children in migrant households has emerged as a vital one across China and not simply in Xinjiang. The highest proportion of families with school age children (79.5 per cent) was to be found among Han Chinese non-migrant households in the sample. However, the proportion of families with children enrolled at school was highest among both migrant sub-groups (88.4 per cent for minorities and 92.5 per cent for Han Chinese). This is a surprising finding given the problems that have typically been faced by migrant families in getting their children into schools. In Urumqi, several District School Boards have taken the initiative of building schools for children in migrant families without Urumqi *hukou* or with only temporary registration. 'They did not want these children not going school because of their lack of *hukou*' (Interview with local education officials, Urumqi, October 1996). There are more than 30 nationalities living in the Shayibake district, and Yamalikeshan has the greatest concentration of about 30 000 migrants. They have come spontaneously from all over the country, have little formal education and are mostly engaged in small trades, service jobs and construction sites. Many of the families had moved from other parts of China 'just to survive', according to some of the children who were interviewed. Their parents are making five or six yuan a day (one US$) from selling vegetables whereas where they had been living before they had had less money.

The school construction projects were the consequence of a realisation that large numbers of Han poor families, whose children needed education, were living on the outskirts of the city. One very small private school existed before the 56th schools were built. The schools were initiated and financed by the local governments where the migrants have settled and they have the same organisation and arrangements as other public schools in the city. These initiatives indicate a commendable willingness on the part of local authorities to assuage the common problem of lack of provision of school services for the children of migrants.

CASE STUDY OF 56ᵗʰ SCHOOLS

The first school was opened in 1988 and in 1996 had 28 classes, with all primary and secondary grades, and three pre-school classes. There were six Uyghur classes, in which the teaching language was Uyghur and pupils started learning Chinese at the third grade. All other classes used Chinese as the teaching language. The 56ᵗʰ school uses the same national curriculum as all other public schools. In 1996, there were 1400 pupils and 61 teachers, among whom there were 21 minority teachers, including Hui, Manchu, Russian, Uyghur, Kazak, Uzbek and other nationalities. Of the teachers, 24 had 15 years of formal education (including teacher training), 35 had special secondary school education, one had senior middle school education and one had junior middle school education. The school had all the advantages of a regular school, such as enough funds, spacious classrooms and good facilities. There is a beautiful teaching building (built at a cost of 2 100 000 yuan), a laboratory, a library with 450 000 books and a sports ground. Children with Urumqi *hukou* go to school free of charge and those without local *hukou* pay 200 yuan tuition per term. However, those who have particular financial difficulties may be enrolled free of charge. Because the tuition fee is very low, all families can afford to send their children to the school.

A second school, the Uyghur nationality school (Xuelian school), was opened by the local government next to the 56ᵗʰ school in 1997. This school enrols Uyghur children both of citizens and migrants. There are 13 classes with 400 pupils and 33 teachers. Among the pupils, 328 do not have Urumqi *hukou*, 50 have temporary Urumqi *hukou* and 14 have formal Urumqi *hukou*. The school teaches in Uyghur and uses Uyghur language textbooks.

Preferred type of schooling is one indicator of nationality identity and signifies concern about the maintenance of language, history and culture. Among the minority migrants there was a stronger preference for children to attend a nationality school (85.2 per cent) than among minority non-migrants (65.4 per cent). It is interesting to note that some Han migrants (18.2 per cent) wanted their children to attend a minority nationality school. Unlike in Inner Mongolia, small proportions of minority migrants and non-migrants indicated a preference for nationality classes in Han Chinese schools. This indicates that some parents are aware of the benefits associated with bilingual classes but the majority do not favour this option. Uyghur migrants elsewhere have indicated the value they place on bilingualism amongst their children so the situation clearly varies by location (Hoy 1996). Linguistic problems identified in this survey may have made some Han parents aware of the advantages connected with their children learning another language. However, in response to the question on preferred languages for their children to learn few Han parents want their children to learn a Chinese nationality language over a foreign language.

Plate 7.4 New school in Shayibake district, Urumqi, 1997 (Photo by R. Iredale)

The question concerning levels of satisfaction with schooling produced interesting results. Minority migrants were on the whole less satisfied than their non-migrant counterparts while the Han Chinese were largely satisfied.

However, the proportion in all cases with 'no idea' is quite sizeable. The reasons for dissatisfaction with schooling are revealed in the next question which deals with problems with schooling. Only 14.8 per cent of minority migrants said that they had no problems with schooling, compared with 44 per cent of Han Chinese migrants, 48.1 per cent of minority non-migrants and 76.3 per cent of Han Chinese non-migrants. The major problems identified by each group were the high cost of educating their children and their lack of local *hukou*. The absence of a nationality school nearby also featured as a problem for minorities and the fact that an appropriate school was too far away was a factor for Han Chinese migrants.

Very few people in the sample had attended university but it seems that many would ideally like their children to do so. Minority respondents overwhelmingly stated they would prefer to see their children attend a University for Nationalities, rather than a Han Chinese university but given that there is no such university in Xinjiang this dream will elude most. Han Chinese migrants want their children to attend a Han Chinese university and as many of these migrants were from provinces other than Xinjiang this may simply mean that they would like their children to attend university in their 'home' province. The one anomaly was the Han Chinese non-migrants who preferred a University for Nationalities over a designated Han university. It may be that these Han regard Xinjiang as 'home' rather than a separate province or they can perceive an advantage for their children if they attend a University for Nationalities. This issue becomes more complex if we then consider the results from the question about 'preferred destination of children after graduation'. Both Han Chinese groups would mostly prefer their children to go elsewhere, especially the non-migrant group (the ones who have been here a long time). Among the minority sub-groups, slightly more migrants (54.1 per cent) would prefer their children to go elsewhere than non-migrants (46.2 per cent). So the Han mostly see their children's future outside of Xinjiang while half of the Uyghur also have this hope for their children.

Relationship of the sampled population to the local community

For all sub-groups, especially the Han Chinese, watching television was the major form of entertainment. Listening to the radio, reading and playing games were also important to varying extents. Activities relating to contact with others were cited rather less frequently but were more important for migrants than for non-migrants. On the whole, the minority groups were more socially active than the Han Chinese. Frequency of contact with relatives and other people are indicators of social cohesion and interaction. Over 75 per cent of minority migrants and over 90 per cent of Han migrants maintained contact of some kind with their relatives. Non-migrants displayed similarly high levels of family contact. The frequency of contact will partially be a function of distance from relatives and it is difficult therefore to base any conclusions about contact and migration on observed differences between the levels of occasional and frequent contact in these populations.

For Uyghurs in Xinjiang, 89 per cent live in rural areas and are unlikely to mix with non-Uyghurs (Ji 1990). Migration brings Uyghurs into greater contact with other nationalities as they move to more ethnically diverse societies. As a consequence, minority cultures may change somewhat. Ren and Yuan (1999) document that minorities change their diet and begin to eat more vegetables, rather than the heavy emphasis on meat, but they do not comment on more significant changes. According to Ji (1992), few Han Chinese speak Uyghur and where Han and Uyghur populations do come into contact with each other the Uyghur are more likely to make movements towards integration than the Han, largely due to their ability to speak Chinese.

Tsui concludes that minority migrants who move to big cities in Xinjiang do not experience a weakening of their ethnic identity and sometimes it even becomes stronger. Tsui used four indicators of ethnicity to determine the manifestation of ethnic identity: who migrants relied on for finding jobs in towns and cities; what kind of jobs they obtained; who they communicated with in the big cities and towns, and the type of education they wanted for their children or themselves. The findings were that most minority migrants relied on relatives or distant family for jobs and they worked in companies, restaurants, etc. managed by Uyghurs. Most did not want to work in businesses managed by non-Uyghurs. Many young Uyghur girls, aged 14 and over, worked as domestics or caring for the children or old folk of kin or relatives. The concept of family/households remains a very important part of ethnic identity. Most minority migrants tended to communicate with other Uyghurs and their language was still an important indicator of ethnicity. Most Uyghurs preferred a nationality school for their children's education and a University of Nationalities was the higher education institution of choice for most parents. Regardless of differences in educational level, age and the nature of the city or town, Tsui believes that Uyghurs do not change their basic identity and they remain strongly attached to their ethnic group. They mostly form separate groups or enclaves in the cities which are increasingly being populated by Han Chinese.

Tsui asks what the government can do to integrate Uyghur young people better into the economy of places such as Urumqi. What ways can be found for young educated Uyghurs to get jobs in the formal sector rather than mainly with their own ethnic group? There are still some preferential policies (targets) but hiring is no longer in the hands of the government. Most hiring is now done by the private sector and there are no preferential policies or targets in place for these new enterprises. Most private sector employers give preference to people with a very good command of Chinese language. Even though an assimilation policy has not prevailed in the region, in theory, in practice the large number of Han cadres means that the reality is quite different. This is manifested in the fact that most official work places operate in Mandarin while small scale minority workplaces operate in nationality languages. The exclusion of Uyghurs from many of the new jobs that are emerging means that previous attempts at affirmative action are no longer operational. Minority cadres have always comprised only a small proportion of all cadres in Xinjiang but this is now being compounded by the labour market profile of the new enterprises.

Government-sponsored migration to Xinjiang has diminished and recent spontaneous Han in-migrants are more business oriented and intend to stay for a long term. Most are arriving for economic gain or just plain survival. While Han in concentrated areas have little interaction with minorities, those who migrate freely, like the people in our sample, are 'usually well adapted to the Uyghur way of life' in terms of language, living style and mode of production (Mao 1999). Some become Muslim but most keep their own folk customs, local gods, etc. Most Han non-migrants in the sample had contact with other nationalities as did almost two thirds of Han migrants. 'The culture of the Han has become diverse, changeable and incorporates many non-traditional elements' that go beyond food and diet (Ren and Yuan 1999, p. 7). Thus we see the gradual process of change taking place that is a consequence of the inter-mixing of groups. But in this case, it is the Han culture which has probably changed the most in response to them being new settlers in what was formerly a predominantly minority region.

Nevertheless, there is no case of intermarriage between Han and Uyghur and most marry locally in their own community. According to Mao (1999), every Han Chinese family has Uyghur friends and Han in rural areas have to learn Uyghur in order to survive. Buying and selling in rural areas must be done in the Uyghur language and the Han have to integrate with Uyghurs. Many Han still think of returning to their place of origin and they pay great attention to their children's education. Often the children of Han have to attend Uyghur primary schools (as there is no Han primary school locally) and they are sent to Han middle schools if they are available. Where Han secondary schools are not available Han children must continue in Uyghur or Kazak schools. As a consequence these Han Chinese students do their entry tests to university in Uyghur or Kazak language. Though this is a small number Tsui believes that anthropologically they are significant as they have acquired minority languages and will serve to break down some of the barriers between Han and minorities.

CONCLUSION

Migration is leading to a greater mixing of ethnic groups and Han but a watering down of minority, especially Uyghur culture, does not appear to have been the outcome. There appears to be a strengthening of ethnic identity and Uyghur migration may even be contributing to this. Migration is a means of transferring information from one region to another, especially from countries to the west of China, as well as from cities and other places within China. The growing pan-Islamic movement has spurred a range of changes in Xinjiang including attempts to keep women out of the workforce and the demand for a ban on a Chinese book considered insulting to Uyghurs. Uyrghur nationalism is a recent phenomenon, inspired both by Muslims in Central Asia and Chinese 'identification' of the Uyghur nationality (Dillon 1995, Gladney 1990). Increased education levels are also putting people in touch with more literature, media reports and other information and they are then better able to become spokespersons for the groups that they represent. But when 'intellectual or cultural expression has threatened the unity of China condemnation has been swift' (Dillon 1995, p. 17). Dillon gives the example of three books by a Uyghur author that have been condemned for portraying Uyghurs and their literature as ethnically and culturally related to Turkic people.

Xinjiang is unique in the degree of planned in-migration since 1949 and the deliberate policies of the central government to influence the ethnic mix of the region. Altering the mixture of Han and minorities in the region was not designed to lead to the assimilation of minorities, except during the Cultural Revolution, but to their integration. Nevertheless, Heberer (1989, p. 98) argues that the 'creation of a Han majority will undoubtedly encourage it [assimilation]'. At this point in time minority languages, cultures and ethnicities remain strong and vibrant, perhaps even more so than before, according to Tsui. The question is will 'modernisation' and the consequent increase in rural-urban migration and spontaneous in-migration from other provinces deliver to the government what planned migration has so far not been able to achieve?

The central government has increased the opening up of Xinjiang to develop the region and to provide resources for the rest of the country. The 'Remake the West Campaign' which was announced in 2000 is expected to become a pivotal component of the 10th Five Year Plan from 2001 to 2005. How much of this is with the support of minority representatives is difficult to know and whether minority autonomy is being respected is questionable. Minority autonomy may again be losing out in the interests of the wider population policy and overall Chinese development.

The following chapter looks at the spontaneous migration of minorities into Beijing. Minorities are joining the large scale movement into Beijing, Shanghai, Guangzhou and other cities of China. The reasons for these movements and how the migrants fare vary significantly across the three ethnic groups under consideration. Each uses migration to Beijing for different purposes and in so doing there are differential impacts on their regions of origin. Chapter 8 will show how what happens internally in each region cannot be separated from what is occurring at the national level. This also raises interesting theoretical questions, at the broader level, regarding social transformation. Urbanisation and international influences are likely to have a major impact on Uyghur culture through the process of migration to cities such as Beijing. However, at the same time we can observe strong local influences through the process of identity-building as a result of the same migration process. Ultimately, the future identities of minorities such as the Uyghur are likely to respond significantly to the interactions of this sort of global/local tension.

8. Beijing's growing ethnic minorities *

INTRODUCTION

Cities manifest all the complexities of contemporary social and economic life. The growth of cities in many developing countries has been associated with severe problems, such as lack of housing and the growth of slums. In China there have been serious attempts to limit the growth of cities and to thereby avoid many of the social problems that are commonly associated with them. Cities such as Beijing and Shanghai are still trying to control the influx in various ways and to militate against too rapid urban change and possible conflict. They are doing this by a range of mechanisms designed to either limit the inflow, deprive 'illegal' migrants of services and access to particular jobs or by sending people back to their places of origin. This is becoming more difficult now with the massive number of people on the move either as part of the floating population or as permanent settlers.

Beijing is described in this chapter as an example of the changes taking place in urban China. Beijing is unique, of course, in that it is the administrative capital, and a higher proportion of its workforce is in the state sector than elsewhere. It is also the showcase for China for official events (for example, the Asian Games in 1990, the bid for the 2000 Olympic Games in 1994, the 50th Anniversary Celebrations in 1999) and the destination for many international tourists/business people. For these and other reasons, there is intense pressure on officials to keep the city ordered and functioning smoothly. Part of this involves improving the transport systems, pulling down old houses and rebuilding modern apartment blocks, upgrading or redeveloping government office blocks, restoring cultural relics and recreation sites and controlling the influx of people.

This chapter is mostly based on data from our *Sample Survey of Ethnic Minority Migration*[1]. The focus is on issues of minority migration to Beijing, especially recent patterns of minority migration and factors associated with such patterns. The survey includes Han and three ethnic minority groups: Mongolian, Tibetan and Uyghur. Mongolians are one of the largest ethnic minority groups in Beijing. Although small in number, Uyghurs have

---

* This chapter has major contributions from Fei Guo and Caroline Hoy.
[1] See Chapter 2 for detailed information about this survey.

become more active in migrating to Beijing in recent years and the well-known 'Xinjiang Village' located in Beijing will be discussed. Tibetans are another interesting group because of their unique history and cultural heritage and they are now coming to Beijing in small numbers.

It was hypothesised that the migration patterns of ethnic minorities would differ from those of Han Chinese, given their different social and economic status and cultural traditions. We consider this hypothesis to see to what extent ethnicity explains people's migration behaviour and whether minorities differ from Han Chinese in pursuing their spatial mobility. Studies of total migration have shown that continuity of the socialist planned system, represented by various institutional elements such as the household registration system (*hukou*) and the labour recruitment system in cities, has been important in determining migrants' social status and economic well-being (Solinger 1999, Goldstein and Goldstein 1991, Guo 1996a). By looking into these institutional factors, this chapter attempts to see whether *hukou* still remains important when ethnicity is taken into account. Though we do not claim that the minority migration patterns to Beijing represent migration patterns elsewhere in the country, our analysis does provide some understanding of migration of ethnic minorities to large cities. The migrant households in the sample had all migrated between 1987 and 1997. The aim of using this time frame was to exclude those very recently arrived migrants who had not yet had sufficient time elapse to deal with employment, housing, children's schooling and so on. Issues raised by the formation of ethnic minority communities in China's cities have so far gone unaddressed but there is growing interest in this topic. This reflected in the joint congress organised by the International Union of Anthropological and Ethnological Sciences (IUAES) and the China Urban Anthropology Association on *Metropolitan Ethnic Cultures: Maintenance and Interaction* which was held in Beijing in July 2000.

POPULATION GROWTH IN BEIJING

As the capital city and an economic and cultural centre of the country, Beijing has attracted a large number of migrants from around the country in past decades. In fact, Beijing is one of the most migrant-attractive regions in China with an official in-migration rate of 6 per cent in the period 1985 to 1990 (State Statistical Bureau of China 1991). As pointed out earlier, this figure only includes those migrants who had been in Beijing for at least one year at the time of the census and those who had changed their *hukou* status. Due to Beijing's strict urban development policy, permanent migration is still tightly controlled and the number of permanent migrants to Beijing has actually decreased in the last two decades. The number of permanent migrants to Beijing in 1980 was about 245 000 but the number decreased to 105 700 in 1997 (Zhuang 1995, Beijing Statistical Bureau 1998). However, starting in the late 1980s, an increasing number of temporary migrants began moving to Beijing for various reasons (mostly for job and business opportunities) and in recent years, the migrant influx has been even more phenomenal. It was estimated in 1991 that long-term migration only comprised about one third of total migration in China (Goldstein and Goldstein 1991). Thus, even though the natural population growth rate was very low in the 1980s Beijing's total population increased from 9.17 million in 1982 to 10.8 million in 1990. Migrants contributed a large share (more than half) of this increase (Li 1987). The Beijing Migrant Census which was conducted in late 1997 shows that the number of migrants who had been in Beijing for at least six months reached 1.46 million, accounting for about one tenth of the total population in Beijing (Beijing Statistical Bureau 1998).

Recent attempts to control population movement to Beijing

Before 1995, Beijing (and Shanghai) municipal authorities and the central government 'did not recognize how influential and profound the rural-urban migration might be. There was not very much done in terms of limiting the number and scale of migrants' (Zhang *et al.* 1998, p. 3). Guangdong authorities had been involved in setting up inter-provincial regulations in 1991 with Sichuan, Hunan and Guangxi to facilitate cooperation between these three sending regions and Guangdong. Shanghai participated in their annual conferences on *Cooperation in Sending and Receiving Rural Labourers in the Cities and Provinces in Southern-East China* and was the first to introduce Temporary Residence Certificates (TRCs) and Work Permits. In addition, in early 1995 Shanghai grouped all occupations into three categories: category A jobs which could be filled by migrant workers after being advertised and not filled; category B jobs which could be filled by migrants but were subject to quotas; and category C jobs which could never be filled by migrant workers (Wu and Li 1996).

In April 1995, the Standing Committee of Beijing People's Congress legislated the *Beijing Regulations for Migrant Labourers and Personnel* or people without *hukou*. A survey undertaken in one migrant village in Beijing in 1994 had found that 91 per cent of migrant employers didn't have a business licence, only four out of 4884 women had signed up with the unit concerned to follow the family planning scheme and 54 per cent of married women had more than one child (Xiang 1999, p. 11). To strengthen the management of rural and other migrant labourers (floating population) from elsewhere, the Beijing Municipal Leading Group of Management for Out-coming Labourers was set up in May 1995. This group consisted of representatives of labour administration, industry and trade, urban planning, construction, finance, family planning, tax, planning, housing and legal offices. They formulated ten regulations which came into effect on 15 July 1995.[2]

Within each regulation there are specific rules to be adhered to. For example, under Regulation number one, people coming to Beijing for work should apply for temporary residence within three days and if they plan to stay for more than one month they should apply for a Temporary Residence Card (TRC) at the same time. The TRC should only be given after the ID card and certificate for status of marriage and child-bearing (for women in child-bearing ages), both issued by public security in their place of origin, are presented. The TRC should be returned on departure after one year or extended if the application is renewed within ten days of expiry. TRCs should be presented on application for a job or business licence. Overall, the regulations were designed to try to gain control of the temporary migrant population but they have not been very effective.

On 6 March 1997 the Beijing Labor Administration Bureau also regulated the sectors and occupations which out-coming labourers (in-migrants) could take up. Rural workers can only get 271 types of job — the dirty and dangerous ones that the urban residents do not want (for example, slaughtering animals, as undertakers and in agriculture, forestry, chemical, metallurgy, building materials and mining industries) or others which are not so dirty and dangerous (such as services and management) but which cannot be filled by Beijingers (Solinger 1995). In spite of the regulations, Beijing's temporary migrant population (that is people without Beijing *hukou* and who had lived in Beijing for more than six months) more than doubled from 700 000 in 1986 to 1.46 million in 1997. This figure includes not only those coming in as floating workers but also people who have come in with the intention of staying permanently but who have done so without permission. The following discussion also includes the third group, albeit small, who have the money or connections to gain urban *hukou* or who have moved to Beijing with official permission.

People without local *hukou* are denied access to health, education, housing, welfare and other services because of their civic, legal and political status. 'Even those who have registered as "temporary city dwellers" still lack the urban *hukou* and so remain disenfranchised' (Solinger 1995, p. 130). Thus the differential treatment of migrants compared to permanent Beijing residents is institutionalised. Temporary in-migrants are unlikely to take any action regarding their situation because of their marginalised position and their lack

---

[2] These ten regulations cover a number of aspects concerning those migrant labours without local *hukou* status. It includes regulations on *hukou* management, renting houses, public security in rented houses, employment management, business and trading engagement, family planning, market place management, domestic service management, designated tasks concerning migrant labourers, and fee levy on business and trading engagement. See Zhang *et al.* 1998, p. 9 and Zou 1996, pp. 289-337 for details.

of political voice and connections. But as we will see in this chapter, this situation is not uniform and some migrant groups in Beijing have good networks and political patronage.

The institutional framework makes analysis of China's migrants' status unique. Most theories of migrant community formation and development and interaction with the host community start from a hypothetical position of legislated or assumed equality. Moreover, models of social policy incorporation range from the 'inclusive', where active social policies are linked to multiculturalism (such as in Australia, Canada, Sweden and the Netherlands), through to societies such as Germany and Switzerland which do not provide equal access by immigrants to services and where the rights of immigrants are not protected by legislation. Minority nationalities within China have legislated equal status to Han but migrants are deemed to be unable to access certain services other than in their place of *hukou*. Within the national setting, therefore, migrants without *hukou* are treated very differently to migrants with *hukou*. But what about ethnic minority migrants with Beijing *hukou*? What sort of settlement patterns have occurred in Beijing among our three ethnic groups? These and other issues will be examined in this chapter.

History of ethnic minorities in Beijing

The history of ethnic minorities in Beijing can be traced to centuries ago, particularly to the Qing Dynasty (1644-1911) when the country was ruled by Manchus. Although they were in the ruling position, the Manchus were a minority group in the population compared with majority Han. In order to strengthen their power, the ruling Manchus moved a large number of Manchu military personnel and their families, also called the Eight Banners, to the Beijing area from a number of north eastern provinces. In 1781, the total population in the Eight Banners reached about 540 000 in Beijing area, in which about 90 000 lived in the inner city area. The total population in Beijing, including urban and surrounding county population and military personnel, was about two million of which Manchus accounted for 26 per cent. The organised migration of Manchu was an important element in Beijing's population increase in the early period of the Qing Dynasty.

From the late nineteenth century, the number of military personnel in the Beijing area decreased as a result of a series of wars with western nations. Many Manchus were forced to migrate to other places and by 1910, Beijing's total population was 2.2 million, of which Manchus were around 430 000 (19 per cent of the total population). In the decades after the end of the Qing Dynasty, migration from other provinces still contributed greatly to population increase in Beijing, but the peak period of migration of Manchu to Beijing was over with the end of Qing Dynasty. The total population in Beijing increased from 2.9 million in 1917 to 3.9 million in 1948 (Li 1987).

Since 1949, Beijing has been the capital city of the new People's Republic and has become a social and cultural centre. The 1953 census shows that there were 38 ethnic minority groups in Beijing, accounting for 92.7 per cent of all officially identified 41 minority nationality groups at that time. Total population in Beijing in 1953 was about 5.02 million and the minority population (about 170 000) accounted for 3.4 per cent of total population. Among the ethnic minority groups, Man (Manchu in the old term) were the largest group with a population of 80 000. Many of them were descendants of the ruling class of Manchus in the Qing Dynasty and military personnel, or the Eight Banners. The other large ethnic groups were Hui and Mongols, with populations of 79 000 and 7 000 respectively. The 1964 census saw a rapid increase in both Han and ethnic minority populations, as a result of both high fertility and migration from other provinces. Total population increased to 7.47 million in 1964 and the ethnic minority component was 285 000 (3.7 per cent of total population). By 1982, the size of the population of ethnic minorities had not changed and they represented 3.2 per cent of the population, but the number of ethnic minorities had increased to 55, indicating significant turnover[3]. The events of the Cultural Revolution outlined in Chapter 3 obviously had an effect. By 1990, the minority proportion had returned to the 1962 proportion (3.8 per cent) and the number of people was 414 036. As pointed out earlier, the overall proportion of minorities in China's population is 8.04 per cent so the Beijing proportion is well below the national average.

Since the proportion of ethnic minorities in the total population of Beijing has remained relatively stable over the past five decades this means that the population growth rate of minorities and Han has been similar, except during the period 1964 to 1982. Both natural increase and migration impact on population growth. Data from the 1982 census show that Beijing minority women's total fertility rate (TFR[4]) was 1.50, which was lower than that of the total population (Li 1987). It is assumed that the mortality rates of the minority population are similar to those of the Han population, and the lower fertility level among the minority population suggests that a larger proportion of the minority population increase was due to migration from other provinces.

---

[3] The increase in the number of ethnic minority groups may be also affected by the re-classification of minorities.
[4] Total fertility rate (TFR) is a measurement of average number of children a woman would have if she follows the age-specific fertility pattern of a given year throughout her life course.

Table 8.1 Han and ethnic minority population in Beijing, 1953-1990

Year	Han		Minority		Total	No. of minority groups
	No.	%	No.	%	No.	
1953	4 854 500	96.6	170 000	3.4	5 024 500	38
1964	7 188 800	96.2	285 000	3.8	7 473 800	53
1982	8 893 300	96.8	285 000	3.2	9 178 300	56
1990	10 405 104	96.2	414 036	3.8	1 0819 140	56

Sources: Li (1987, pp. 330-1), Yuan (1995 , p. 149).

CONTEMPORARY MINORITY MIGRATION TO BEIJING

The 1990 census provides details on the populations of ethnic minorities in Beijing. Over 414 000 people were registered as members of an ethnic minority in 1990: 214 000 males and 199 000 females (State Population Census Office 1993, Vol. 1, p. 300). Almost half the ethnic minority population in Beijing were recorded as members of the Hui nationality and many of these would have been indigenous to Beijing. The second largest ethnic minority is Manchu (population 165 000) and they account for about 40 per cent of the total minority population in Beijing. Mongolian is the third largest minority group in Beijing (16 833), accounting for about 4 per cent of total minority population. Uyghur (2020) and Tibetan (1329) account for very small proportions (0.4 per cent and 0.3 per cent respectively).

Although relatively small in numbers, the population of the three ethnic groups in this study has increased significantly since 1982. Mongolians have almost doubled, Uyghurs have more than doubled and Tibetans have increased by more than 60 per cent in the period of less than ten years.[5] Migration from other provinces has obviously contributed to these increases. The movement of these three ethnic groups to Beijing is relatively new and for this reason it makes the study of their movement and settlement very significant. This is substantiated by a 1994 migrant survey conducted by the Beijing Statistical Bureau (Zou, 1996) which showed that Han migrants accounted for 96.8 per cent of total migrants in Beijing and minorities for 3.2 per cent. Manchus accounted for 1 per cent of migrants, followed by Uyghurs

---

[5] The figures of nationality in the censuses only include those who are defined as usual residents of Beijing, which include those who have local *hukou*, those who have been away from their place of registration for at least one year, and those who don't have registration anywhere. Temporary migrants or floaters are not included. For discussions in the following section about the results from the survey, migrants (both Han and minority) include both those who have local *hukou* and those who don't have a local *hukou* but have moved to Beijing within 1987-97.

(0.54 per cent), Hui (0.44 per cent), and Mongolians (0.36 per cent). Other minority groups accounted for only 0.28 per cent of total migrants.

Similar proportions of all Han and all minority migrants in China went to Beijing in this period: 6.21 per cent for Han and 5.84 per cent for minorities. Figure 8.1 shows the source of migrants to Beijing between 1985 and 1990. Minority migrants came mostly from the neighbouring province of Hebei, the northern provinces of Inner Mongolia, Liaoning, Jilin and Heilongjiang, and from Guangxi in the south. The number coming from Inner Mongolia, Tibet and Xinjiang was 4300, 200 and 600 respectively. On the other hand, Han migrants came from a much wider range of provinces and 19 200 came from Inner Mongolia, 1400 from Tibet and 12 800 from Xinjiang.

Social-demographic characteristics of the sample

The Beijing migrant sample consisted of 398 households: 101 Han Chinese, 99 Mongolian, 98 Tibetan and 99 Uyghurs. As pointed out earlier, the three groups are quite diverse on a range of indicators and therefore it would be anticipated that they represent a spectrum of minorities rather than minorities of one particular category (such as religion, level of education, socio-economic status, etc). Nevertheless, in order to explain the overall migration processes and the differences between Han and minorities in the sample in a more statistical fashion, regression analysis was conducted. The size of the sample made this feasible whereas in the case of the other samples they were not large enough to conduct similar analysis and the studies are more indicative or exploratory . Regression analysis is a commonly used technique to examine the interrelationships among variables in a certain environment. Factors that are not of primary interest can be held constant to see the impact of variables (factors) of interest (Chatterjee and Price 1991). Logit regression was used in the analysis, as the dependent variables were dichotomous (that is only two possibilities).

Among the sampled ethnic minority population, 71.9 per cent were male and 28.1 per cent were female. Among the Han sample, 59.5 per cent were male and 40.5 per cent were female. Over half of the sampled population for each group were aged 20 to 29, which is the premium age for labour participation. The Mongolian and Uyghur samples were comprised largely of singles while the Tibetan and Han samples had higher proportions that were married. Overall, only a quarter of the minority sample was married compared to 34 per cent of the Han sample. The high single rate (66.3 per cent) of the full sample is quite typical of the pattern of migration to Beijing. Single people mostly move first and may later be joined by family or may return home.

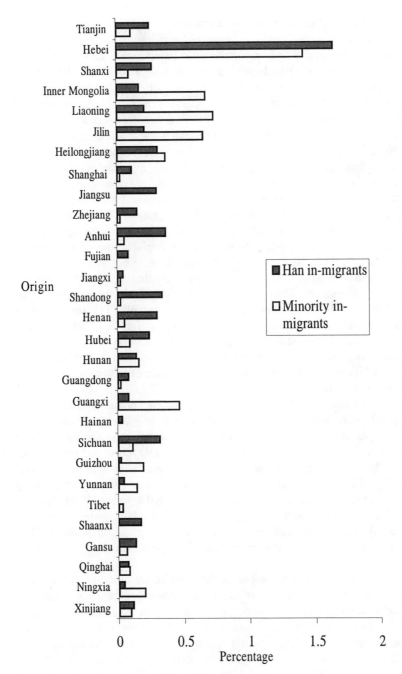

Source: State Population Census Office (1993, Vols. 1 and 4).

Figure 8.1 Minority and Han movement to Beijing by origin, 1985-90

As pointed out earlier, the government has tried to limit the influx of people to large cities in past decades. The household registration system (*hukou*) has been one of the most effective policies ever implemented in regulating and controlling people's spatial movement. Although not so effective in controlling people migration nowadays, *hukou* still is an important factor in determining people's access to labour markets and public facilities and services. In the sampled population, only 20.6 per cent had a local *hukou* status and the majority of them were in Beijing without a local *hukou* status. Among all four ethnic groups, including Han, Tibetans are the only group that has a large proportion (52 per cent) of locally registered migrants. They are a special group that includes a high level of government-sponsored migration, including student enrolment and allotment and officials assigned to Beijing. This is typical of the pattern of Tibetan migration to Beijing where half belong to this type of planned migration. There are some spontaneous Tibetan migrants in Beijing, mostly selling artefacts and animal bones. Almost all Uyghurs (98 per cent) in the sample were not locally registered. There are also Ugyhur officials and students in Beijing but they are not captured in the survey. Only 12 per cent of Mongolians in the sample had local *hukou* as did only 16 per cent of the Han sample. The proportion of locally registered males was similar to that for females. Better-educated migrants have a better chance of getting a local *hukou*. Among 66 migrants with education of 15 years and above, almost half of them possessed a local *hukou*, while among 105 migrants with education of seven to nine years, only 13 per cent had a local *hukou*.

The educational composition of the sampled population shows that, compared with minority migrants, more Han migrants had obtained a university level education. Education levels of minorities in the sample were concentrated at the lower middle school, higher middle school and professional school levels. The proportion of people without any schooling among minority migrants was negligible. In addition to formal education, the survey also included information on migrants' work-related training. Both Han and minority migrants showed similar patterns. More than half of the migrants in the sample had not received any work-related training and only one third of migrants had received some work training for a period of one year to three years.

Compared to Han people in the sample, minority migrants had a higher proportion (40 per cent) of 'living together with more than five people' in Beijing. Other fieldwork[6] in a Han migrant community in Beijing suggests that Han migrants, especially those who are single and young, tend to migrate in a group of three to five if they don't have any family members or close relatives to depend on after their arrival in the destination. Young

---

[6] Fieldwork in a migrant community in Beijing in 1997 and 1998 by Guo Fei supported by an Andrew Mellon post-doctoral fellowship.

Han migrants tend to live together and due to the nature of their occupations, many live in collective households (such as dormitories in factories and temporary shelters at construction sites) provided by their employers. Why minority migrants congregate in larger households is not clear. It may be associated with their social distance from the host society or their social exclusion (which Han are also subjected to but perhaps to a lesser extent).

Migration process of the sample

In a traditional society where the labour market is not well developed and where information channels from society are not available to a majority of its members, family networks are an important source of information about the destination and prospective job market (Harbison 1981). Given the fact that China is still a traditional society in many aspects, even though it has experienced rapid social transformation in recent years, it is interesting to see how minority migrants compare with Han on this aspect. The results from the survey show that 74.9 per cent of the migrants in the sample moved to Beijing alone, 19.2 per cent with family and the remainder with family and friends or others. Among the Uyghur sample, 93.8 per cent came alone, followed by 79.4 per cent for Mongols, 66 per cent for Tibetans and 60 per cent for Han. The Uyghur and Tibetan groups came largely from cities, 85 per cent and 64 per cent respectively, while the Mongolians (64 per cent) came mainly from rural areas. The Han sample originated from a diverse range of sources, about one third from cities, 27.3 per cent from rural areas, 25.3 per cent from small towns and 12.1 per cent from large towns.

　　　　Table 8.2 lists the means of the variables used in the regression analysis. Except for the variable 'age', all other variables are categorical variables, eg. a migrant's *hukou* status is defined as whether the migrant has a local *hukou* or not, and ethnicity is defined as whether the migrant is a Han Chinese or not.

　　　　As shown in Table 8.2, more than half (58 per cent) of migrants in the sample received help from others in their migration to Beijing. Table 8.3 shows the logistic regression coefficients of whether migrants received any help from others in their move to Beijing. Six independent variables were included in the analysis, and four were statistically significant. A migrant's *hukou* status (whether locally registered or not), ethnicity (whether Han or non-Han), education level (whether having a higher education level) and place of origin (whether from an urban area or not) all had a significant effect on whether the migrant received any help from others in their migration to Beijing. A migrant who was able to register his/her *hukou* in Beijing was less likely to rely on others' help in their migration to Beijing. A Han migrant was less likely to rely on others' help to facilitate his/her migration suggesting that compared with Han Chinese, minority migrants were more

Table 8.2 Means and standard deviation of variables included in regression analysis (N=335)

Variables	Mean	Standard Deviation
After-moving personal income *(monthly income 800 yuan and above coded as 1, otherwise as 0)*	0.3425	0.4752
Hukou status *(locally registered as 1, otherwise as 0)*	0.2060	0.4050
Sex *(male coded as 1, female as 0)*	0.6890	0.4636
Ethnicity *(Han coded as 1, non-Han as 0)*	0.2538	0.4357
Occupation in Beijing *(informal sectors coded as 1, otherwise 0)*	0.2613	0.4328
Education *(professional school/university coded as 1, otherwise as 0)*	0.4121	0.4928
Age	27.8300	8.9800
Original places *(city and town coded as 1, otherwise as 0)*	0.7362	0.4413
Get help from others for moving *(yes coded as 1, no as 0)*	0.5879	0.4928

Source: Data from *Sample Survey of Ethnic Minority Migration (1997-98)*.

likely to receive help from relatives, friends or family members already in Beijing. Because of language and cultural difference, a minority migrant may need more help from his/her friends or relatives to adjust himself/herself to a new place. Minority migrants may be more willing to help each other and the familial and other ties may be stronger. If we rely on literature on migrant communities in other parts of the world we see a strong tendency among many ethnic groups to support and promote the migration of people from their own family, village or town as a means of building up their community in the destination. In this way they have a better chance of retaining their language and culture and surrounding themselves with familiar faces, foods, customs, etc.

The results also show that a migrant with a higher education level was less likely to receive help from others in his/her migration process. In many societies better-educated people are more capable of coping with changes, including migration, and he/she may be more able to land a job and have the financial resources for a place to live by him/herself. The results show that if other factors are the same, a migrant from a rural origin was less likely to receive any help from others for their moving, while a migrant with urban origin was more likely to receive help from others in their migration process.

Table 8.3 Logistic regression coefficients of whether migrants received any help from others in their move to Beijing

Variables	Coefficient	Standard error	Significance
Hukou (locally registered=1)	-0.8617	0.3317	**
Sex (male=1)	0.0788	0.2563	
Ethnicity (Han=1)	-0.9412	0.2711	**
Age	-0.0119	0.0146	
Education (higher education=1)	-0.5698	0.2541	**
Original places (urban orgin=1)	0.1328	0.2691	**
Constant	1.3359	0.4597	

Note: The dependent variable is whether the migrant received any help from others for their moving to Beijing, yes is coded as 1, and no as 0. ** significant at p<0.05.

Source: Data from *Sample Survey of Ethnic Minority Migration (1997-98)*.

This may indicate that people from urban origins are more likely to have family or social contacts in Beijing while people with rural origins are less likely to have such contacts.

Employment and income of the sample

Current employment status of the sampled population showed that the majority of migrants, regardless of their ethnic background, moved to Beijing for economic-related reasons. About 80 per cent of migrants were either employed or looking for a job. There are a large number of educational institutions in the Beijing area, from primary to university level, which may have attracted people from other provinces. It is interesting to observe that in the sampled population, although more than 17 per cent of minority migrants claimed that they were currently attending school, there were actually only about 4 per cent reported as students. This suggests that many people attending school in Beijing are either part-time students or are in various training programs. Similarly, about 13 per cent of Han migrants claimed they were currently attending school but no one reported as a student in the sample.

In terms of current labour force status, minority and Han migrants had a similar pattern. Among the sampled population, about 40 per cent of both Han and minority migrants reported that they relied on agricultural or semi-agricultural activities as their livelihood before moving to Beijing. Interestingly, 13.4 per cent of male and 8.3 per cent of female minority migrants had already had experience in engaging in business before moving to Beijing, while only 4 per cent of Han male and 2.9 per cent of Han female migrants had such experience before moving. Engaging in business activities is seen as an involvement in the market-oriented economy and in this area the minority sample was more active.

Studies of migrants' occupational attainment in China show that rural migrants in cities tend to take jobs in informal sectors, such as street vendors or domestic maids, or as temporary workers in formal sectors, such as construction workers, mainly because access to permanent jobs in formal sectors is not available (Yang and Guo 1996). The conditions imposed on migrants without *hukou* by the Beijing officials reinforce this pattern. The sampled population in this survey also show that migrants in Beijing tend to concentrate in small business and service sectors. Female migrants are especially likely to work in the service sector compared with their male counterparts. About 60 per cent of female minority migrants were in the service sector while only about 30 per cent of male minority migrants were in these sectors. Compared with minority migrants, Han migrants had a larger proportion in professional/technician/manager categories, which are considered high-level occupations.

As already described, migrants who don't have a local *hukou* are denied equal access to the employment market in Beijing. Local government policies restrict people without local *hukou* to 271 types of jobs. Most of the jobs available to temporary migrants are in the informal sector. A logistic regression was used to isolate the factors that affect whether or not the migrants in the sample had a job in the formal sector. Migrants' *hukou* status, sex, ethnicity, age, education level were used in the analysis.

Table 8.4 Logistic regression coefficients of whether migrants had a job in the formal sector in Beijing

Variables	Co-efficient	Standard error	Significance
Hukou (locally registered=1)	1.0436	0.3572	**
Sex (male=1)	0.2913	0.3493	
Ethnicity (Han=1)	0.3071	0.3442	
Age	0.0718	0.0177	**
Education (higher education=1)	1.3744	0.3274	**
Constant	-4.6850	0.6534	

Note: The dependent variable is whether the migrant has a job in the formal sector in Beijing. Jobs in formal sectors include jobs as professional/technician, managers, and clerk, which are coded as 1, otherwise as 0. ** significant at $p<0.05$.

Source: Data from *Sample Survey of Ethnic Minority Migration (1997-98).*

The result shows that migrants' *hukou* status, age and education level had a significant effect on whether the migrant had a job in the formal sector in

Beijing, while migrants' gender and ethnicity did not have any significant effects. Compared with temporary migrants, permanent migrants were more likely to have a job in the formal sector in Beijing. Local government regulations that restrict temporary migrants' access to the formal labour market have no doubt played a role in shaping the occupational pattern of the sampled population. The results confirm that *hukou* remains an important factor in determining migrants, access to formal job markets in Beijing, even when the factor of ethnicity is considered. Minorities' access to jobs in the formal sector does not differ significantly from that of Han migrants if their *hukou* status in Beijing is the same. In other words, when these two institutions, ethnicity and *hukou*, are considered at the same time, the role of *hukou* in determining migrants' access to the formal job market is more significant. As described above, the majority of migrants are of prime labour force participation age. If all other factors are the same, younger migrants are less likely to access the formal job market than older migrants. Migrants' educational level was also significant in that a migrant with vocational school level and above was more likely to be in the formal sector.

To further understand migrants' economic well-being, the relationship between migrants' income and other associated factors was analysed using logit regression analysis. Migrants' monthly income after migration was used as the dependent variable (having a monthly income above 800 yuan or not) and six independent variables were: migrants' *hukou* status in Beijing (locally registered or not), sex, ethnicity (Han or non-Han background), occupation (in formal sector or not), age and educational level (having a higher than vocational school education or not).

Table 8.5 Logistic regression coefficients of whether a migrant has a higher income

Variable	Coefficient	Standard error	Significance
Hukou (locally registered=1)	0.1431	0.3575	
Sex (male=1)	1.0604	0.2968	**
Ethnicity (Han=1)	1.0076	0.2884	**
Occupation (formal sector jobs=1)	-0.0978	0.3403	
Age	0.0310	0.0154	**
Education (higher education=1)	-0.2581	0.2866	
Constant	-2.4448	0.4924	

Notes: Personal monthly income after moving is used in the analysis. Monthly income 800 yuan and above is categorised as high income, coded as 1, and lower than 800 yuan as low, coded as 0. ** significant at $p<0.05$.

Source: Data from *Sample Survey of Ethnic Minority Migration (1997-98)*.

Results from this analysis show that migrants' gender, ethnicity and age had significant effects on their personal income after migration. When other variables were held constant, a male migrant had a higher chance of earning more than 800 yuan a month. Ethnicity shows some significant effects on income in that a Han migrant had a relatively greater possibility of earning a high income than a minority migrant. Minorities' reduced likelihood of earning a high income may reflect their difficulties in adjusting to the predominantly Han society in Beijing, even though they are equally capable of landing a job in formal sectors compared with their Han counterparts. Age was another significant variable that had an effect on migrants' income. A younger migrant was more likely to earn a higher income than an older one. Surprisingly, *hukou* status, which was expected to have a significant effect on people's income, did not show up. The analysis in the previous sections shows that *hukou* is often a very important factor in determining whether migrants received any help from others, including whether they are able to land a job in formal sectors. When migrants' income is concerned, it seems that *hukou* does not have any significant impacts. This seemingly contradictory result indicates *hukou*'s limited effects on migrants' well-being in today's more market-oriented economic system in China. On the one hand, *hukou* determines the likelihood of migrants' access to jobs in formal sectors which may also partially determine their benefits and rights in Beijing, such as job security or subsidised housing. A migrant with a local *hukou* is more likely to access a job in the formal sectors. On the other hand, *hukou* does not effect income level. A migrant who does not have a local *hukou* may not necessarily earn less than what a migrant with a local *hukou* earns. When their *hukou* status is the same, a Han migrant is more likely to earn a monthly income higher than 800 yuan compared with their minority counterparts. Ethnicity shows significant effects on well-being when personal income is concerned.

Social/personal aspects of migration for the sample

Migration is a means of pursuing economic gains, residential satisfaction and an improvement in social and economic status. The majority of migrants in the sample felt that their current economic status was average or above average level. While more than 90 per cent of Han migrants in the sampled population regarded their economic status in Beijing as average or above, about 78 per cent of minority migrants had the same perception. Among minority migrants, about 75 per cent claimed that their current economic status was better than that of other migrants in Beijing. Less Han migrants felt this way. The results suggest that the majority of minority migrants were able to satisfactorily pursue their economic objectives in Beijing and compared with Han migrants, minority migrants were no worse off in terms of both economic performance and self-perception. It is encouraging that the majority of migrants felt that their current economic status was at average and above average level, regardless of their ethnic background.

In the current conditions in China, pursuing residential satisfaction through migration is not realistic for many migrants in urban areas as the urban housing market is simply not an option for them. Urban residents are allocated their apartments through their work units and the ownership of apartments is still largely in the hands of either work units or the state. Only recently, with the housing reform, have urban people been able to purchase apartments or houses either from the private market at very high prices or from their employers at subsidised prices. Those migrants who don't have formal employment status or *hukou* status, are unable to purchase subsidised housing at affordable prices. Results from our survey show that more than half the Han migrants in the sample rented places from private owners, 24 per cent lived in work unit provided housing, and the rest either borrowed from other people or obtained housing through other sources. Compared with Han migrants, minority migrants were better off in terms of access to public housing. More than half (52.9 per cent) the ethnic minority migrants lived in work unit provided housing, about 38 per cent rented places and only a small proportion (8.9 per cent) had to rely on other sources.

Being able to save some money to send or take back home for a house is often regarded as a feasible objective for many migrants. While 70 per cent of Han migrants reported that they were able to save some of their earnings in Beijing less than 40 per cent of ethnic minority migrants claimed the same. For minority migrants, therefore, having an average or above average economic status did not mean they were able to save. Another possibility is that people were sending money straight back home and this did not show up as savings.

Among all migrants in Beijing, 98 per cent claimed that their health status was either average or above average. This is partially due to the young age structure of the sample migrant population. More than 80 per cent were younger than 40 years old and most of them were in the labour force participation ages. Migration is a selective process in which only those who are capable of moving and surviving at the place of destination will go. Those who are not capable of this will either not move or would have returned to their original place. The fact that the majority of migrants claimed that they were in good health does not necessarily indicate that they have access to health care services in Beijing. Fieldwork in Beijing and the above outline show that migrants' access to urban facilities, including affordable housing, school and health care, is very limited. The urban health care system is designed to meet the needs of employees of urban work units. Without employment status with a formal work unit, it is difficult for migrants to access affordable health care services.

Relationship of the sample population to the local community

The conditions that are conducive to 'successful' resettlement, including harmonious interaction with the host community, are not easily defined. Some of the factors that are seen to be important are: whether there is any cultural compatibility between migrants and the local population; public opinion; whether the receiving society aspires to assimilation or pluralism; the occupational and social skills of the migrants, and whether a community of migrants from the same source already exists (Robinson 1999, p. xxvii). To this set of general factors the policy environment must be added, especially in China.

Contact between migrants and members of the host community is an important step for migrants to integrate or assimilate to the host society. The results from the survey show that more than half of the minority migrants in the sample claimed that they mainly use their own ethnic language and about one third were able to use both their own language and *Putonghua* (official spoken language) in their daily life. Interestingly, only a small fraction (1 per cent) of minority migrants claimed that *Putonghua* was their first language. All Han Chinese in the sample claim that their first language was *Putonghua*. The continuation of ethnic minorities' languages is clear from the results of the sample. The bilingual or multi-lingual ability of some ethnic minority migrants indicates the possibility of interaction with the host community in Beijing.

The results also show that the most popular form of recreational activity among the sampled population was watching TV. More than one third of both Han and minority migrants spent their leisure time in this way. Going to movies and reading were also popular among migrants. This pattern is typical of many Beijingers. In terms of who they mix with, a large proportion (91 per cent) of minority migrants said that they communicated with people of other nationalities while less than 70 per cent of Han migrants communicated with people from other nationalities. This difference is understandable since Beijing is largely a Han society. On the surface, the data indicate a high level of interaction between minority migrants and the dominant Han but the nature and depth of this interaction cannot be detected from the survey.

THE IMPACTS OF MINORITY MIGRATION ON BEIJING

The socio-economic impacts of minority movement to Beijing include not only the consequences of migration for the city, its economic structure and its inhabitants, but also the impacts on the migrant communities themselves and their relationships with both Beijing inhabitants and the people who remain at home. The focus here is on the social and economic life of Beijing and on the way in which the minority groups establish their living and working spaces. The contemporary movement of minority migrants also has political consequences and these will be touched upon.

The movement of minorities into Beijing is, in some ways, not very different from the movement of Han from other provinces. They are all affected by government policy in that it is an explicit determiner of class order — that is, people with urban *hukou* get access to services and those without do not, on the whole. Unless, of course, migrants have the connections (*guangxi*) or money to purchase an urban *hukou*[7] or to exist well without it. Solinger (1995, p. 120) argues that:

> the 'ethnic' division in the eyes of the localistic — and, in response even to their fellow non-local Chinese, one might go so far as to say xenophobic — Chinese, is chiefly defined by place of origin. In these terms certainly extra-provincialities but even rural people from the same province are viewed as foreign.

Floaters are commonly referred to as 'country bumpkins' because of their skin colour, dress or dialect. As a consequence of this social and political differentiation many cities, including Beijing, have an array of 'villages' housing out-of-towners. This is not to say that some migrants have not merged into the general community and become difficult to locate. Some 'villages' are governed by their own special 'co-ethnic' chiefs who mediate the negotiations between residents and local authorities. Solinger (1995, p. 122) argues that this tendency segments the migrants as well as cutting them off from the stable urban population and thus it is 'a force that obstructs integration, and possibly mobility too for the ex-peasant residents of cities'. While acknowledging that Solinger's arguments still stand to a large extent today, we have started to see changes in some migrant communities in China. Although the majority of migrants in cities, particularly those with a rural origin, are not able to integrate into city life and are not able to climb the ladder of the city hierarchy, some migrants do progress out of their very marginalised position and eventually become wealthy business people.

Xiang's ground-breaking work in Beijing highlights variations in the nature and operation of villages in Beijing. Villages are named either after the province of origin (though in fact people may come from only one village in that province) or the major product that the peasants deal with. There are four major 'villages' in Beijing though they are not necessarily concentrated in space — Anhui (vegetable vending, rubbish collection and domestic and cleaning work), Henan (rubbish collection), Xinjiang (food stalls and restaurants) and Zhejiang (clothing manufacturing). There is also 'eyeglass

---

[7] According to Solinger (1999, p. 91), the fee for a Beijing urban *hukou* in the centre of the city was about 100 000 yuan in the mid-1990s.

village' (peasants from Dongyan, Zhejiang and Zhangjiagang, Jiangsu) and 'lumber village' (peasants from Putian, Fujian) in the eastern suburbs, and Enjizhuang area in the west where migrants from Wenling, Zhejiang are concentrated, and sell plastic products. The two Xinjiang villages, where Uyghurs have concentrated, are the only two 'truly ethnic enclaves' in Beijing (Xiang 1999, p. 63).

Xiang (1999, p. 10) describes Zhejiang village, which consists of 14 000 Pekingese and 96 000 migrants, as the largest such 'village' in any Chinese city. It actually consists of 26 'natural villages' whose residents are still legally peasants though they have transferred from agriculture to the garment industry. It is not only a community, with the usual (poor) water, sanitation and public facilities, but it is a 'business space ... embedded in a national and even an international network'. In 1995, official sales of garments to northeastern and northern China as well as overseas (especially Russia, Mongolia and eastern Europe) amounted to 1.5 million yuan (US $300 000). The village started in the 1970s and in the last decade has moved from being merely a destination for migrants to work to a more complete community.

Plate 8.1 Henan village rubbish collectors in Beijing, 1997 (Photo by Xiang Biao)

New enterprises have emerged, such as a kindergarten in 1988, a food marketplace in 1989 and clinics, barber shops and repair shops since 1990. Most notable is the construction of a number of very large retailing outlets. From 1992, rich migrants began to pool their savings and invested in the building of 'big courtyards' (*dayuan*), in cooperation with the local administrative bodies. These courtyards, which are supplied with water, electricity, sewerage systems, postal services and educational and recreational facilities, accommodated about 30 000 migrants in 1998. The courtyard owners also manage public security that is normally a function of local government administrators. The patronage networks open to members of the Zhejiang village have been built up over time and are obviously very good to have enabled the structures that now exist to be built. Money has obviously been an important element in enabling Zhejiang villagers in Beijing to buy permission to build and operate their businesses. The level of graft and corruption and the opportunities available to officials to make money from in-migrants are well documented by Solinger (1999).

> In the words of the migrants, these courtyards were built by people with 'money, influence and prestige' ... Government organizations at different levels and lots of people of the municipality have all been involved in one way or the other in the interaction with this community. (Xiang 1998, p. 14)

Although not fully integrated into the life of Beijing, Zhejiang village provides an example of a migrant community that may be able to survive well, outside of the space of the state and formal institutions in Chinese cities. Given the size of the community and the scale of its production in the garment industry, the impacts of Zhejiang village on Beijing cannot be easily ignored. Has the same thing happened to Uyghurs in the Xinjiang village? Have they received the same patronage and access to the structures of power or have they relied on their own ethnic network to build up their businesses in Beijing? How do they fare in Beijing society and are they accepted in the same way as the Zhejiang villagers? Or are they treated more like people in the Henan and Anhui villages who tend to be more loosely connected to the urban society, except in their functions as trash collectors or vegetable sellers? How do Mongolians and Tibetans interact with Beijing society and the economy? Do they congregate together and do they have a sense of community among themselves?

INTEGRATION AND SEPARATION IN BEIJING

This section draws on a range of sources and fieldwork to compile a profile of the three minority communities under investigation. There is a very uneven balance between the picture provided for Uyghurs compared with that for Mongolians and Tibetans. The first reason for this is that little work has been done on the latter two populations in Beijing. Second, Mongolians are longer term residents of Beijing and many people assume that they have assimilated or integrated, through intermarriage, education and employment, and no longer exist as an identifiable group. This is largely the case, from our fieldwork, even though Mongolians and Han are culturally dissimilar. The long period of interaction in Inner Mongolia that was detailed in Chapter 5 has resulted in a high degree of mixing. Mongolians and Han are similar from a socio-economic point of view and there are no distinctly Mongolian jobs or businesses in Beijing. Moreover, Mongolians are held in high regard by the Han, on the whole, primarily because of their strong place in Chinese history. This has resulted in their getting educational and other resources that have not been available to other ethnic groups. Third, Tibetan movement into Beijing is relatively recent and mostly consists of temporary students and officials who are granted local *hukou* and live in small concentrations around the Himalaya Hotel in the western part of Beijing. Uyghurs represent the opposite in terms of their separate living spaces and economic activities, and they have been the subject of some study even though much of it is unpublished. The bulk of the material on Uyghurs and the Xinjiang villages is attributable to Caroline Hoy and Ren Qiang's work.

Minority communities in Beijing: Uyghurs as an example

The aim of this section is to outline and explore ways in which ethnic minority groups have attempted to integrate into Beijing, both socially and economically, and ways in which they have remained separate. We will concentrate on various socio-economic impacts: living space, commerce, education, food and marriage. It is to be hoped that wider lessons can be drawn from these identified subjects. The Uyghur community in Beijing is used as an example.

A mere 0.5 per cent of Beijing's minority population (1736 people) was registered as members of the Uyghur population in 1990. This was probably a significant underestimate of the number of Uyghurs in Beijing at the time as this is a highly mobile population and it is likely that many chose to be absent during the census period. The two Xinjiang villages are geographically compact with Xinjiang restaurants and food stalls and a distinct Uyghur atmosphere. Shop signs are in both Chinese and Uyghur languages and the restaurants, shish kebab, bread and fruit sellers now cater to a wide variety of customers. In fact, Hoy and Ren (1996) located respondents in six areas in total during their fieldwork: Ganjiakou, Haidian district; Weigongcun, Haidian district; Madian in Haidian District; Jintai Lu, Chaoyang district; Hepingli, Dongcheng district; and Tianqiao, Xianwu district. The first two are by far the largest. Local Han estimates of the number of Uyghurs living in Ganjiakou in 1997 were more than 1000 even though there were only 500 people who were temporarily registered and 700-800 in Weigongcun area (Xiang 1999). Hoy points out that concerns about the nature of the Uyghur population may also cause their numbers to be over-estimated at times. But an additional factor is that around 3000 people per year come to Beijing from Xinjiang to apply for a visa to go to Mecca (Xiang 1999, p. 64). The larger village, in Ganjiakou area, has around 27 restaurants (about one-third of the total number of Uyghur restaurants in Beijing) and five bakeries making Uyghur bread (*nang*). The smaller one has about 15 restaurants. There are two village chiefs in the Ganjiakou village, one appointed by the public security office of the district and who serves as the liaison between the village and the district government, and the other elected by the Uyghurs to handle their own internal affairs.

These two villages grew up in these areas because of the earlier need to house cooks from the Xiyuan Hotel (built in the 1950s to accommodate Chinese Muslims and the Beijing Office of the Xinjiang government) which is located nearby. The original cooks came as permanent migrants but later ones came on an informal basis. The cooks originally stayed in the hotel but as their numbers increased they moved to apartments built specifically for them in Ganjiakou and Weigongcun. The proximity of the Central Nationality University, where many Muslim students come to study, to Weigongcun also partly explains its growth. Young men also came and set up braziers on the sidewalks, selling shish kebabs. Live sheep were kept on the side of the road in Weigongcun area till the meat was needed for cooking. Local officials have now banned sidewalk braziers as they claim they are too polluting. The smoke from the coal fires was certainly a problem but it had enabled people to set up a small business without much capital. Recent observations in Beijing in 1999 indicate that many of these sidewalk vendors have now moved off the main streets into small lanes and shopfronts and they are selling a variety of Uyghur foods from a wider range of locations. So they have adjusted their businesses to the new laws. This pattern of infiltrating a city, or 'colonisation', is part of the Uyghur strategy of spreading out across China (Hoy and Ren 1999).

A high sex ratio exists among the Uyghur population (195 males to 100 females) indicating that differences in migration opportunities by sex are in operation. This is quite a common pattern but there are also regions in China where particular ethnic groups (such as the Miao) or particular streams are more heavily female (Iredale 2000). It is very common for young, unmarried men to migrate to Beijing, mostly from villages in southern Xinjiang, in order to obtain work experience for a couple of years and then return home to Xinjiang. One young Uyghur male, aged 20 and working in a restaurant, had decided that five years hence would be soon enough to marry and at that date he would return to Xinjiang in order to marry. He doubted that he would be able to return to Beijing, as his parents would be reluctant to let him do so. The owner of one restaurant outlined his recruitment procedure as following: if labour was needed word would be sent back to his village and the bus and train fares of recruits to Beijing would be paid for by the owner of the restaurant. Most of the restaurants are now owned by migrants from cities in Xinjiang, predominantly from Urumqi, the capital, and Kashi, in the far west of Xinjiang. The restaurateurs pay 250 to 900 yuan per month, with room and board provided by the owner (Xiang 1998, p. 7).

Marriage patterns, as recorded in the 1990 Census and outlined in Table 8.6, show that almost two thirds of Uyghur men and half of Uyghur women were single. The equivalent percentages amongst the Han and, for comparison, several minority populations, Hui, Manchu (Man), Kazak, Miao and Tujia, are also shown in the table. The Uyghur population lies towards one end of a spectrum of the proportion of single people in Beijing. Only the Kazak minority has a higher percentage of unmarried people. These patterns suggest that differing social strategies may be taking place between and within the minority populations. Anecdotal evidence, such as that supplied by the young restaurant worker discussed above, points to the use of Beijing as an 'escalator' region for younger members of the Uyghur population, especially males, who are expected to return to Xinjiang after a period of work experience or apprenticeship and marry with their parents' guidance. To a limited extent this may also be true of the females. However, as yet, there are no data available by which we can test this assumption.

Table 8.6 The unmarried population (15 and over) in selected nationalities in Beijing, 1990 (%)

Nationality	Male	Female
Uyghur	63.4	50.4
Han	44.4	17.9
Hui	23.1	17.7
Man	27.4	24.9
Kazak	69.8	64.4
Miao	52.1	46.1
Tujia	51.3	27.9

Source: State Population Census Office (1993, Volume 1, p. 176).

In 1990, 54 per cent of the recorded Uyghur population in Beijing were registered as employed: 58 per cent for men and 47 per cent for women. The majority of the Uyghur population was engaged in what the authorities defined as 'commerce, public catering trade, supply and marketing of commodities and storage' (State Population Census Office 1993, Vol. 4, p. 543). Smaller numbers worked in education and the arts, and in government or party-related posts. The commerce and food industries represent the most obvious manifestations of Uyghur industry in Beijing as the restaurants have a tendency to cluster around two or three areas in the city. But these businesses also have connections with others that are rather more hidden — for example, grape transportation from Xinjiang and the illicit drug trade. Uyghurs return to Xinjiang with clothes, fabrics and daily goods to sell. Beijing is not identified as a particularly important locale for Uyghurs, as pointed out in Chapter 6, but pressure for success exists and movement to Beijing is part of the wider expansion of Uyghur interests. The pattern of 'colonisation', whereby small braziers are followed by smaller then larger groups of inhabitants, is an important strategy and it has been used in Beijing to link the city into a wider system of trade routes (Hoy and Ren 1999, p. 13).

Uyghurs and their relationship with Beijing society

The social relationships between migrants and Beijingers and with other migrants are very important. Intermarriage, one indicator of interaction, is a common phenomenon in many societies subject to migration. The question of whether intermarriage has increased in China as a result of increased mobility has not yet been answered (Fan and Huang 1998, Lee 1998). Marriages between people of different ethnic origins present a slightly more complex case. The assimilation of the Hui, a second Muslim minority in China, has been explained with reference to intermarriage with the Han. Jankowiak (1993) argues that the subject of intermarriage is a sensitive one and one which is affected by the demographic structure of ethnic groups in particular places and whether a mate of the desired ethnic group is available. The acceptability or otherwise of intermarriage may also have been influenced by government policy which has promoted positive discrimination for members of ethnic minorities and meant that members of the Han community marrying into minority communities are more likely to accept that their children are brought up within the minority's heritage. But it seems that the attractions of positive discrimination identified in some areas (e.g. Hohhot) are not necessarily shared by the residents of other areas. For example, Gladney (1998) argues that the ethno-religious revival in China among the Muslim population has ensured that the Muslim populations continue to be perceived as 'other' in Chinese society, negating any form of social interaction, let alone the kind of permanent one marriage would offer.

In previous sections we identified locations in which members of the Uyghur ethnic population were living and it is worth returning to the subject of location as sites in which migrants gather, especially if they have achieved a high profile within the city such as the Uyghurs in Ganjiakou or migrants from Zhejiang based in Big Red Gate in Fengtai in southern Beijing. A common factor in urban minority villages appears to be the general lack of household space. From information supplied it appears that Uyghur migrants accept a decline in living standards in terms of available space: those who remain in Xinjiang live in an average of 4.5 rooms while those in Beijing inhabit an average of two. It also seems that migrants from Xinjiang live in more crowded conditions than Han migrants from other parts of China and also live in larger co-resident groups compared to Han migrants. While some may prefer to live in close association with friends and family, such cramped conditions are also a reflection of the space made grudgingly available in Beijing. Many people, especially men, are the only members of their family in Beijing and are accommodated in already cramped living quarters with friends, family or in hostels (Hoy 1996).

Like the Zhejiang village or Big Red Gate area in the south, little or no planning has taken place as the Xinjiang village areas have grown. Individual restaurant owners have made improvements to their own restaurants, such as paint, pictures, televisions etc. Ma and Xiang (1998) noted the reluctance of Beijing authorities to improve conditions in this and other migrant villages across Beijing and suggest that any improvements may be interpreted as an invitation for more migrants to come to Beijing. We have seen, however, that improvements have been permitted and in fact supported in Zhejiang village. Ma and Xiang (1998 p. 567) also note that given 'the sensitive political issues related to the Uyghurs a larger Uyghur base in the capital would certainly not be in the best interests of the local or national government'.

Plate 8.2 Xinjiang street, Beijing, 1997 (Photo by Xiang Biao)

Plate 8.3 Uyghur restauranteurs, Xinjiang village, Beijing, 1997 (Photo by R. Iredale)

A high profile tends to attract the attention of the city government and can result in severe measures against the targeted population. This first occurred with the razing of 'Zhejiang village' in southern Beijing in 1995-96. The Beijing City Committee moved over 18 000 people, nearly 10 000 buildings were demolished and many stalls cleared away. Solinger (1999, p. 86) maintains that in total 100 000 people were affected. The Zhejiang village issue had been considered at the highest levels, notably by the then Premier, Li Peng. The task of razing the village proved to be the responsibility of the Beijing Public Security Bureau not the local authority of the Big Red Gate area in which Zhejiang village was based. The operation involved over 5000 cadres and 3000 police and armed police for two months in December to January, 1995-96. This was a large operation in which the CPC put great emphasis on successful implementation. It is clear that the government felt threatened by the scale of the village as it housed some 37 000 migrants who worked under less than desirable conditions and churned out fake brand-name products. Tax evasion was also a problem as were criminal offences, and the huge size of the population reportedly presented severe medical problems.

This razing was repeated when one area of Uyghur restaurants was demolished in the west of Beijing in March 1999, ahead of the 50th Anniversary of the founding of the Republic. Despite pleas from the owners and claims of their contribution to the city the action went ahead. The official reason giving for clearing the village was that a new highway was to go through the area. But it has been suggested that the razing measure was part of a larger agenda on the part of the Beijing government to see many migrants deported from Beijing and the areas they have made their own destroyed (Kuhn 1999). One restaurant owner was quoted as saying 'We may not be Beijingers but we are Chinese and we have rights ... the truth is that they just don't want a Xinjiang village in Beijing'. It appears that Beijing residents and officials felt that the government had lost control over these areas and that they had become centres of vice (Kuhn 1999). It is also notable that the Chinese government has become concerned about increasing levels of violence in Xinjiang and the razing of Uyghur areas in Beijing may be part of an effort to send messages to secessionists that ideas of separateness whether expressed through violence in Xinjiang or discrete areas of inhabitation and economic activity in Beijing, will not be tolerated. However, the razing of one concentration of Uyghurs in Beijing has led to their dispersal not their elimination. Restaurants and shops have mostly moved elsewhere and it is unlikely that people have returned to Xinjiang.

Plate 8.4 Uyghur woman preparing food in Xinjiang village, Beijing, 1997 (Photo by Xiang Biao)

Plate 8.5 Uyghurs socialising in Xinjiang village, Beijing, 1997 (Photo by R. Iredale)

Uyghurs remain very separate from the Beijing population. Hoy and Ren (1999) found a sense of hostility identifiable on both sides. Most Uyghur economic dealings are with Han migrants, with the latter being used as a buffer between Uyghurs and the wider Han residential community. Uyghurs maintain the social structure of their origin and their interaction with other minority groups is limited. Intermarriages between Uyghurs and others are very rare, a point illustrated with a Uyghur proverb: *Shan Han, mie Hui* or 'kill the Han and destroy the Hui'. Among Uyghurs interviewed in Beijing there was only one case of inter-nationality marriage. The wife was a Uyghur from Xinjiang and her husband was a Hui, who was originally born in Gansu but who had moved to Xinjiang while still an infant. On the other hand, one individual remarked that in principle there was no reason why there should not be marriages between the Beijing population and the Uyghurs but 'Beijing people were Beijing people and the Uyghur people were a minority; there would be no objection if they were willing, but generally it does not happen'. It is likely that any marriage between a Uyghur and a Beijing resident would face significant problems of acceptance.

The Uyghur inhabitants of the Xinjiang villages do not have the same sort of political patronage as the Zhejiang villagers even though they also pay money to set up and maintain their businesses. There is much more fear and anxiety promulgated about the dangers of entering Xinjiang villages

in Beijing and signs have been erected by the local police bureau about the
danger of pickpockets. The present authors are not aware of similar signs
being erected in any other parts of Beijing. On the whole, Uyghurs are much
more marginalised and they are excluded from the wider society not only by
factors such as their lack of urban *hukou* but also by clear signs of ethnic or
race discrimination. Thus while all in-migrants are marginalised there is a
hierarchy in this marginalism. Solinger (1999, p. 242) states that those at the
'top of the hierarchy of noncitizens benefited from having cash or other
capital, a well-endowed community, and most of all, informal connections
with state cadres; those progressively lower down the social pyramid lacked
some or all of these sources of strength'. She does not cover ethnic minorities
in cities and therefore ignores the impact of ethnic difference on
marginalisation.

*Plate 8.6 Police sign warning about pickpockets, Xinjiang village, Beijing,
1997 (Photo by Xiang Biao)*

Castles and Miller (1998, pp. 232-3) point out that 'phenological difference
may coincide with recent arrival, with cultural distance, with socio-economic
position, or, finally, it may serve as a target for racism'. Any of these may
provide the explanation for the extreme marginalisation of certain ethnic
minorities but the most significant explanation lies in 'practices of exclusion
by the majority populations and States'. In the case of Uyghurs in Beijing,
they are more recent arrivals and they are culturally quite different from the
majority of the residents of Beijing. But these explanations are not the full
story. The political sensitivities surrounding Uyghurs in China are very great.

Moreover, there is a great deal of suspicion about their activities and they are frequently accused of having high crime rates in theft, trafficking in drugs, involvement in underground activities, and generally being a threat to urban public security. Harassment, either by officials or the public generally, tends to reinforce further their ethnic minority formation and forces them into defensive strategies. Racism 'may lead to various types of self-organisation and separatism' (Castles and Miller 1998) and for Uyghurs in Beijing this appears to be the case. Stopping this unwanted migration to Beijing is impossible and the development of strategies for the social and economic incorporation of Uyghurs would be much more productive. Education is one way in which this may happen and the following analysis will look at how ethnic minorities have been integrated into Beijing's education systems.

MINORITIES AND EDUCATION IN BEIJING

The role of education as a means of achieving social and occupational mobility, especially for ethnic minorities, has already been discussed in Chapter 3 and the previous case study chapters. In Beijing this has operated in two ways. First, mobility for education in Beijing (and elsewhere) is one means of raising the education level of ethnic minority groups, and preferential or affirmative action policies have been used to provide educational opportunities in Beijing. This is especially the case for regions where there is no University for Nationalities, such as Inner Mongolia and Xinjiang. On the other hand, many people realise that educational opportunities are much better in Beijing and part of their reason for moving may be to access these better facilities for themselves or for their children. Beijing is undisputedly the education capital of China and it operates as a magnet for people aspiring to higher levels of education, in particular. This is evidenced in the number of students enrolled in higher education per 10 000 inhabitants. The figure for Beijing is 355 compared to 173 for Shanghai, the next highest, and 151 for Tianjin (Department of Development and Planning 1999, p. 68). Enrolments per 10 000 inhabitants in specialised secondary schools are also higher than elsewhere. At the general senior level, Shanghai outnumbers Beijing but in vocational schools the two are on an equal par for first.

Almost one third of the sample interviewed gave education as the reason for moving to Beijing, with Tibetans and Uyghurs having the highest proportions. For Tibetans this is approved migration for education and training purposes. As we saw in Chapter 6, there is also 'official' migration for attendance at middle school. For Uyghurs it is not approved and people may give education as their reason when the real reason is broader. The fact that two Uyghurs had local *hukou* and only one out of 99 was a student indicates that education is regarded more widely than formal schooling. Planned migrants who have local *hukou* and are formal members of the city enjoy compulsory education in nearby schools. In Beijing except for some nationality schools, such as Korean nationality schools, Chinese and formal textbooks issued by the People's Educational Publishing House are used. Consequently most official minority migrants and non-migrants send their children to nearby schools where they learn alongside of Han children.

The popular perception is that many children of migrants do not attend school because parents treat the matter lightly or cannot afford the education. On the contrary, many minority migrant parents emphasise the importance of educating their children and make special efforts to get their children into schools. Without a Beijing *hukou* of two years standing, parents must pay a minimum of 480 yuan per year, as well as an additional fee which depends on the quality of the school, to get their child enrolled.[8] Our sample contained mostly single people but for Uyghurs in general Hoy (1996) found that this emphasis was often prompted by a pragmatic understanding of the importance of China to the economy of the Uyghurs. Uyghur parents feel that their children should be thoroughly grounded in both Uyghur and Chinese society, with the emphasis firmly on the ability to speak fluently in both Chinese and Uyghur. Gladney (1990) has documented that many parents feel that opportunities for becoming fully bilingual while attending school in Xinjiang are few and this could prejudice a child's later chances of social mobility and economic interaction in the Chinese speaking world. A better education for their children is clearly one motivation for migration.

But they often face considerable opposition in Beijing to their children being enrolled. One Uyghur interviewed used personal connections to get her elder child into a school in Beijing at a reduced fee of 700 yuan per year. A second child attended the same school at the full fee of 1200 yuan. Another couple took action after their children were refused access to a school. They had brought their children to Beijing when it became clear that no-one would be available to look after the children in Xinjiang. The Beijing school which the parents identified as suitable refused to take the children due, they claimed, to the children's poor understanding of Chinese. After the parents took legal action the school agreed to educate the children on the condition that they pass an entrance examination. The two elder children failed the examination and had to remain at home but the younger child passed and was put into the first grade, though by age he should have been in the third grade. The parents paid the school 1000 yuan each year for his education. The nature of the examination used is not known nor is it open to scrutiny. Decisions about enrolments are in the hands of the principals. Also the educational disadvantage that has been experienced by children is used as a reason for

---

[8] Even Han Chinese with a Beijing *hukou* must pay 10 000 to 30 000 yuan, depending on the quality of the school, for the six years of primary schooling.

excluding them rather than being used to make special provision to enrol them. It appears that prejudice is at work here as children are rejected on the basis of their ethnicity not their inability to pay.

In the case of Tibetans, a large proportion of our sample were officials whose children have gained access to local schools by dint of their having a Beijing *hukou*. A Tibetan school, operated by the Beijing government, exists in Beijing to provide for the children of these officials as well as for other children who are sent from Tibet to board at the school. Another twelve such schools exist in major cities of China. There are no Mongolian schools in Beijing and all Mongolians in the sample who had their children in school had them in mainstream schools.

Those who cannot gain access to Beijing's public schools may be forced to enrol their children in private schools. In some concentrations of migrants, there are a few private schools run by local citizens. These schools operate as small home schools where the teachers are all old teachers who have retired from public schools. There are some very expensive private boarding schools for wealthy pupils but these are not located in centres where migrants have concentrated.

As we saw in Urumqi, Xinjiang, local education officials had set up special schools for migrant children without *hukou* on the outskirts of the city. These schools are similar to other public schools but only migrant children are enrolled. These schools solve the problem of migrants' children attending school and are a good measure. Even though it is recognised that 'well educated children will in the near future make a better contribution and be less trouble to the locality', no such schools have been set up in Beijing (Wang 2000, p. 9).

One option that has emerged in Beijing is that migrants have set up schools by and for themselves in areas of heavy migrant concentrations, especially where house prices are low and most houses are temporarily built in farmland or unused suburban fields. These people cannot afford to send their children to public or expensive private schools. Migrants who have been educated in high schools and middle schools may establish primary schools. Many of the teachers were originally teachers in hometown schools or have other experience. The schools, though not formally licensed by local districts, are agreed to by local authorities and migrants. These private schools want less money than public ones, about 60 yuan ($7 dollars) per month, which migrants can easily afford even for two children. The textbooks they use are either the same as in Beijing public schools or the same as those of the province that they originated from.

Almost every migrant centre in Beijing has this type of school. For example, at Wukesong region of Haidian district in Beijing, there are three schools of this type for some thirty thousand rural migrants. On the whole, these schools are not formally managed, and have bad conditions, are short of necessary equipment and do not reach the standards laid down by the government. The education identity (attainment) cards of the pupils may not be acknowledged by other schools or universities for further education purposes. In spite of these difficulties, this is regarded as a common way in Beijing of successfully overcoming the problem of education for migrant children and what is needed is to support them and standardise them quickly (Wang 2000, pp. 9-10). There is no such school for Uyghur children even though it is reported that a private Muslim school has emerged in Beijing for Hui children.

The Xingzhi school is unique in that it was the first such school to be set up and it has attracted considerable attention and funds. Most migrant children's schools do not get the same attention and they teach in simple, crude houses. Many of them teach lessons to only four grades and they do it in shifts or they put pupils of different grades and ages together. The curricula are more casual and lessons are conducted in Chinese and arithmetic only.

CASE STUDY OF XINGZHI MIGRANT CHILDREN'S SCHOOL IN BEIJING [9]

Xingzhi school is situated in LiangJia village of Haidian district. It was established on 1 September 1994 by a migrant named Li-Sumei who was a teacher in peasant schools before migrating to Beijing. As outlined in Chapter 3, there are two kinds of teachers — official or formal teachers and *minban* teachers. The former enjoy welfare benefits and cannot be discharged but they must have teacher training. Because of the shortage of official teachers in rural areas, *minban* or peasant teachers exist and they have few rights and poor conditions. Li-Sumei was a peasant teacher for ten years in Xi county, Henan. She was not permitted to become a formal teacher and she became angry, left the school and came to Beijing. Li-Sumei had eight brothers who were migrants to Beijing and they had many children who were not attending school. Before long she started teaching the children words and arithmetic and soon neighbours also began sending their children to her. Gradually, the number of children increased and she established a temporary house in a very small vegetable plot in Wukesong area, Haidian district. At first, it was a simple school and she was

---

[9] Tao-Xingzhi is the name of a well known teacher and educationalist in modern China who called for the setting up of schools all over the country. He advocated teaching the common people.

the only teacher but the number of pupils increased and word spread. In October 1995, after just one year of operation it became too busy for one woman to manage and her husband resigned his job in their hometown and came to Beijing to help her.

TEACHERS

By 2000 the school had developed into a large primary school with six grades and 1336 pupils from 24 provinces and regions. In addition, there was a small junior middle school with two grades and 66 students. There were seven nationalities in the schools, including Han, Manchu, Mongol, Hui, Uyghur, Miao and Daur. Most of them were Han so the teaching language was Chinese. The school had 62 teachers and other subsidiary workers. One quarter of them had been trained in teacher colleges or universities and the remainder mostly had senior middle school education. Most, 80 per cent, came from outside Beijing. The school hires teachers through door-knocking and introductions and by issuing advertisements. Teachers' wages are from 500 to 1000 yuan per month, which is in the middle level income range for Beijing, and the school also provides accommodation and food. These conditions are favourable to students who have just graduated from universities and senior middle schools but there is a high turnover of staff. As most of them do not come from a Teachers University or teacher training schools, most teachers lack experience. They do not have knowledge about the psychology of children and they especially lack training in subjects such as music, physical training and art. There are five important universities in Beijing — Beijing University, Beijing Teachers' University, Capital Teachers' University, China Center of Finance and Economics University, and China Youth Politics College — and they are all sending some students to the school as temporary volunteers to teach music, art and physical training. These volunteers are not only getting knowledge and experience but they are also helping the school to overcome the shortage of teachers. The school also invites good teachers from nearby schools to give lessons to its teachers about teaching methods as well as sending some teachers to nearby schools for training. These activities all enhance the quality of teachers but there is still a great difference between public schools and this school in respect of teachers' attitudes to their occupation and pupils' educational experiences. In public schools pupils learn to think independently but in this school teachers mainly teach from the textbook.

CURRICULUM

There is almost no difference between Xingzhi school and nearby public schools in curriculum and other activities. Its curriculum includes Chinese, mathematics, music, physical training and art, and extra-curricula activities are similar. The textbooks used are the official textbooks decided by the Education Department. The school has similar examinations to local schools and uses test papers from nearby public schools for final examinations. In this way Xingzhi school officials can both check on pupils' learning progress and evaluate any differences with public schools, so as to change or improve teaching arrangements. They have good relations and cooperation with nearby public schools, such as Yingding Street school, Railway Teacher's subsidiary school, Liangmajia school.

FUNDS

As with many schools, funds are a major problem. There are two sources of funds for the school, tuition fees and donations. Tuition fees are only 300 yuan per term, which is well below other public schools' financial allocation from the government, the tuition fee of public schools for migrant children or other private schools for citizens' children. It is estimated that after deducting all other expenses the average migrant saves 1000-3000 yuan per year so even these low tuition fees are still a substantial amount for them to find. In China, donations to schools are comparatively rare but reports in the mass media about the school led to a couple of American Chinese donating 200 000 yuan in 1996. A charitable institution in Hong Kong also donated 100 000 yuan and there are teachers, doctors, entrepreneurs and family nurses on the donation list.

In spite of these developments, for many migrant parents there is still no possibility of enrolling their children in a Beijing school. In early 1998, the central government made a policy announcement in relation to the provision of education for the children of 'floaters'. The 'Provisional Method of Migrant Children Going to School' is a national strategy for improving access to education for the children of floating migrants. In Beijing it has not led to any new developments so far but rather to authorities allowing existing migrant schools to continue to operate on their own.

Attendance at a Beijing school can have unexpected results, the most obvious of which is a change in the language of communication between parents and children. Several Uyghur children were observed speaking to their parents in Chinese rather than Uyghur. For this reason as well as the difficulty of enrolling children in local schools many Han and minority nationalities feel that they can't get a good school education for their children in big cities and so many of them send their children back home. This particularly seems to be the case for minorities, most of whose children are sent back in order to receive an education in their own language and culture. The expense of supporting pupils is very high for migrants and it seems that if there are people willing to care for children back home (especially boys as education is still often subject to gender bias among minorities) they will be sent home for several years to ensure fluency in their language. Also, for Uyghurs, a comprehensive inculcation of history and tradition remains important.

CONCLUSION

Little legislation exists outside the PRC's constitution for protecting migrant rights. Zhang *et al.* (1998) maintain that Shenzhen has moved on from regulations governing migrants to the 'rights' of migrants. Shenzhen, in Guangdong, was one of the earliest regions of China to develop and open up to the outside world and is often seen as the leader in social change. Compared with the Beijing Regulations for Out-coming Labourers and Personnel, Shenzhen now has more concrete rules about the rights of in-coming labourers and fewer concrete rules about the requirements of in-coming labourers. This may be the way forward in the future but for the moment Beijing, and most cities in China, are still focussed on how to control unwanted in-migrants (without urban *hukou*). Most come from poor areas, they can't get access to many jobs and either compete with locals for low skill jobs or get jobs in the informal sector. They are denied access to most urban services unless they have the money or connections to buy *hukou* or access.

Findings from our survey and other sources suggest that to a certain extent the movement of minorities into Beijing is not fundamentally different from the movement of Han from other provinces. As a big city as well as the country's capital, Beijing is very attractive to people from other provinces. Permanent movement to Beijing, however, has been strictly controlled in the past decades. The movement of ethnic minorities was sometimes organised and supported by governments in various ways, such as recruiting students from minority regions (who would eventually return to their regions) and training ethnic minority officials in Beijing. In the recently emerged massive voluntary migration process, largely driven by market forces, ethnic minorities seem to be following a similar pattern to that of Han migrants. As we have seen, institutional factors, especially the household registration (*hukou*) system, still have significant effects on the migration process and migrants' occupational status. A permanent migrant (who is able to have a local *hukou* registration) is less likely to rely on traditional personal networks and is more likely to land a job in formal sector. *Hukou* also determines whether migrants have access to public housing and other facilities and services in Beijing.

While sharing many similarities, ethnic minorities differ from Han migrants in that minorities are more likely to rely on help from their social and personal network in the migration process and they are less likely to land a job in the formal sector. However, minority migrants in Beijing are somehow worse-off than their Han counterparts in terms of economic well-being. The survey results suggest that minorities are less likely to have a high income compared to Han. Migrants from other provinces, especially those from rural origins, are often seen as 'foreign' by local residents in urban areas. All migrants are 'minorities' compared with local residents but ethnic minority migrants in Chinese cities appear to bear a 'double minorities' image, both in terms of their ethnic background and their residence status.

Article 4 of the constitution of the PRC states that 'All nationalities in the People's Republic of China are equal. The state protects the lawful rights and interests of the minority nationalities and upholds and develops a relationship of equality, unity and mutual assurance among all of China's nationalities. Discrimination against and oppression of any nationality is prohibited; any act which undermines the unity of the nationalities or instigates division is prohibited'. But the case study of Uyghurs in Beijing shows that this ethnic group has a very different profile and level of integration in Beijing society. The impact of the Uyghurs on Beijing is most marked in that due to their exclusion from the formal job market they have set up trading nodes and restaurants. They live in cramped, separate housing and their access to services, especially education, is very limited. The harassment of Uyghurs by officials is constant and most recently evident in the razing of one of their villages in 1999. This type of strategy is unproductive in the long term and may simply lead to further marginalisation and counter activity by the Uyghurs. A more productive path needs to be found as the chances of stopping in-migration are small. Separate enclaves are not necessarily a problem but enclaves that are isolated and excluded from the mainstream of society may lead to further separatism. The development of policies and strategies for the social and economic incorporation of Uyghurs and other ethnic minority groups is needed.

9. Conclusion

China's history and the communist government's approach to the identification of *minzu* or nationalities have created a situation where even though it was intended that minorities would be equal to the Han majority this has not eventuated in many respects. Before 1949 there was a policy of assimilation and the Cultural Revolution which started in 1966 saw a temporary worsening of ethnic relations and breaching of previous ethnic policies. This was followed by a revival of ethnic identities after 1976 and money (often subsidies from the central government) was directed by autonomous governments into the development and maintenance of minority schools, language resources, TV and radio programs, etc., as well as into economic development. This official support for ethnic minorities led to a spectacular upsurge in the number of people identifying as belonging to a minority ethnic group from the early 1980s, mostly a result of 'category-shifting' — from Han to minority (or between minorities).

In the 'communist project' (Harrell 1994), everything was supposed to be different but ingrained prejudice and dogmatic adherence to a belief in the five stages of history, both an integral part of Confucian philosophy and ideology, thwarted the 'project'. Harrell (1994, pp. 25-6) refers to this as the 'Confucian co-optation of the communist project'. Repeated statements by high ranking officials about the value of minority cultures and Deng Xiaoping's concept of 'two civilisations' (the simultaneous development of the material and spiritual sides of socialism) did little to change this situation. Many minority leaders were cynical about these statements and they argue that 'traditional culture [was] invoked and symbolised for political ends, and [was] therefore useful as state capital' (Bilik 1996b, p. 135). The value of non-Han cultures is not really understood or appreciated and the Han sense of superiority continues to prevail. Most Han Chinese remain ignorant about the cultures, values, education, history, religions and other aspects of minorities' lives. In spite of the 'image-correction' efforts of officials who work in nationality affairs departments at both central and local levels, Han Chinese know minorities only for their 'strong build', their 'militant inclination' and their singing and dancing. Material about minorities is not included in mainstream curricula and lack of education about minorities means a lack of appreciation of alternate national or ethnic identities and of the merit of retaining minority cultures and languages. The drive for economic modernisation began to take place in many minority regions from the late 1980s and through the 1990s. This trend is likely to continue as international engagement and incorporation into the processes of globalisation both increase. Areas that were left largely to their own devices are now gradually being incorporated into the economic development process. The government is also encouraging the expansion of local initiatives that are outside state control. They may be private or village/town but they all allow for the re-emergence of income differentials. Market reform processes could potentially bring about a rapid integration of minority groups into mainstream cultures, as the drive for economic development often ignores or negates the value of non-economic aspects. In time it may lead to 'homogenisation' or 'amalgamation' as minority members perceive the adoption of Chinese culture and the abandonment of their cultural and linguistic heritage as the only way to ensure that their standard of living improves at a rate commensurate with that of Han Chinese. This process is aided by the fact that most successful minority cadres and intellectuals are trained in Chinese and this has become a symbol of social promotion and economic gain. Limited attention to the promotion of minority languages, as well as political feasibility, have led to today's language landscape and the predominance of the Han Chinese.

Thus the market economy with its narrow vision and economic rationalism poses a threat to minority cultures and values by failing to take account of culture, social systems and the environment. For example, in the case of the Ewenki minority in the northern part of Inner Mongolia state subsidies were used to settle reindeer herders in forestry settlements, as this was perceived as economic advancement. But the provision of housing, a timber mill and other services was not sufficient to persuade the herders to remain permanently in the new development and after a while some returned to their mountain habitat. The policy makers had not realised that 'emotions and social values are inseparable from the ethnic economy and its products and commodities' (Bilik 1996a, p. 68). By taking away their traditional livelihood they threatened the Ewenki culture. Thus, at the micro or local level, failure to take account of culture both sabotaged this economic development project and destroyed the local culture for those who did not return to their original habitat. In future, painstaking efforts must be made on a case-by-case basis to ensure the survival and adaptation of minority cultures.

Cultural pluralism, the state's policy since 1976, was meant to tolerate (but not necessarily celebrate) different ethnic groups and their cultures and to bring them into the mainstream of Chinese society and economy. It was anticipated that minorities would eventually amalgamate or assimilate with the Han and ethnic differences would largely disappear. But the communist plan for equality has also had the unintended consequence of strengthening some ethnic identities and has led to a continuation or even upsurge in ethnic politics. For example, Mongolians in rural areas have a renewed ethnic identity that relies on elements of the past but updates them to include the present — thus 'Mongols on horseback' have become 'Mongols on wheels'. This was partly with the assistance of Mao Zedong who saw reference to the great hero, Chinggis Khan, as one way of leading Mongolians to believe in the unity of China. This is only one case but there are many instances that demonstrate this outcome. On top of this, the migration patterns of the last 20 years are adding another dimension to the concept of ethnic identity.

MIGRATION BEHAVIOUR OF THE THREE GROUPS

Within the above context, we sought to understand the contemporary movements of ethnic minorities. Their experiences and the consequences for ethnic identity have been examined by looking at three minority groups — Mongolians, Tibetans and Uyghurs. They differ vastly and provide fascinating case studies of different patterns and experiences in the process of social transformation. Education was given particular attention as it is often the stepping stone to socio-economic mobility and integration. Both the implications of education for mobility and the effects of mobility on education have been discussed. The impacts on sending areas have not been examined in depth but implications for receiving areas, especially Beijing, have been a focus. The transformation that is taking place in China's large towns and cities is even more interesting and complex when groups of minority migrants are settling or staying temporarily.

On the whole, ethnic minorities appear to have been somewhat slower than Han Chinese to start moving in significant numbers. This finding is not conclusive, however, and may be partly a matter of definitional issues and data collection mechanisms. From both census and survey data, it is apparent that the movement of minorities is a trend to urban rather than non-urban areas. With the full introduction of the household contract system by 1984 the land was carved up among existing households. It has become impossible for anyone to acquire land in rural areas without local *hukou*, but it can be rented from existing landholders. Renting of land is not a common practice amongst some minority groups and marriage migration provides the most common reason for movement to non-urban areas.

The large surplus labour force of rural areas in particular is being enabled or even encouraged to move to provide the workforce for much of the new activity inherent in economic reform. Much of this movement is into low skilled 3D (dirty, dangerous and difficult) jobs or into small scale entrepreneurial activities. Segmentation of the job market in major cities such as Beijing and Shanghai is reinforced by rules and regulations. On the other hand, we have also seen that numbers of skilled minority migrants have moved with official sanction and by means of obtaining an urban *hukou*. They are elite migrants who are selected or whose movement is facilitated to achieve specific purposes. Solinger (1999, p. 91) likens them to the 'designer' migrants who are allowed to enter Australia, Canada, etc., as long as they pass a points test.

Market reforms have softened the official attitude to spatial mobility and have often led to officials 'turning a blind eye', giving positive support to movement and to migrant communities in cities, or giving approval (permanent or temporary *hukou*). Similarly, the movement of ethnic minorities has largely been ignored but this has also meant that their special circumstances have not attracted the attention required. The movement of minorities seems to have been ignored in some instances (Mongolians) and their integration into city life has not been assisted in any particular way, as has occurred for example with Zhejiang villagers in Beijing. For Tibetans, mobility is being promoted for educational purposes, the training of officials and the staffing of government offices. This, in turn, has lead to some unofficial movement that has again largely been ignored. For Uyghurs, mobility seems to have prompted extreme action in terms of the closing down of their enterprises and razing of one of their areas in Beijing. We must remember that this also happened to Zhejiang village in Beijing but this was some years ago and these people have been supported in the redevelopment of the area. The fact that each group is treated differently highlights the political sensitivity attached to the group as well as the socio-economic and cultural characteristics of the group.

Most streams of minority migrants consist of young people moving for education or jobs or for the better life or bright lights of cities and large towns. The opportunities available in urban areas are much greater than in rural areas and they operate like a magnet to young people, in particular. The open, more accepting environment of cities also provides greater freedom from familial control and more room for difference. In particular, we have seen that this is appealing to young minority women in Xinjiang and Tibet and even though they may have few job skills they acquire domestic jobs that provide a springboard to other openings. This is in line with Hoy's findings that both married and single women use migration either as a means of empowerment or as part of the perpetuation of strong patriarchal families (Hoy 1999). Tsui's in depth fieldwork in Xinjiang has also shown the importance of individual behaviour and the fact that migration provides an opportunity to expand one's horizons while at the same time reinforcing the importance of ethnic networks. Thus, the perception of migrants as 'victims' that underlies much migration research is not confirmed by our study. Migration provides new opportunities and options as well as being a means for alleviating poverty.

In all flows we have seen the vital importance of kinship, ethnic and native place or hometown networks. These appear to be even more important for minority migrants than for Han migrants. Reliance on the ethnic group for support, contacts, employment, housing, social life and personal relationships was particularly strong among the Uyghurs who tended to be migrants without *hukou*. Analysis of the Beijing sample survey data showed that all migrants were 'minorities' compared with local residents, but this was especially the case if they lacked Beijing *hukou*. Such minority migrants experienced a double disadvantage due to their residency status and their ethnic background.

MIGRATION AND ETHNICITY

Ethnicity takes many forms and is closely linked to history, politics, economics, emotions and culture. Anthropologists' common tendency to 'fix' identity is now seen as outdated and even Anderson's notion of identity and 'imagined communities' may serve to revive old notions of bounded spaces and cultures (Meyer and Geschiere 1999, p. 6). Other-definition and self-definition are continual practices that do not stop at ethnic boundaries. Rather, they happen at different levels, outside and inside a particular ethnic group. It is important to keep in mind that a person's identity is not fixed. Identity is a 'moveable feast', formed and transformed according to the cultural systems surrounding the person (Hall 1992). People assume different, even contradictory, identities at different times. Moreover, at times of rapid social and cultural transformation ethnicity can be highly politicised and issues of culture, identity and community may take on great significance both for minorities and majorities. The question of identity must be seen in this context rather than in a context that is fixed and immutable.

The overriding question is whether movement, both spatially and occupationally (as a result of education), can go hand-in-hand with the maintenance of good ethnic relations. Migration introduces a new set of factors into an individual's or group's self-definition. Departure from a minority region is resisted by many as they do not want to leave their ethnic group. Uyghurs, for example, are concentrated in compact communities and enjoy a relatively homogeneous culture grounded in the economies of oasis agriculture and trade and reinforced by a strong language identity and Islamic ties. Many Tibetans and Mongolians also do not want to leave the environment of their ethnic group. But others move for a variety of reasons and with a range of outcomes. The widening of people's experiences, especially by migration, often leads to the occurrence of multiple identities which consist of an urban or other ethnic identity as well as the original ethnic group identity. In urban areas, for example, Mongolians have not lost their ethnic identity but common descent and endogamy have come to be the important markers in separating them from the Han. Migration not only leads to multiple identities but they also become more conspicuous or obvious.

It is clear that Uyghurs who migrate give up very few, if any, of their ethnic markers. Uyghurs who move to Urumqi or Beijing retain their ethnic identity and it may even be strengthened while at the same time they acquire urban or regional sub-identities. They settle in communities where they are able to maintain many of their practices and customs — religion, informal meetings in the street or market place, language, etc. Their isolation from the mainstream in Beijing appears to strengthen their ethnic identity. Within Xinjiang, those who move to Urumqi and other cities work and play together with very little contact with Han Chinese. Separation from families and marginalisation from the new jobs that are being created both serve to drive them closer together. Relations between Han and Uyghurs are marked by distinctive cultural differences that have been increasingly strengthened by the rising trend of Islamic globalisation. Intermarriage is virtually non-existent and social interaction is minimal, even among educated Uyghurs.

Minorities moving to mainly Han areas rarely seem to come to identify themselves as Han. On the other hand, intermarriage or moving into a Uyghur or Mongolian environment has been shown to lead some Han to identify themselves as belonging to that ethnic group. This is both a pragmatic response to better educational opportunities for their children and looser family planning provisions and other advantages, and the result of a desire to integrate into the community for economic reasons. For example, some Han Chinese who have moved into the grasslands areas of Inner Mongolia have become herders, often because they have no other means of earning a living. They learn the language and for all intents and purposes become 'Mongolian'. As we saw this process has not occurred in Tibet where economic motives are not strong enough to overcome the reluctance of most Han Chinese to stay permanently.

At the same time, we have seen that the increasing number of Han Chinese in minority regions impacts on minority cultures. Pasternak and Salaff (1993, pp. 4-5) discuss the 'homogenising power of the Chinese state' but conclude in Inner Mongolia that there is a 'give and take between Han and Mongols on the grasslands, while the Chinese Way prevails in the villages'. The arrival over time of Han Chinese has also gradually meant that

Mongolian herders have been forced to leave many areas of grassland and have been forced back onto poor drier land to continue their herding. This has led to resentment, and increased attention has come to be paid by Mongolian cadres to ecology and the maintenance and enhancement of the grasslands, to enable a continuation of the Mongolian life style, albeit mostly in a settled form. The 'get rich quick' approach that has already led to widespread environmental damage in other parts of China may have the same results in minority regions. The challenge is to curtail similar developments in fragile environments and to avoid the widespread ecological displacement of ethnic minorities.

The situation is compounded further by globalisation and the changing ethnicities that come about as a result of the transformation in people's life experiences. In general, globalisation often leads to the re-emergence of ethnic identities as groups and individuals strive to single themselves out from the mass. This is a worldwide phenomenon and not one that is confined to China. We have seen that Tibetans who have begun trading in Tibetan culture have undergone a change which in turn is impacting on the education system, and Uyghurs trading and communicating with regions to the west of Xinjiang, in the Middle East, have brought home changes in the practice of their religion and other aspects of their lives.

The economic integration and inclusion of autonomous regions in the overall national goals and framework in the 1990s, is a means of gaining greater control. Increased centralisation is both a response to the 1989 Tiananmen Square event, where regional differences were seen as one of the causes of the crisis, and a result of increased emphasis on unity. The break up of the USSR and Yugoslavia served as sober reminders of what could happen in socialist states if the economy was not run properly. But economic development or 'planned inclusion' of minority regions is a two-edged sword. On the one hand, it appears equitable in terms of raising the living standards of all residents of China. The exclusion or neglect of minority peoples and regions could reasonably attract criticism as a form of racism. Exclusion could also lead to greater unrest and more dissatisfaction with the central government. On the other hand, inclusion like colonisation often has the effect of negating the values, lifestyles and cultures of the people who are incorporated. Greater economic development enables greater control of minority regions and less real autonomy. The challenge is to find a balance between the two.

MIGRATION AND EDUCATION

The level of educational achievement among minority groups is diverse and for the three groups we studied this is the case, in spite of special minority education policies since 1952. Attention did not really begin to be focused on this issue till the early 1980s and since then there have been various attempts to raise the education levels of particular minority groups. The motivation for this was both to raise the level of socio-economic development in minority regions and to train minority cadres and teachers.

Education was chosen as a particular focus in this study as it often is the means by which migrant groups, everywhere, find a bridge to affiliation with and eventual acceptance by the host society. How this is occurring for minority groups in China is complex. First, we have seen that educational status affects the propensity to migrate and minorities with higher education levels are more likely to move as well as being more likely to get an urban *hukou*.

Second, educational acquisition has become a major motivation for movement. We have seen that economic reasons predominate as the major motivating force for mobility of the population as a whole but for those with more than 12 years of education many move for either higher education or a better job. Minorities have joined this stream and we saw that young Uyghur and Mongolian migrants moved either for education purposes or after the completion of their studies, as they sought out better opportunities in the cities in their region or elsewhere. Education is a high priority for Mongolians and consequently it is an important factor promoting mobility. The level of formal education among Uyghurs has been much lower but major efforts in Xinjiang have led to significant improvements in schooling rates in the last two decades. As a consequence young Uyghurs with secondary or tertiary education are now moving to find 'better' lifestyles though not necessarily better jobs. Education in Tibet started from a very low base in the 1950s and suffered serious setbacks during the 1960s and 1970s. Improvements have occurred since then but the difficulties inherent in developing a good school system led to the decision in the early 1980s to send some children out for education in other provinces.

The movement of minorities for education has often been associated with particular strategies and policies. For example, the location of Universities of Nationalities influences educational mobility. In addition, there are preferential education policies — if they cannot get into universities through the normal examination process (in competition with Han) they can fill the quotas assigned to minorities (with lower examination results). This leads to significant mobility as students move from high minority density areas to low density areas in the central and eastern regions.

There are differences between intra-provincial migration and inter-provincial migration for the purposes of seeking education. Mongolians appear much more likely to go to Beijing for educational purposes than Uyghurs. Inner Mongolia is quite near to Beijing and there is good transport. In addition, many Mongolians speak Chinese and so living in Beijing is relatively straightforward. Mongolians are relatively integrated into Beijing society and have access to officials and connections. Xinjiang is situated in the northwest of China and most Uyghurs do not speak Chinese. So movement to universities in Beijing is limited but is still the main reason for education-based migration. Language, culture and distance all appear to affect the level of inter-provincial migration for education reasons, with the important caveat that this is overridden by policy considerations in particular instances.

Third, there are major consequences for educational systems if a significant number of people move. The movement of large numbers of non-*hukou* migrants, and increasingly their children, is impacting on the creation of new educational institutions and education policies. The 1985 decision on reforms to the education system stipulated that nine years of schooling was compulsory but floaters' children were often not covered. A conflict between the maintenance of the *hukou* system and 'illegal' migration arose. The exclusion of migrant children from schools is quite exceptional in the history of the way that most countries have dealt with similar situations of 'outsiders'. In China's case, however, these are nationals that are excluded and even the former USSR did not go to these lengths to deny its children the right to education. At the same time, however, the emergence of privately-run migrant children's schools and the purchase of enrolment or an urban *hukou*, as we saw in Beijing, were either tolerated or ignored. The provision of schools for the floating population's children by local government authorities, such as those in Urumqi, was also permitted. Often distance from the centre enables considerable autonomy that is either with or without the sanction of the central government. In this case, it is clear that the central authorities knew about these schools and in fact saw them as an innovative approach to solving the problem of providing migrant children's schooling. The question must be asked though whether such schools would have been provided if there had not been large numbers of Han non-*hukou* migrants in a minority region.

The 1998 policy change, the 'Provisional Method of Migrant Children Going to School', is a significant breakthrough as it is a national strategy for improving access to education for the children of floating migrants. It overrides both the *hukou* system and the total autonomy vested in principals from 1985. Because migrant children's education is often neglected, they fall behind their peers in terms of achievement. This makes integration into the appropriate class for their age group difficult and they generally need extra assistance. City classes are already oversized with 50-60 students and the addition of children with special needs and from rural backgrounds poses a heavy burden. In the past, schools wanted compensation from the government or from parents to the value of 2000 to 10 000 yuan per child. The 1998 policy outlaws the practice of principals charging high fees and puts pressure on locations with large numbers of in-coming migrants to enable children to attend school.

Individual provinces are developing their own means of dealing with the new policy, ranging from sanctioning private schools and incorporating them into the public school system, creating additional classes in existing schools, and creating new schools or allowing existing migrant schools to continue to function without government interference. The latter is the case in Beijing where there are around 100 such schools. But these schools must be incorporated into the state system in other than a sporadic and *ad hoc* fashion. The provision of adequate numbers of teachers for coping with students from a diverse range of ethnic and rural backgrounds represents a major challenge. Tuition in languages other than Chinese is important as is the placement of students in classes appropriate to their needs, rather than their chronological age. Unless curricula are specially designed to meet the children's needs both their participation and their drop-out rates will differentiate them from students with *hukou*. The development of a multi-tiered education system is not conducive to social inclusion or social and occupational mobility. Shanghai is going a different route by allowing migrants to establish schools but the schools must be registered with (and presumably financed by) the officials in the place of origin. This is obviously difficult as migrants do not all come from the one place to the area of the schools. The policy is a manifestation of the commitment of the Shanghai Municipal government to controlling unofficial in-migration.

We saw that in relation to minority children, there is often a desire to send children home to their place of origin for schooling. In the past this was a response to both limited educational access in urban areas and to the desire for education to be in the minority culture and language. This continues, especially for Uyghur children, and is part of the maintenance of a strong Uyghur identity. Only one minority (Hui) school has emerged spontaneously in Beijing and this probably reflects a number of factors: the number of school aged children, the absence of minority teachers and fear of harassment by local officials.

The 1998 policy sees the sending home of children to guardians in the place of origin as the first option and it is only if this is not available that migrant children are to be accommodated in urban schools. Obviously this solution will ensure consistent contact and visits between family in the origin and those in the destination. This high level of communication is conducive to the transfer of information and may in turn lead to further mobility. The impact on the sending area in other ways, such as the promulgation of new ideas and products and the remittance of money and the uses to which it is put, are an important part of the migration system that needs to be addressed.

The impact of educating Tibetan children in provinces outside of Tibet also needs to be investigated for its role in social transformation. It is assumed that most of these children return home at the end of their education and training but there are no data available on this. Their place and role in the changes taking place in Tibet, including Tibetan identity, warrant investigation.

THEORETICAL IMPLICATIONS

Since the late 1970s, internal mobility has been increasing across the whole of China in response to the widening economic and social divide between regions. Migration is multi-directional and motivated by a range of factors. It was previously segmented into two distinct migration systems: the officially sanctioned movement of people for education, higher skill jobs and resettlement projects in frontier areas, and the 'floaters' who were not sanctioned to move but who went nevertheless. The rigid divide between these two migration streams has been breaking down since the late 1980s and this trend escalated in the 1990s. For example, some non-*hukou* movement is with direct government input (organised temporary labour migrants) while some is with the government's tacit or implicit agreement. Other non-*hukou* migrants have been able to buy a permanent or temporary urban *hukou,* or through their networks (*guangxi*) they have been able to become urban residents with access to a wide range of services. The dual labour market still pertains, to some extent, and in many instances non-*hukou* migrants are still characterised by the same features that are ascribed to international labour migrants. But the introduction of private businesses and the arrival of TVEs in cities means that there are ways of circumventing the rigid divide, and non-*hukou* migrants increasingly manifest characteristics of official migrants in terms of their access to wealth, status and government connections.

The neo-classical and modernisation theories of migration partly explain what is occurring. In particular, many non-*hukou* migrants are operating 'like "free" migrants do in market economies, subject to only certain (obviously, more in the Chinese case) administrative and economic constraints' (Kam 1999, p. 67). On the other hand, *hukou* or official migrants are generally no longer moving against their wishes as often occurred in the past. In most instances there is a high degree of correlation between the wishes of the state (or individual cities, SEZs, etc.) and individuals. On the whole, it is safe to say that much migration is for economic gain, as described in the individualistic approach proposed by Todaro. The geography of non-*hukou* migration is also consistent with neo-classical predictions (Kam 1999, p. 67). But it is also clear that complex migration systems and forces have emerged that generate further migration and that are much broader than economics. Social, political, cultural and environmental factors are playing a major role in contemporary movements within China while the role of the state in dictating or preventing migration has diminished.

The migration systems theory approach incorporates settlement outcomes and patterns as part of the model. The place where the state's policies are still most influential is in the settlement outcomes for non-*hukou* migrants. The *hukou* system, albeit in a weakened form, still prevails and its role is still, as originally intended, to exclude migrants without permission from urban services. It was designed to discourage or stop migration but because people now circumvent the system, it has led to the creation of urban spaces that are disadvantaged. We agree with Pieke (1999, p. 11) that *hukou* migrants are 'at the top of the pile in the destination area' but the findings of this study do not support his view that 'here ethnicity neither has much relevance nor is allowed room to develop'. Perhaps by 'ethnicity' he means place of origin or 'native' place and he is referring to Han Chinese. In this case the statement may be correct but as a general statement it does not hold.

Mongolians in Beijing appear to have integrated into the wider society but the ethnic group still has strong markers, including an emphasis on common descent and origins. Tibetan migrants in Beijing also tend to be *hukou* migrants but their ethnicity and areas of concentration are very noticeable. They do form ethnic communities and ethnic organisations, even though they may be informal. We found that the predominantly non-*hukou* Uyghur migrants have a double disadvantage which is contingent on their lack of *hukou* and their ethnicity. Their experience in Beijing (and elsewhere) mirrors that of other non-*hukou* migrants in many ways but they also attract particular negative attention from officials, the media and the general public. The level of antagonism and prejudice towards the Uyghurs has few parallels in China. This is not to say that it is at the same level as the treatment of African Americans, Australian Aborigines, some Indian tribes and castes and European guest workers and asylum seekers, but it does need to be taken seriously.

Recent moves by the state to 'allow' migrant schools to emerge and more importantly the 1998 policy announcement enabling migrant children to get better access to schools are a significant indication that the state is starting to deal with some of the consequences of massive, non-*hukou* migration. The major question is whether the government will abandon the *hukou* system altogether. Only time will tell but there is currently a great deal of debate on this topic with conservatives pushing for its maintenance, as a means of controlling the population, while others argue for its removal and the operation of a free labour market which would be consistent with market reform. Whatever happens, the increase in migration cannot be stopped. State policies need to be developed that incorporate all migrants into mainstream society. Relying on governments in migrants' areas of origin to administer schools or birth control policies (Hoy 1996) is unmanageable and short sighted. User-pays, personal taxation or some other means need to be found to cover the costs of services to migrants.

Our study has found that there appears to be a hierarchy of ethnic groups, especially in their settlement outcomes. We have seen how cultural difference and ethnic prejudice towards Uyghurs in Beijing, in particular, have led to their isolation from the mainstream and utilisation of the urban space for their own goals. Close relations and inter-marriage with the Han are a long way off but in the meantime a situation of less official harassment and greater receptivity to admitting Uyghur children into Beijing schools needs to be found. Simply ignoring the needs of minority communities in Beijing and elsewhere will not aid future ethnic relations. The rate of internal migration in China has escalated since China's opening up and incorporation into the global economy. Globalisation, in turn, leads to increased uncertainty by challenging the 'true' identity of people. Thus new ways need to be found to incorporate and provide for changing identities without leading groups to the extreme position of using ethnic violence as the ultimate means of ethnic identification (Meyer and Geschiere 1999).

Clearly individuals are motivated to move by a wide range of factors and this study has highlighted the need to look at migration systems as more than impersonal phenomena where groups of disassociated individuals are grouped together 'for some external analytical purpose' (Pieke 1999, p. 15). The migration systems theory emphasises the need for analysis of both individual and social and political factors and, therefore, we do not agree with Pieke (1999, pp. 15-16) that a new 'migration configuration' approach which is actor centred, is necessary. Such a cultural approach, as Pieke terms it, has not so much been excluded by the migration systems theory approach but rather has been neglected by many geographers and demographers. In this study we have tried to integrate discourses of belonging and separation and the consequences for identity of migration. Pieke (1999, p. 16) proposes that anthropologists should now be studying mobility as a 'discursively constituted event ... rather than just as an adjunct of, say, the inequalities of the world economic system, modernization, or simply the workings of the national or international labour market'. This proposal is admirable but separating individuals from their context is impossible and migration studies must be interdisciplinary in order to understand the full set of forces at work.

POLICY IMPLICATIONS

The general situation whereby migrants without *hukou* are excluded from access to services is beginning to change, though not uniformly. Change is often incremental in China but national policies that include migrants in mainstream society are needed. Solinger (1995) calls for assimilation as the ideal outcome while Pieke (1999, pp. 21-22) proposes a different model based on a concept of self-managed integration. Pieke's solution relies on using a mixture of the elite or professional associations in migrant communities as self-governing agents (as he says occurred in the past and is currently occurring in overseas Chinese communities) and 'origin' governments, in the administration and delivery of services. Migrant associations have played a vital role in service delivery in many societies but usually in supplementing the provision of mainstream services by the government. They have not taken on a full range of service provision except in extreme circumstances of total exclusion, as we saw in Zheijiang village in Beijing. Strand (1995, pp. 412-13) advocates a considerable degree of self government with government recognition of professional associations.

This model seems unworkable in relation to China's minorities in the current context. The government is already diminishing minority self-government in autonomous regions and is unlikely to re-establish self-government in urban areas. Han Chinese migrant communities may have the connections and *guangxi* to establish much of their own infrastructure but it is unlikely that the same applies to ethnic minorities. Integration is the best solution but with state provision of most services. Services can still be ethno-specific and tailored to meet particular needs but the onus for providing schools, housing, health facilities, etc. must not reside with the ethnic group. Otherwise services will be dependent upon the size, affluence and political affiliations of the group and the right of access to basic services may not be met. The crucial point for ethnic minorities is that they have special needs as well as special characteristics, and these need to be built into policy development.

The solution to China's hierarchy of ethnic groups lies partly in the education of the Han majority about the nature and value of minority cultures — their attributes, attitudes, cultural capital — not only to counter negative stereotypes but to appreciate the value of a rich cultural diversity. Curricula which are inclusive of minorities and their issues and which do not ignore them as part of China's history, society and development are required. A mechanism should be created to enable Han people to 'imagine' what it is like to be a minority member. At the same time, the number of minority anthropologists, sociologists, musicians, poets, ethno-musicologists, writers, historians and other social scientists should be increased to ensure a much greater output of material that documents and presents the cultures of minorities. The number of centres for cultural anthropology and minority cultures and languages needs to be increased to address the need for power and representation among minorities. This should not just be in special institutes or as enclaves in mainstream universities. A way also must be found to promote and celebrate the ethnic diversity of China in a more meaningful manner.

Han Chinese and minorities should work together, in direct dialogue, to overcome the problems of marginalisation or exclusion. They will have more space for negotiation and understanding if they can interact both as group members and as individuals. The only way to accommodate ethnic differences and maintain peaceful co-existence is by negotiation. Ethnic boundaries are built and re-built through continual negotiations where compromise is necessary from all sides. This would also help to alleviate tensions between ethnic groups. According to Dikotter (1992, p. 195) 'it would be wrong to underestimate [the] pervasiveness and tenacity' of ethnic group conflicts, even if they have seldom been translated into practice in China, as they have in certain western countries. But there is no one solution to ethnic problems and flexibility and a variety of approaches are needed.

In the past, preferential employment policies (quotas) were one means of promoting minority employment in work units (*danwei*) but they have not been adjusted to keep pace with the changing economic and social environment. Many employment opportunities in the formal sector are not open to minorities, both because of their lower levels of Chinese competency and their lack of urban *hukou*. As a consequence they are being excluded from many of the new jobs in the emerging private sector. More attention also should be paid to the non-economic aspects of these policies and the way they function in the current context. Affirmative action or preferential policies have an important role to play as long as they are updated and are flexible enough to deal with different circumstances. The most important point is to guard against unintended negative side effects.

Migration is serving to heighten the level of intergroup communication and mixing and what the outcomes of this speeded up process will be is not clear. More tolerance and inclusion of Uyghurs in the city life of Beijing is needed to minimise the tendency to anti-social behaviour. Migration is only one of the processes at work, however. International migration and tourism, overseas study and the expansion of the media, internet and other information networks, are all changing the dynamics of ethnic identity. It is evident that increased diversification rather than homogenisation is occurring and ways need to be found to accommodate ethnic groups as they and China adjust to the forces of globalisation. Special policies continue to be needed to ensure good community relations and the maintenance of cultural diversity and social capital. The preferential policies of the past have played an important role but they need to be constantly updated to ensure that they are leading to the best possible outcomes. Social transformation is a complex process and China has a massive task ahead to ensure that unity and diversity are both maintained.

References

Alatan, Sun Qing, Hua Xinzhi and Qi Xiaoping (1989), *Lun minzu (On Nationality)*, Beijing: Minzu chubanshe.

Anderson, B. (1983) or (1991), *Imagined Communities: Reflections on the Origin and Spread of Nationalism* (2nd Edition), London: Verso Press.

Banister, J. (1987), *China's Changing Population*, Stanford: Stanford University Press.

Banks, Marcus (1996), *Ethnicity, Anthropological Constructions*, London: Routledge.

Baomingzhi, Surina (1997), 'Analysis of Minority Education in Tibet, compared with Inner Mongolia', in Institute of Sociology and Anthropology, Beijing University, and Center of Tibetan Studies of China (eds), *Study of Social Development of Tibet*, Beijing: Tibetan Studies Publishing House, pp. 279-308.

Barth, Fredrik (ed.) (1969), *Ethnic Groups and Boundaries. The Social Organisation of Culture Difference*, Bergen/London: University Forlaget/Allen and Unwin.

Basang, Loubu (1991), 'A view of the new structure of Tibetan culture', *Xizang yanjiu*, 2, 126-31.

Beijing Statistical Bureau (1998), *1997 Beijing shi wai lai ren kou pu cha zi liao (Data of 1997 Beijing migrant survey)*, Beijing.

Bilik, Naran (1996a), 'Culture, The Environment and Development in Inner Mongolia', in Caroline Humphrey and David Sneath (eds), *Culture and Environment in Inner Asia*, Cambridge: The White Horse Press, pp. 134-46.

Bilik, Naran (1996b), 'Emotion Gets Lost, An Ewenki Case', *Inner Asia*, Occasional Papers, 1 (1), 63-70.

Bilik, Naran (1998a), 'The Mongol-Han Relations in a New Configuration of Social Evolution', *Central Asian Survey*, 17 (1), 69-91.

Bilik, Naran (1998b), 'Language, Education, Intellectuals and Symbolic Representation, Being an Urban Mongolian in a new configuration of Social Evolution', in William Safran (ed.), *Nationalism and Ethnoregional Identities in China*, Special Issue of *Nationalism and Ethnic Politics*, 4 (1 and 2), 47-67.

Bodde, D. (1959), *China's Cultural Tradition, What and Whither?*, New York: Rinehart and Company.

Borchigud, W. (1994), 'The Impact of Urban Ethnic Education on Modern Mongolian Ethnicity, 1949-1966', in S. Harrell (ed.), *Cultural Encounters on China's Ethnic Frontiers*, Hong Kong: Hong Kong University Press, pp. 278-300.

Brandt, C., Schwartz, B. and Fairbank, J. (eds) (1952), *A Documentary History of Chinese Communism*, London: Allen and Unwin.

Brown, L. A. and Sanders, R. L. (1981), 'Toward a development paradigm of migration, with particular reference to Third World settings', in G. De Jong and R. Gardner (eds), *Migration decision making: multidisciplinary approaches to microlevel studies in developed and developing countries*, New York: Pergamon Press, pp. 149-69.

Brown, M. J. (ed.) (1996), *Negotiating Ethnicities in China and Taiwan*, China Research Monograph 46, Institute of East Asian Studies, Berkeley: University of California.

Bu, Zhang (1998), 'The research on the status of temporarily-staying population engaged in industry, business and service trades in China', presentation at the *Labour Mobility and Migration in China and Asia Conference*, Institute of Asia-Pacific Studies (Chinese Academy of Social Sciences) and International Institute of Asian Studies (Leiden), Beijing, 17-18 April.

Buhe, Lin, W., Liu, Y., Tegshi and Fang, C. (eds) (1991), *Great Dictionary of Inner Mongolia*, Hohhot: Inner Mongolia People's Publishing House.

Cadwallader, M. (1992), *Migration and residential mobility, macro and micro approaches*, Madison: University of Wisconsin Press.

Cai, Fang (1998), 'Regional Characteristics of Labor Migration in China's Transitional Period', presentation at the *Labour Mobility and Migration in China and Asia Conference*, Institute of Asia-Pacific Studies (Chinese Academy of Social Sciences) and International Institute of Asian Studies (Leiden), Beijing, 17-18 April.

Cao, Min (1995), 'Worker Influx must be tidy', *China Daily*, 11 February, p. 1.

Castles, S. (1996), 'The racisms of globalisation', in E. Vasta and S. Castles (eds), *The teeth are smiling . . . But what of the heart?*, Sydney: Allen and Unwin, pp. 17-45.

Castles, S. (1999), 'Development, Social Transformation and Globalisation', in Kavoos Mohannak (ed.), *Analysing Social Transformation*, Proceedings of the CAPSTRANS Planning Workshop, June, CAPSTRANS Working Paper No. 1, Centre for Asia Pacific Social Transformation Studies (CAPSTRANS), Wollongong, pp. 1-18.

Castles, S. and Miller, M. (1998), *The Age of Migration*, second edition, London: Macmillan.

Chan, Kam Wing (1994), 'Urbanisation and rural-urban migration in China since 1982 — a new baseline', *Modern China*, **20** (3), 243-81.

Chao, Emily (1996), 'Hegemony, Agency, and Re-presenting the Past, the Invention of Dongba Culture among the Naxi of Southwest China', in Melissa J. Brown (ed.), *Negotiating Ethnicities in China and Taiwan*, China Research Monograph 46, Institute of East Asian Studies, Berkeley: University of California, pp. 208-39.

Chatterjee, S. and Price, B. (1991), *Regression Analysis by Example*, New York: John Wiley and Sons.

Chen, C. Z. (1990), *Preliminary Studies on Deng Xiaoping's Educational Thought*, Beijing: Educational Research Press.

Cheng, K. M. (1995), 'Education, Decentralization and the market', in Linda Wong and Stewart MacPherson (eds), *Social Change and Social Policy in Contemporary China*, Hong Kong, Department of Public and Social Administration, City University of Hong Kong, pp. 70-87.

Cheng, H. (1999), Sex and Age Profile of Lhasa Floating Population in Lhasa', *Journal of China's Minority Population*, **3**, 6-8.

China National Institute for Educational Research (1999), Data supplied to the authors, Beijing.

Clarke, G. E. (1994), 'The Movement of Population to the West of China, Tibet and Qinghai', in J. M. Brown and R. Foot (eds), *Migration, The Asian Experience*, Oxford: St Martin's Press, pp. 221-37.

Connerton, P. (1989), *How Societies Remember*, Cambridge: Cambridge University Press.

Daniels, D. (1984), 'Affirmative Action in Education in Inner Mongolia, People's Republic of China', *Canadian Journal of Native Education*, **11** (2), 14-26.

Daniels, D. (1986), 'The Coming Crisis in the Indigenous Rights Movement, From Colonialism to Neo-colonialism to Renaissance', *Native Studies Review*, **2** (2), 97-115.

Davin, D. (1999), *Internal Migration in Contemporary China*, London: Macmillan Press.

Day, L. H. (1994), 'Introduction' in L. H. Day and Ma Xia (eds), *Migration and Urbanization in China*, Studies in Chinese Environment and Development, An East Gate Book, New York: M. E. Sharpe, pp. 1-18.

Day, L. H. and Ma Xia (eds) (1994), *Migration and Urbanization in China*, Studies in Chinese Environment and Development, An East Gate Book, New York: M. E. Sharpe.

De Jong, G. and Gardner, R. W. (1981), 'Introduction and overview', in G. De Jong and R. W. Gardner (eds), *Migration decision making multidisciplinary approaches to microlevel studies in developed and developing countries*, New York: Pergamon Press, pp. 1-10.

Deng, Xiaoping (1987), *Fundamental Issues in Present China*, Beijing: Foreign Language Press.

Department of Planning and Construction, Ministry of Education (1998), *Educational Statistics Yearbook of China 1997*, Beijing: People's Education Press.

Department of Development and Planning, Ministry of Education (1999), *Essential Statistics of Education in China 1998*, Beijing: People's Education Press.

Dicks, A. (1990), 'New Lamps for Old, The Evolving Legal Position of Islam in China, With Special Reference to Family Law', in Chibli Mallat and Jane Connors (eds), *Islamic Family Law*, London: Graham and Trotman, pp. 351-80.

Dikotter, F. (1992), *The Discourse of Race in Modern China*, 1st edition, Hong Kong: Hong Kong University Press.

Dikotter, F. (1996), *The Discourse of Race in Modern China*, 2nd edition, Hong Kong: Hong Kong University Press.

Dikotter, F. (ed.) (1997), *The Construction of Racial Identities in China and Japan*, London: Allen and Unwin.

Dillon, M. (1995), *Xinjiang: Ethnicity, Separatism and Control in Central Asia*, Durham East Asia Papers 1, Durham: University of Durham.

Dogan, M. and Pelassy, D. (1984), *How to Compare Nations, Strategies in Comparative Politics*, New Jersey: Chatham House.

Dojiecaidan and Jiangchunluobu (1995), *Concise Economic History of Tibet*, Beijing: China Tibet Study Press.

Dreyer, J. T. (1976), *China's Forty Millions, Minority Nationalities and National Integration in the People's Republic of China*, Cambridge Mass. and London: Harvard University Press.

Dwyer, A. M. (1998), 'The Texture of Tongues, Languages and Power in China', in William Safran (ed.), *Nationalism and Ethnoregional Identities in China*, Special Issue of *Nationalism and Ethnic Politics*, **4** (1 and 2), 68-85.

Ebrey, P. (1996), 'Surnames and Han Chinese Identity', in Melissa J. Brown (ed.), *Negotiating Ethnicities in China and Taiwan*, China Research Monograph 46, Institute of East Asian Studies, Berkeley: University of California, pp. 19-36.

Economist (1996), 'How Poor is China?', 12 October, pp. 27-9.

Elkin, A. P. (1951), 'Reaction and Interaction, A Food Gathering People and European Settlement in Australia', *American Anthropologist*, **53** (2), 164-86.

Euromonitor PLC INC (1994), *China, A Directory and Sourcebook 1994*, London: Euromonitor PLC.

Fan, C. C. (1996), 'Economic Opportunities and Internal Migration, A Case Study of Guangdong Province, China', *The Professional Geographer*, **48** (1), 28-45.

Fan, C. C. and Huang, Y. (1998), 'Waves of rural brides, female marriage migration in China', *Annals of the Association of American Geographers*, **88** (2), 227-51.

Feng, Jianjiang (1993), Zai xibei xiao chengzhen de mangliu (Blind movement in small urban areas of the north-west), *Renkou Yanjiu* (Population Movement), **2** (80), 57-61.

Gladney, D. (1990), 'The ethnogenesis of the Uyghur', *Central Asian Survey*, **9** (1), 1-28.

Gladney, D. C. (1991), *Muslim Chinese, Ethnic Nationalism in the People's Republic of China*, Cambridge: Harvard University Press.

Gladney, D. (1993), 'Ethnic Identity in China, The New Politics of Difference', in William A. Joseph (ed.), *China Briefing, 1994*, Boulder, Colorado: Westview Press, pp. 171-92.

Gladney, D. C. (1995), 'China's Ethnic Reawakening', *Asia Pacific Issues*, Analysis from the East-West Center, Hawaii, January.

Gladney, D. C. (1996), *Muslim Chinese, Ethnic Nationalism in the People's Republic*, Cambridge: Harvard University Press.

Gladney, D. C. (1998), *Ethnic Identity in China, The Making of a Muslim Minority Nationality*, Case Studies in Cultural Anthropology, Orlando: Harcourt Brace and Company.

Goldscheider, C. (1987), *Urban migrants in developing nations, patterns and problems of adjustment*, Boulder, Colorado: Westview Press.

Goldstein, A. and Wang, Feng (eds) (1996), *Changing Population of China*, Boulder, Colorado: Westview Publishers.

Goldstein, S. (1990), 'Urbanization in China, 1982-1987, Effects of migration and reclassification', *Population and Development Review*, **16** (4), 673-702.

Goldstein, S. and Goldstein, A. (1991), *Permanent and temporary migration differentials in China*, Paper of the East-West Population Institute, No. 17, Hawaii: East-West Center.

Goldstein, S. and Goldstein, A. (1994), 'Permanent and Temporary Movement Differentials', in L. H. Day and Ma Xia (eds), *Migration and Urbanization in China*, Studies in Chinese Environment and

Development, An East Gate Book, New York: M. E. Sharpe, pp. 43-66.

Grunfeld, A. T. (1996), *The Making of Modern Tibet*, revised edition, An East Gate Book, Armonk, New York: M. E. Sharpe.

Guo, F. (1996a), *China's Internal Population Migration since the 1980s, Origins, Processes and Impacts*, Unpublished Ph.D. Dissertation, University of Hawaii, Honolulu.

Guo, Z. (1996b), Director, Institute of Population Research, People's University of China, Beijing, Personal interview, 14 October.

Guo, F. (1998), Analysis of the 1990 Chinese Census of Population, Australian National University, Canberra.

Hall, S. (1992), 'The Question of Cultural Identity', in S. Hall, D. Held and T. McGrew (eds), *Modernity and its Futures*, Cambridge: Polity Press, pp. 273-325.

Hao, S. Y. (1999), 'Introductory Comments', *Workshop on Minority Migration, Education and Ethnic Boundaries in China*, 5-6 October, Beijing.

Haribson, S. (1981), 'Family Structure and family strategy in migration decision making' in G. De Jong and R. Gardner (eds), *Migration Decision Making:* Multidisciplinary *Approaches to Micro Level Studies in Developed and Developing Countries,* New York: Pergamon Press.

Harrell, S. (1988), 'Joint Ethnographic Fieldwork in Southern Sichuan', *Chinese Exchange News*, **16** (3), 8-14.

Harrell, S. (1989), 'Ethnicity and Kin Terms Among Two Kinds of Yi', in Chien Chiao and Nicholas Tapp (eds), *Ethnicity and Ethnic Groups in China,* Hong Kong: Don Bosco Printing Co., pp. 179-97.

Harrell, S. (1993), *China's Civilizing Project*, Seattle: University of Washington Press.

Harrell, S. (1994), 'Introduction' in S. Harrell (ed.), *Cultural Encounters on China's Ethnic Frontiers*, Hong Kong: Hong Kong University Press, pp. 3-36.

Harrell, S. (1996), 'Introduction' in Melissa J. Brown (ed.), *Negotiating Ethnicities in China and Taiwan*, China Research Monograph 46, Institute of East Asian Studies, Berkeley: University of California, pp. 1-18.

Harvie, C. and Turpin, T. (1996), 'China's Market Reforms and its New Forms of Scientific and Business Alliances', in C. Tisdell and J. C. H. Chai (eds), *China's Economic Growth and Transition,* Brisbane: University of Queensland Press, pp. 481-502.

Heberer, T. (1989), *China and Its National Minorities: Autonomy or Assimilation?,* An East Gate Book, New York: M. E. Sharpe.

Higgins, A. (1997), 'Jiang gambles on more state job losses', *The Jakarta Post*, 19 September, p. 5.

Hinton, W. (1990), *The Great Reversal, The Privatization of China 1978-1989*, New York: Monthly Review Press.

Hobsbawn, E. (1983), 'Introduction', in Eric Hobsbawn and Terence Ranger (eds), *The Invention of Tradition*, Cambridge: Cambridge University Press, pp. 1-10.

Hoy, C. S. (1996), *The Fertility and Migration Experiences of Migrant Women in Beijing*, China, Unpublished Ph.D. thesis, University of Leeds, United Kingdom.

Hoy, C. (1999), 'Issues in the fertility of temporary migrants in Beijing', in Frank N. Pieke and Hein Malle (eds), *Internal and International Migration: Chinese perspectives*, Richmond, Surrey: Curzon, pp. 134-56.

Hoy, C. and Ren, Q. (1996), Information supplied by Ren Qiang, Population Research Institute, Xinjiang University, Urumqi, 4 October.

Hoy, C. and Ren, Q. (1999), 'Socio-economic impacts of Uyghur movement to Beijing', Paper prepared for the *Workshop on Minority Migration, Education and Ethnic Boundaries in China*, Beijing, 5-6 October.

Huang, P., Guo, Y., Yang, Y., Jing, T., Cheng, W., Xu, P., Xie, S. and Feng, S. (1995), *Rural Migration and Rural development, A Report on the Field Investigation of Eight Villages from Four Provinces in China*, Beijing, Institute of Sociology, Chinese Academy of Social Sciences.

Hurelbaatar, A. (1996), *Mongols in Present-Day China*, Institute of Mongolian Language and Literature, Unpublished paper, Inner Mongolia Normal University, Hohhot.

Imrie, R., Pinch, S. and Boyle, M. (1996), 'Identities, Citizenship and Power in Cities', *Urban Studies*, 33 (3), 1255-61.

Iredale, R., Fox, C. and Sherlaimoff, T. (1994), *Immigration, Education and Training in New South Wales*, Canberra: Australian Government Publishing Service.

Iredale, R. (2000), 'China's Labour Migration Since 1978', in Charles Harvie (ed.), *Contemporary Development and Issues in China's Economic Transition*, London: Macmillan Press, pp. 212-37.

Jagchid, S. and Hyer, P. (1979), *Mongolia's Culture and Society,* Boulder, Colorado: Westview Press.

Jankowiak, W. R. (1993), *Sex, Death, and Hierarchy in a Chinese City*, New York: Columbia University Press.

Jenkins, A. (1996), 'Defining and defending the Chinese state, geopolitical perspectives', in Terry Cannon and Alan Jenkins (eds), *The geography of contemporary China: The impact of Deng Xiaoping's decade*, London and New York: Routledge, pp. 266-90.

Ji, P. (1990), 'Migration and Socioeconomic Stratification between Ethnic Groups, A Case of Xinjiang Uygur Autonomous Region of China', Draft Paper for the Population Association of America Conference, Sociology Department, Brown University, New York.

Ji, P. (1992), 'Ethnic inequality and social structural assimilation, the Xinjiang autonomous region of China', in Calvin Goldscheider (ed), *Migration, Population Structure and Redistribution Policies*, Brown University, London: Westview Press, pp. 117-35.

Kam, Wing Chan (1999), 'Internal Migration in China: A dualistic approach', in Frank N. Pieke and Hein Mallee, *Internal and International Migration Chinese Perspectives*, Richmond, Surrey: Curzon Press, pp. 49-72.

Karmel, S. (1996), 'The Neo-authoritarian Dilemma and the Labor Force, control and bankruptcy vs freedom and instability', *Journal of Contemporary China*, **5** (12), 111-33.

Kaup, Katherine Palmer (2000), *Creating the Zhuang, Ethnic Politics in China*, Boulder, Colorado: Westview Press.

Khan, A. (1994), 'Chinggis Khan', in Stevan Harrell (ed.), *Cultural Encounters on China's Ethnic Frontiers*, Hong Kong: Hong Kong University Press, pp. 248-77.

Kuhn, A. (1999), Beijing starts razing Muslim Area, http, //www.future-china.org/tw/spcl_rpt/ uygr19990316.html.

Lary, D. (1999), 'The "static" decades, Interprovincial migration in pre-reform China', in Frank N. Pieke and Hein Malle (eds), *Internal and International Migration: Chinese Perspectives*, Richmond, Surrey: Curzon, pp. 29-48.

Lee, Ching Kwan (1998), *Gender and the south China miracle, two worlds of factory women*, Berkeley: University of California Press.

Leiberthal, K. (1995), *Governing China: from revolution through reform*, New York and London: Norton.

Lewin, K. M., Xu, H., Little, A. W. and Zheng, Z. (1994), *Educational Innovation in China: Tracing the Impact of the 1985 Reforms*, Essen: Longman Cheshire.

Li, M. (ed.) (1987), *Zhongguo Renkou, Beijing Fenche (China's Population, Beijing Volume)*, Beijing: Zhongguo caizheng jingji chubanshe (Chinese Financial and Economics Press), pp. 330-31.

Li, R. M. (ed.) (1989), 'Migration in China's Northern Frontier, 1953-1982', *Population and Development Review*, **15**, 503-38.

Li, W. L. and Li, Y. (1995), 'Special characteristics of China's interprovincial migration', *Geographical Analysis*, **27** (2), 137-51.

Lipset, S. M. and Zetterberg, H. L. (1967), 'A theory of social mobility', in R. Bendix and S. Lipset (eds), *Class, status, and power, social stratification in comparative perspective*, New York: The Free Press, pp. 561-73.

Liu, T. T. and Faure, D. (eds) (1996), *Unity and Diversity: Local Cultures and Identities in China*, Hong Kong: Hong Kong University Press.

Long, G. Y. (1999), 'China's changing regional disparities during the reform period', *Economic Geography*, **75** (1), 59-65.

Lyons, Thomas P. (1998), 'Intraprovincial disparities in China, Fujian Province, 1978-1995', *Economic Geography*, **74** (4), 405-17.

Ma, Rong (1987), *Migrant and Ethnic Integration in Rural Chifeng, Inner Mongolia Autonomous Region, China*, Ph.D. Dissertation, Brown University.

Ma, Rong (1991), 'Han and Tibetan Residential Patterns in Lhasa', *China Quarterly*, **128**, 814-35.

Ma, Rong (1997), 'Migration of Population in Tibet Autonomous Region', in Institute of Sociology and Anthropology, Beijing University, and Center of Tibetan Studies of China (eds), *Study of Social Development of Tibet*, Beijing, Tibetan Studies Publishing House, pp. 237-67.

Ma, Xia (1994), 'The Survey, Objectives and Organization' in L. H. Day and Ma Xia (eds), *Migration and Urbanization in China*, Studies in Chinese Environment and Development, An East Gate Book, New York: M. E. Sharpe, pp. 9-24.

Ma, L. J. and Xiang, B. (1998), 'Native place, migration and the emergence of peasant enclaves', *China Quarterly*, **155**, 546-81.

Mackerras, Colin (1994), *China's Minorities Integration and Modernization in the Twentieth Century*, Hong Kong: Oxford University Press.

Mao, Y. F. (1999), 'Han Settlement in Uygur populated regions in Xinjiang', Paper presented at *Workshop on Minority Migration, Education and Ethnic Boundaries in China*, Beijing, 5-6 October.

Massey, D., Arango, J., Hugo, G., Kouaouci, A. and Taylor, J. (1993), 'Theories of international migration, a review and appraisal', *Population and Development Review*, **19** (3), 431-66.

Mauldin, W. P. and Berelson, B. (1978), 'Conditions of Fertility Decline in Developing Countries', *Studies in Family Planning*, **9**, 89-148.

Meyer, B. and Geschiere, P. (1999), 'Introduction' in Meyer, B. And Geschiere, P. (eds), *Globalization and Identity: Dialectics of Flow and Closure*, Oxford and Malden: Blackwell, pp. 1-15.

Naughton, B. (1988), 'The Third Frontier, Defense industrialisation in the Chinese interior', *China Quarterly*, **115**, 351-86.

Neimenggu dacidian (Compiling Committee) (1991), *A Grand Dictionary of Inner Mongolia (Neimenggu Dacidian)*, Hohhot: Inner Mongolia People's Publishing House.

Oberai, A. S. (1983a), 'Introduction', in A. S. Oberai (ed.), *State Policies and Internal Migration Studies in Market and Planned Economies*, London: Croom Helm, pp. 1-10.

Oberai, A. S. (1983b), 'An Overview of Migration-Influencing Policies and Programmes', in A. S. Oberai (ed.), *State Policies and Internal Migration Studies in Market and Planned Economies*, London: Croom Helm, pp. 11-26.

Pasternak, B. and Salaff, Janet W. (1993), *Cowboys and Cultivators: The Chinese of Inner Mongolia*, Boulder: Westview Press.

Pepper, S. (1990), *China's education reform in the 1980s, policies, issues and historical perspective*, Berkeley: University of California Press.

Phan, B. G. (1996), 'How Autonomous are the National Autonomous Areas of the PRC? An Analysis of Documents and Cases', *Issues and Studies*, **32** (July), 83-108.

Pieke, F. (1999), 'Introduction: Chinese and European perspectives on migration', in Frank N. Pieke and Hein Malle (eds), *Internal and International Migration: Chinese perspectives*, Richmond, Surrey: Curzon, pp. 29-48.

Ping, He (1995), 'Perception of Identity in Modern China', *Social Identities*, **1** (1), 127-54.

Piore, M. J. (1979), *Birds of passage, migration labor in industrial societies*, Cambridge: Cambridge University Press.

Postiglione, G. A. (1992), 'China's National Minorities and Educational Change', *Journal of Contemporary Asia*, **22** (1), 20-44.

Poston, D. L. and Shu Jing (1987), 'The Demographic and Socioeconomic Composition of China's Ethnic Minorities', *Population and Development Review*, **13** (4), 703-22.

Poston, D. L. and Yaukey, D. (1992), *Population of Modern China*, Plenum Series on Demographic Methods and Population Analysis, New York: Plenumm Press.

Renmin Ribao (1976), 'Developments in the Tibet Autonomous Region', September, p. 6.

Ren, Q., Yuan, X. and Ma, H. (1998), 'Floating Population in Xinjiang', *Journal of Population Research (Beijing)*, **22** (6), 31-40.

Ren, Q. and Yuan, X. (1999), 'Population Migration to Xinjiang since the 1950s, Social, cultural, economic and environmental impacts', Paper presented at the *Workshop on Minority Migration, Education and Ethnic Boundaries in China*, Beijing, 5-6 October.

Robinson, V. (1999), 'Introduction', in V. Robinson (ed.), *Migration and Public Policy*, Northampton, Cheltenham, UK and Northampton, MA, USA: Edward Elgar, pp. xii-xxxiv.

Roosens, E. (1996), 'The Primordial Nature of Origins in Migrant Ethnicity', in Hans Vermeulen and Cora Govers (eds), *The Anthropology of Ethnicity*, Amsterdam: Het Spinhuis, pp. 81-104.

Rudolph, L. I. and Rudolph, S. H. (1967), *The Modernity of Tradition: Political Developments in India*, Chicago: University of Chicago Press.

Salt, J. (1996) 'International migration at the end of the 20th century: recent changes, characteristics and policies', Paper presented at 28th *International Geographical Congress*, The Hague, 4-10 August.

Sarula, Cao Renxiang (1999), 'Exploring of Economic Issues of Tibet population', *Journal of China Minority Population*, **1**, 6-12.

Schoenhals, M. (1993), 'Introduction', in W. Woody (ed.), *The Cultural Revolution in Inner Mongolia*, Occasional Paper 20, Center for Pacific Asia Studies at Stockholm University, Stockholm: University of Stockholm, pp. 1-11.

Seymour, J. (1976), *China, The Politics of Revolutionary Reintegration*, New York: Thomas Y. Crowell.

Shaw, J. (1989), 'Some Current Trends of Ethnology in China', *New Asia Academic Bulletin*, Special Issue on Ethnicity and Ethnic Groups in China, **8**, 41-63.

Skehan, C. and Hutcheon, S. (1996), 'The handshake China tried so hard to prevent', *Sydney Morning Herald*, 27 September, p. 1.

So, A. Y. (1990), *Social change and development, modernization, dependency and world-systems theories*, Sage Library of Social Research, Vol. 178, Newbury Park, California: Sage Publications.

Soled, D. (ed.) (1995), *China, A Nation in Transition*, Washington DC: Congressional Quarterly Inc.

Solinger, D. (1995), 'The floating population in the cities, chances for assimilation?', in Deborah S. Davis, Richard Kraus, Barry Naughton and Elizabeth J. Perry (eds), *Urban Spaces in Contemporary China, The Potential for Autonomy and Community in Post-Mao China*, Cambridge: Woodrow Wilson Center Press and Cambridge University Press, pp. 113-39.

Solinger, D. J. (1999), *Contesting Citizenship in Urban China, Peasant Migrants, the State, and the Logic of the Market*, Berkeley, CA: University of California Press.

Spence, H. (1993), *British Policy and the 'Development' of Tibet 1912-1933*, Unpublished Ph.D. Thesis, Wollongong, University of Wollongong.

Stafford, C. (1993), 'The Discourse of Race in Modern China', *Man, the Journal of the Royal Anthropological Institute*, **28** (3), 609.

Stalin, Joseph V. (1953), *Works 1907-1913, Vol. 11,* Moscow: Foreign Languages Publishing House.

State Population Census Office and State Statistical Bureau (1993), *Tabulation on the 1990 Population Census of the People's Republic of China*, Vols. 1-4, Beijing: Zhongguo Tongji Chubanshe (China Statistical Press).

State Population Census Office, Xinjiang (1992), *Tabulation on the 1990 Population Census*, Vol. 3, China Statistical Press.

State Statistical Bureau of China (1988), *Tabulation on the 1987 one per cent sample survey*, Beijing: China Statistical Press.

State Statistical Bureau of China (1991), *Tabulation of China 1% Population Sample Survey*, National Volume, Beijing: China Statistical Press.

State Statistical Bureau of China (1996), *China Statistical Yearbook*, Beijing: China Statistical Publishing House.

State Statistical Bureau of China (various years), *Social and Economic Statistical Yearbook of Tibet*, Beijing: China Statistical Publishing House.

Stein, R. A. (1972), *Tibetan Civilization*, Stanford, California: Stanford University Press.

Strand, D. (1995), 'Conclusion: Historical Perspectives', in Deborah S. Davis, Richard Kraus, Barry Naughton and Elizabeth Perry (eds), *Urban Spaces in Contemporary China: The Potential for Autonomy and Community in Post-Mao China*, Cambridge: Woodrow Wilson Center Press and Cambridge University Press, pp. 394-426.

Sun, J. (1994), *China's Zang Population*, Beijing: China Statistics Press House.

Sun, L. (1996), 'Conflict between Tibetan Traditional Culture and Modern Culture', *Journal of China Tibetan Studies*, **4**, 3-13.

Sun, L. M. (1998), 'Rural labourers in China's cities', Paper presented at *China Migration Research Network Workshop,* Beijing, 28-29 March.

Thornberry, P. (1987), *Minorities and Human Rights Law*, London: Minority and Human Rights Group.

Thul bstan, Mkhas grub (1993), 'Tibetan traditional culture and modernization', *Xizang yanjiu*, **1**, 159-62.

Todaro, M. P. (1969), 'A model of labor migration and urban unemployment in less-developed countries', *The American Economic Review*, **59**, 138-48.

Todaro, M. P. (1976), *Internal migration in developing countries, a review of theory, evidence, methodology, and research priorities*, Geneva: International Labor Office.

Tsui, Y. H. (1999), 'The Ethnic Identity of the Rural Uyghur Population moving to Towns in Xinjiang and its Cultural Implications', Paper presented at the *Workshop on Minority Migration, Education and Ethnic Boundaries in China*, Beijing, 5-6 October.

Tumen and Zhu Lidong (1995), *Kang Sheng yu Xin Neirendang yuanan (Kang Sheng and the unjust case of Inner Mongolian People's Revolutionary Party)*, Beijing: Central Party School Press.

Upton, J. L. (1996), 'Home on the Grasslands? Tradition, Modernity, and the Negotiation of Identity by Tibetan Intellectuals in the PRC', in Melissa J. Brown (ed.), *Negotiating Ethnicities in China and Taiwan*, China Research Monograph 46, Institute of East Asian Studies, Berkeley: University of California, pp. 98-124.

Vermeulen, H. and Govers, C. (eds) (1994), 'Introduction' in *The anthropology of ethnicity, beyond ethnic groups and boundaries*, Amsterdam: Het Spinhuis, pp. 1-9.

Wang, D. (1998a), 'The East Turkestan Movement in Xinjiang, A Chinese Potential Source of Instability?', *EAI Background Brief No. 7*, East Asian Institute, Singapore: National University of Singapore Press.

Wang, K. (1997), Personal interview, Chinese Academy of Sciences, Changsha, Hunan.

Wang, Su (1998b), *Education for Minority Nationalities in China, Its Development and Policies*, Unpublished paper, China National Institute for Educational Research, Beijing.

Wang, S. (1998c), 'Mobile Population and Socioeconomic Development in Lhasa City of Tibet', *Journal of Population and Economics, 6*, 3-9.

Wang, Su (2000), 'Education and Mobility', Paper presented at the *Workshop on Minority Migration, Education and Ethnic Boundaries in China*, Beijing, 5-6 October.

Wang, W. (1994), 'An Overview of the Pattern of Internal Migration and Reasons for Migrating', in L. H. Day and Ma Xia (eds), *Migration and Urbanization in China*, Studies in Chinese Environment and Development, An East Gate Book, New York: M. E. Sharpe, pp. 24-42.

Wood, C. H. (1982), 'Equilibrium and historical-structural perspectives on migration', *International Migration Review*, **16** (2), 298-319.

World Bank (1996), *Poverty in China: what do the numbers say?*, New York: World Bank.

World Bank (1999), *China Western Poverty Reduction Project*, Summary Paper, 2 June, Washington: World Bank.

Wu, D. (1990), 'Chinese Minority Policy and the Meaning of Minority Culture, The Example of the Bai in Yunnan, China', *Human Organization*, **49** (1), 1-14.

Wu, H. X. (1994), 'Rural to urban migration in the People's Republic of China', *The China Quarterly*, **139**, 669-98.

Wu, H. X. and Li, Zhou (1996), *Research on Rural-to-Urban Labour Migration in the Post-reform China, A Survey*, Chinese Economy Research Unit, Adelaide: University of Adelaide.

Xiang, B. (1998), 'A Community without Boundary: The Basic Structure of a Migrant Enclave in Contemporary China', paper presented at the *Labour Mobility and Migration in China and Asia Conference*, Institute of Asia-Pacific Studies (Chinese Academy of Social Sciences) and International Institute of Asian Studies (Leiden), Beijing, 17-18 April.

Xiang, B. (1999), 'Expanding with Congregating, Studies on Migrant Communities in Beijing', in Stephen Fitzpatrick (ed.), *Work and Mobility: Recent Labour Migration Issues in China*, Asia Pacific Migration Research Network, Wollongong: University of Wollongong, pp. 61-79.

Xiaodong, N. (1996), 'Mao Zedong and Deng Xiaoping, A Comparison of Educational Thought', *Canadian and International Education*, **25** (1), 61-85.

Yan, R. and Wang, Y. (1992), *Poverty and development — A Study of China's Poor Areas,* Beijing: New World Press.

Yan, X. (1996), 'Study on China's International Migration since the late 1970s', Paper presented at 28th *International Geographical Congress*, The Hague, 4-10 August.

Yang, Q. and Guo, F. (1996), 'Occupational Attainments of Rural to Urban Temporary Economic Migrants in China, 1985-90', *International Migration Review*, **30** (3), 771-87.

Yu, Z. (1999), *Modernization of Tibet*, Beijing: Central Minority University Press.

Yuan, Q. (1990), 'Population changes in Xinjiang Uyghur Autonomous Region (1949-1984)', *Central Asian Survey*, **9** (1), 49-73.

Yuan, R. (1995), 'Zhongguo shaoshu minzu renkou fengbu yu fazhan' ('Population distribution of minority Chinese and economic development'), in Population and Labour Statistics Department of State Statistical Bureau (ed.), *Monograph on the 1990 Population Census of the People's Republic of China*, Beijing: China Statistical Publishing House, pp. 134-92.

Zang Population in Tibet Group (ed.) (1997), *Zang Population in Tibet*, Beijing: China Statistical Publishing House.

Zelinsky, W. (1971), 'The hypothesis of the mobility transition', *Geographical Review*, **61**, 219-49.

Zhang, Q. (1987), *Huji shouce* (Registration Handbook), Beijing: Masses Press.

Zhang, T. (1997), *Population Development in Tibet and Related Issues*, Beijing: Foreign Language Press.

Zhang, Y., Ma, C. and Huang, P. (1998), 'The Change of Regulations on Rural-Urban Migration in China', Paper presented at *Asia Pacific Migration Research Network Second Conference*, 23-25 Feb, 1998, Hong Kong.

Zheng, Y. (1999), *Discovering Chinese Nationalism in China: Modernization, Identity, and International Relations*, Cambridge: Cambridge University Press.

Zhuang, Y. (1995), *Zhongguo renkou qianyi shuju ji (Migration data of China)*, Data User Service, CPIRC/UNFPA, Beijing: Zhongguo Renkou Chuban She (China Population Press).

Zou, L. (1996), *Beijing de liudong renkou (Beijing's Migrant Population)*, Beijing: Zhongguo Renkou Chuban She (Chinese Population Publishing House).

Index